# REPORT ON THE
# STEEL STRIKE OF 1919

A Da Capo Press Reprint Series

# CIVIL LIBERTIES IN AMERICAN HISTORY

GENERAL EDITOR: LEONARD W. LEVY

*Claremont Graduate School*

# REPORT ON THE
# STEEL STRIKE OF 1919

By The Commission of Inquiry,
The Interchurch World Movement

DA CAPO PRESS • NEW YORK • 1971

A Da Capo Press Reprint Edition

This Da Capo Press edition of
*Report on the Steel Strike of 1919*
is an unabridged republication of the
first edition published in New York in 1920.

Library of Congress Catalog Card Number 73-139200
SBN 306-70081-6

Published by Da Capo Press
A Division of Plenum Publishing Corporation
227 West 17th Street, New York, N. Y. 10011

# REPORT ON THE
# STEEL STRIKE OF 1919

# REPORT ON THE STEEL STRIKE OF 1919

BY

## THE COMMISSION OF INQUIRY,
## THE INTERCHURCH WORLD MOVEMENT

BISHOP FRANCIS J. McCONNELL
*Chairman*

DANIEL A. POLING
*Vice-Chairman*

GEORGE W. COLEMAN             NICHOLAS VAN DER PYL
ALVA W. TAYLOR               JOHN McDOWELL

MRS. FRED BENNETT

*Advisory* { BISHOP WILLIAM MELVIN BELL
{ BISHOP CHARLES D. WILLIAMS

HEBER BLANKENHORN
*Secretary to the Commission*

With the technical assistance of
THE BUREAU OF INDUSTRIAL RESEARCH, NEW YORK

NEW YORK
HARCOURT, BRACE AND HOWE
1920

THE QUINN & BODEN COMPANY
RAHWAY, N. J.

## TO THE PRESIDENT

[Following is the essential part of the letter addressed by the officers of the Commission of Inquiry to President Wilson in presenting a copy of the Report.]

Authorized by the Interchurch World Movement to investigate industrial unrest in general and the steel strike in particular, the Commission, of which the undersigned are Chairman and Vice-Chairman, respectively, has gone forward with its work for a little more than seven months. The publication of its completed report has been authorized. It is the very earnest desire of the Commission that since this report ventures to suggest certain actions by the Federal Government, it should come first to the President of the American people.

The Commission finds in the iron and steel industry conditions which it is forced to describe as not good for the nation. It fails to find any federal agency which, with promise of early result, is directly grappling with these conditions.

Unless vital changes are brought to pass, a renewal of the conflict in this industry seems inevitable. The report suggests the appointment of a special commission to bring about immediately free and open conference between employee and employer. This commission to go forward on the precedents of the presidential commission for the bituminous coal industry, named by you after a strike, and of the anthracite commission, appointed to avert a strike. . . .

The conviction has grown upon this Commission that it should not fail to recommend a practical suggestion of peace for an industry drifting toward unrestricted warfare. As Christians we can do no other.

FRANCIS J. McCONNELL, Bishop Methodist Episcopal Church,
*Chairman,* Commission of Inquiry.
DANIEL A. POLING, Associate General Secretary, Interchurch World Movement,
*Vice-Chairman,* Commission of Inquiry.

[The White House received the copy of the Report on July 27, 1920.]

# CHRONOLOGY OF THE INVESTIGATION

Establishment of an independent, representative Commission of
Inquiry by the Industrial Relations Department of the
Interchurch World Movement . . . Oct., 1919.
Personnel: Bishop Francis J. McConnell (Methodist)
Dr. Daniel A. Poling (United Evangelical)
Mr. George W. Coleman (Baptist)
Dr. Alva W. Taylor (Disciples)
Dr. John McDowell (Presbyterian)
Dr. Nicholas Van der Pyl (Congregationalist)
Mrs. Fred Bennett (Presbyterian)
Advisory [1]
Bishop William Melvin Bell (United Brethren)
Bishop Charles D. Williams (Protestant Episcopal)

Field investigation . . . . Oct., 1919—Feb., 1920.
(Mediation effort, Nov. 28,—Dec. 5, 1919.)
Report adopted unanimously by the Commission of Inquiry
March 29-30, 1920.
Report received by the Executive Committee of the Interchurch
Movement . . . . . . . . . . May 10
Recommended for publication by Sub-committee of Executive
Committee . . . . . . . . June 25
Personnel: Dr. Hubert C. Herring, (Congregationalist);
Bishop James Cannon, Jr., (Methodist South); Mr. Warren S.
Stone (Congregationalist).
Adopted unanimously by the Executive Committee of the Inter-
church Movement . . . . . . June 28, 1920

[1] The advisory members did not take part in the active field investigation but signed the report after full examination of it and the evidence
on which it was based.

# CONTENTS

# REPORT ON THE STEEL STRIKE, 1919

## MAIN SUMMARY

NOTE.—This volume presents the Summary of industrial facts as drawn from all data before the Commission and adopted as the Report of the Commission. On it a sub-committee of the Commission based the Findings, from the Christian viewpoint, which are printed at the conclusion of the book.

Another volume will be required for the supporting reports and exhibits by the staff of field investigators: George Soule, David J. Saposs, Miss Marian D. Savage, M. Karl Wisehart, and Robert Littell. Heber Blankenhorn had charge of the field work and later acted as Secretary to the Commission.

The principal sub-reports, frequently quoted in this Summary and awaiting full publication, deal with the following topics:

Civil Liberties.
Welfare Work, Pensions, Etc.
Discharges for Unionism.
The Press and the Strike.
The Pulpit and the Strike.
The Strike in Johnstown.
The Strike in Bethlehem.
Family Budgets and Living Conditions.
Intellectual Environment of Immigrants.
Rank and File View.
Under-cover Men.
History of the National Committee.
The Steel Corporation's Labor Policy.
The Negro in the Steel Industry.

# MAIN SUMMARY

## I

## INTRODUCTION

SUMMARIZED CONCLUSIONS. RECOMMENDATIONS

THE steel strike of September 22, 1919, to January 7, 1920, in one sense, is not over. The main issues were not settled. The causes still remain. Moreover, both causes and issues remain uncomprehended by the nation. The strike, although the largest in point of numbers in the history of the country up to the first date, exhibited this extraordinary phase; the basic facts concerning the work and lives of the 300,000 strikers were never comprehensively discovered to the public.

The strike's real issues were swallowed up in other issues, some just as real as the actual causes of the strike, some unreal but in general quite characteristic of American industrial development.

Moreover the little-known working conditions, which caused the strike, persist in the steel industry. Also the engulfing circumstances, nationally characteristic, persist.

The following report, therefore, in attempting to analyze and publish the facts, though belated, finds peculiar justification in a central phase of the strike and of conditions left after the strike. If the steel industry is to find a peaceable way out of its present state, it must do so on the basis of a general understanding of such facts as are here set forth. If the country is to find peaceable ways out of the present industrial tension it must find them through an enlightened

3

public opinion based upon a more general understanding of those national conditions and trends here analyzed.

In the months after the close of the strike no effort was being made to settle the issues raised by the strike in the steel industry through reasoned public discussion of the basic facts. Employers and employees began to wait for "the next strike"; they and the public wondered, careless rather than fearful, whether "the next strike" would come in months or years, and whether it would be "without violence" as in 1919 or with guns and flame as at Homestead in 1892. The steel industry continued in the same state as in the past, a state of latent war. It was expected that the next outbreak would be precipitated as was the last, by efforts for workmen's organization and collective bargaining. Meanwhile the civil liberties of entire communities were subordinated to the "necessities" of this state of war and the situation in the steel industry continued, in a peculiar way, to threaten the industrial peace of the nation.

Rank and file strikes of such spontaneity, intensity and duration as to slow up the industry of the whole nation characterized the period succeeding the steel strike. Labor unions which had been striving toward internal reform by democratizing their organizations and by defining their responsibilities to the public; employers who were working toward plans for industrial cooperation; those few government agencies and social institutions which had been at work on the nation's after-war industrial problem—all felt a set-back. Conditions of industrial disorganization set in, directly related to events in the steel industry.

Put tersely, the public mind completely lost sight of the real causes of the strike, which lay in hours, wages and conditions of labor, fixed "arbitrarily," according to the head of the United States Steel Corporation, in his testimony at a Senatorial investigation. It lost sight of them because it was more immediately concerned with the actual outcome of the great struggle between aggregations of employers and aggregations of workers than it was with the fundamental circumstances that made such a struggle inevitable. This investigation and report deal primarily with the causative facts,—with abiding conditions in the steel industry—and only secondarily with conflicts of policies and their influence on national institutions and modes of thought.

Out of the first set of undisputed facts, these may be cited in the beginning:

(a) The number of those working the twelve-hour day is 69,000. (Testimony of E. H. Gary, Senate Investigation, Vol. I, p. 157.)

(b) The number of those receiving the common labor or lowest rate of pay is 70,000. (Letters of E. H. Gary to this Commission.)

This means that approximately 350,000 [1] men, women and children are directly affected by the longest hours or the smallest pay in that part of the industry owned by the United States Steel Corporation, which fixes pay and hours without conference with the labor force.

Since this corporation controls about half the industry, it is therefore a reasonably conservative estimate that the working conditions of three quarters of a million of the nation's population have their lives determined arbitrarily by the twelve-hour day or by the lowest pay in the steel industry.

This nub of the situation, the Commission found, was subordinated, and after the strike remained subordinate, to the industry's warfare over collective bargaining. Both sides were enmeshed. The huge steel companies, committed to a non-union system (and offering no alternative) and the masses

[1] The average American family, the so-called statistical family, consists of five persons.

of workers, moving as workers do traditionally, seemed both to be helpless. Espionage replaced collective bargaining or cooperative service.

*Inauguration of Inquiry:*

The data for this report were obtained by and for an independent Commission of Inquiry appointed at the request of the Industrial Relations Department of the Interchurch World Movement of North America after a National Industrial Conference in New York on October 3, 1919. The Conference rejected a resolution condemning one party to the strike for refusing to adopt the principle of collective bargaining but unanimously supported a resolution directing a thorough investigation of the strike and publication of the reports of the investigators.

Those parts of the evidence obtained directly by the Commission were secured through personal observation and through open hearings held in Pittsburgh in November, supplemented by inspection trips in Western Pennsylvania, Ohio, Indiana and Illinois. More technical and detailed data were obtained by a staff of investigators working under a field director from the Bureau of Industrial Research, New York. Other evidence was obtained directly by the Bureau of Industrial Research, by the Bureau of Applied Economics in Washington, by a firm of consulting engineers, and by various other organizations and technical experts working under the direction of the Commission.

The results are presented in a Main Report with subsidiary supporting reports. Pertinent phases of other investigations and surveys, including governmental studies, the recent findings of the Senate Committee on Labor, evidence on the limitation or abrogation of civil rights, before and during the strike, have been collected and analyzed. The relation of " welfare work " to the workers was determined, chiefly by the analysis of available statistics.

A detailed analysis was made of the relation of the press and of the pulpit to the strike, fields hitherto neglected; and a similar analytical study was made of companies' " under-cover men " and " labor detective agencies." A body of over five hundred affidavits and statements from striking and non-striking steel workers was collected and analyzed.

The chief effort at intensive study was limited to the Pittsburgh district, including Johnstown and Youngstown. The evidence may be said to center in the plants of the United States Steel Corporation and particularly its plants in the Pittsburgh district.

Difficulties in obtaining evidence were expected;—they exceeded expectations. In certain quarters the Commission of clergymen were charged with being " Bolshevists " and " anarchists "; their investigators were rebuffed as " Reds "; one was " arrested." Formal action was finally necessary to combat the circulation in written form of charges whose only basis, apparently, was that any persons had ventured to make any investigation. In other quarters great courtesy was accorded, coupled with inability to furnish the desired statistics. Moreover the lack of up-to-date and available statistics which should have been possessed by union officials, the over-supply of unverified complaints from strikers and the reluctance to impart any information on the part of the companies combined to lengthen unduly the period of field investigation. The Commission's effort was in itself a reve-lation of the lack of authoritative means for acquainting the public with industrial information at a time of industrial crisis.

At one period, investigation was delayed by an effort of the Commission to settle the strike. The Commission, hav-ing been urged to do so in a manner impossible to refuse, actually formulated a plan of mediation which was formally accepted by the leaders of the strike but was definitely rejected by the Steel Corporation.

*Scope and Method:*

The scope of the inquiry was delimited by applying two simple questions:

(a) What workers constituted the bulk of the strikers?

The answer is not disputed: the backbone of the strike consisted of the mass of common labor and the semi-skilled, constituting roughly three-quarters of all employees, and mostly " foreigners."

By " foreigners " the steel industry means not all immigrants or sons of immigrants, but only the " new immigration," consisting of the score of races from southeastern or eastern Europe. About half of these " foreigners " had citizenship papers.

In many places all the skilled struck; in a few places the skilled went out and many unskilled stayed in the mills.

The foreigners had never been organized before; hitherto they had been looked upon by the unions as potential strike breakers, " stealing Americans' jobs and lowering the American standard of living."

(b) What was the chief factor on the employers' side?

The answer is not in dispute: the U. S. Steel Corporation was the admittedly decisive influence.

Whatever the Steel Corporation does, the rest of the industry will ultimately do; whatever modifications of policy fail to take place in the industry fail because of the opposition of the Steel Corporation.

Throughout the report great emphasis is laid on Mr. Gary's testimony, partly because he was almost the sole spokesman for the industry during the strike and partly because officials, corporation and " independent," referred investigators to Mr.

Gary and often limited their own testimony to reading extracts from Mr. Gary's statements or approving his policies.

The *scope* of the inquiry, therefore, included chiefly representative cross-sections of the mass of low-skilled "foreigners" in the Pittsburgh and Chicago district plants of the Steel Corporation.

Of the Corporation's 268,000 employees, 80,000 are miners, railworkers and dockmen, ship crews and shipyard workers, who were untouched by the strike and are therefore excluded.

The *method* was to carry the inquiry to the steel workers themselves, strikers and non-strikers. Effort was made to get beyond the debates of Mr. Gary and Mr. Gompers. The statements and affidavits of 500 steel workers carefully compared and tested, constitute the rock bottom of the findings, the testimony of the leaders on both sides being used chiefly to interpret these findings.

Effort was made to keep in mind, that a strike is not merely a *call* to strike, it is a *walk-out,* frequently without a call. Everything,—Mr. Gary, Mr. Gompers, the Corporation's labor policies, Mr. Foster's record,—was viewed in the light of whether or not it had or had not a relation to the separation of 300,000 men from their jobs.

The Commission and its investigators went to the steel workers with two main questions:

A. Why did you strike? (Or why refuse to strike?)

B. What do you want?

Answers to A. were found to deal with things that existed, —schedules of hours, wages, conditions, grievances, physical states and states of mind.

Answers to B. were found to deal with a method (hitherto non-existent in the steel industry), for changing A.; the strike leaders called it collective bargaining and the right to organization; the steel employers called it the closed shop and labor autocracy.

Therefore, the first half of the inquiry concerned, primarily, conditions of labor.

The second half concerned, primarily, methods for changing the conditions revealed by the first half.

The second line of inquiry was found to stretch back with decisive effect over the first half; in short, the key to the steel industry, both before and during the strike and now, was found in following to its furthest implications this question: What means of conference exist in the steel mills? Both sides agreed that the *occasion* of the strike, leaving aside for the moment its relation to any fundamental cause, was the denial of a conference, requested by organized labor and refused by Mr. Gary.

The inquiry into the means of conference was pursued through the three possible forms of conference: (a) through individuals; (b) through shop committee or company unions; (c) through labor unions.

The complete scope of this phase of the inquiry might be restated as follows:

(A) Investigation of a system of denial of organization and collective bargaining (the policy of the Steel Corporation).

(B) Investigation of a system or systems of non-union collective bargaining (existent in certain "independent" plants where strikes had once existed or were feared).

(C) Investigation of a movement for collective bargaining and organization of the traditional trade union kind (initiated by the American Federation of Labor and fought by the Steel Corporation).

Inquiry B. was not sufficiently completed to be presented in this report, except as a sidelight on the main conditions. The plans in operation or attempted in the Pueblo plant of the Colorado Fuel and Iron Company, the Midvale-Cambria

Company, the Bethlehem, Inland and International Harvester plants, etc., did not suggest to the dominant factor, the Steel Corporation, any modification of its policy.

*Summarized Conclusions:*

Sufficient data were analyzed to warrant the following main conclusions concisely stated here and discussed at length in this report and the sub-reports.

1. The conduct of the iron and steel industry was determined by the conditions of labor accepted by the 191,000 employees in the U. S. Steel Corporation's manufacturing plants.
2. These conditions of labor were fixed by the Corporation, without collective bargaining or any functioning means of conference; also without above-board means of learning how the decreed conditions affected the workers.
3. Ultimate control of the plants was vested in a small group of financiers whose relation to the producing force was remote. The financial group's machinery of control gave it full knowledge of output and dividends, but negligible information of working and living conditions.
4. The jobs in the five chief departments of the plants were organized in a pyramid divided roughly into thirds; the top third of skilled men, chiefly Americans, resting on a larger third of semi-skilled, all based on a fluctuating mass of common labor. Promotion was at pleasure of company representatives.
5. Rates of pay and other principal conditions were based on what was accepted by common labor; the unskilled and semi-unskilled force was largely immigrant labor.
6. The causes of the strike lay in the hours, wages and control of jobs and in the manner in which all these were fixed.
7. *Hours:* Approximately one-half the employees were subjected to the twelve-hour day. Approximately one-half of these in turn were subjected to the seven-day week.

Much less than one-quarter had a working day of less than ten hours (sixty-hour week).

The average week for all employees was 68.7 hours; these employees generally believed that a week of over sixty hours ceased to be a standard in other industries fifteen to twenty years ago.

Schedules of hours for the chief classes of steel workers were from twelve to forty hours longer per week than in other basic industries near steel communities; the American steel average was over twenty hours longer than the British, which ran between forty-seven to forty-eight hours in 1919.

Steel jobs were largely classed as heavy labor and hazardous.

The steel companies professed to have restored practically pre-war conditions; the hours nevertheless were longer than in 1914 or 1910. Since 1910 the Steel Corporation has increased the percentage of its twelve-hour workers.

The only reasons for the twelve-hour day, furnished by the companies, were found to be without adequate basis in fact. The increased hours were found to be a natural development of large scale production, which was not restricted by public sentiment or by organization among employees. The twelve-hour day made any attempt at "Americanization" or other civic or individual development for one-half of all immigrant steel workers arithmetically impossible.

8. *Wages:* The annual earnings of over one-third of all productive iron and steel workers were, and had been for years, below the level set by government experts as the *minimum of subsistence* standard for families of five.

The annual earnings of 72 per cent. of all workers were, and had been for years, below the level set by government experts as the *minimum of comfort* level for families of five.

This second standard being the lowest which scientists are willing to term an "American standard of living," it fol-

lows that nearly three-quarters of the steel workers could
not earn enough for an American standard of living.

The bulk of unskilled steel labor earned less than enough
for the average family's minimum subsistence; the bulk
of semi-skilled labor earned less than enough for the average family's minimum comfort.

Skilled steel labor was paid wages disproportionate to the
earnings of the other two-thirds, thus binding the skilled
class to the companies and creating divisions between the
upper third and the rest of the force.

Wage rates in the iron and steel industry as a whole are
determined by the rates of the U. S. Steel Corporation.
The Steel Corporation sets its wage rates, the same as its
hour schedules, without conference (or collective bargaining), with its employees.

Concerning the financial ability of the Corporation to pay
higher wages the following must be noted (with the understanding that the Commission's investigation did not include analysis of the Corporation's financial organization):
the Corporation vastly increased its undistributed financial
reserves during the Great War. In 1914 the Corporation's
total undivided surplus was $135,204,471.90. In 1919 this
total undivided surplus had been increased to $493,048,-
201.93. Compared with the wage budgets, in 1918, the
Corporation's final surplus after paying dividends of
$96,382,027 and setting aside $274,277,835 for Federal
taxes payable in 1919, was $466,888,421,—a sum large
enough to have paid a second time the total wage and
salary budget for 1918 ($452,663,524), and to have left
a surplus of over $14,000,000. In 1919 the undivided sur-
plus was $493,048,201.93, or $13,000,000 more than the
total wage and salary expenditures.[1]

[1] Detailed figures on the Corporation's surpluses, accumulation of
which was begun in 1901, are:

| | |
|---|---|
| 1913—Total undivided surplus .............. | $151,798,428.89 |
| 1914—Total undivided surplus .............. | 135,204,471.90 |
| 1915—Total undivided surplus .............. | 180,025,328.74 |
| 1916—Total undivided surplus .............. | 381,360,913.37 |
| 1917—Total undivided surplus .............. | 431,660,803.63 |
| 1918—Total undivided surplus .............. | 466,888,421.38 |
| 1919—Total undivided surplus .............. | 493,048,201.93 |

Increases in wages during the war in no case were at a sacrifice of stockholders' dividends.

Extreme congestion and unsanitary living conditions, prevalent in most Pennsylvania steel communities, were largely due to underpayment of semi-skilled and common labor.

9. *Grievances:* The Steel Corporation's arbitrary control of hours and wages extended to everything in individual steel jobs, resulting in daily grievances.

The Corporation, committed to a non-union system, was as helpless as the workers to anticipate these grievances.

The grievances, since there existed no working machinery of redress, weighed heavily in the industry, because they incessantly reminded the worker that he had no " say " whatever in steel.

Discrimination against immigrant workers, based on rivalry of economic interests, was furthered by the present system of control and resulted in race divisions within the community.

10. *Control:* The arbitrary control of the Steel Corporation extended outside the plants, affecting the workers as citizens and the social institutions in the communities.

The steel industry was under the domination of a policy whose aim was to keep out labor unions. In pursuit of this policy, blacklists were used, workmen were discharged for union affiliation, " under-cover men " and " labor de-

---

This report does not go into the long dispute over the Corporation's financing, a controversy which blazed up during the strike but not as a part of the issue. A typical criticism printed about this time was the following from the *Searchlight*, commenting on Basil Manly's analysis of Senate Document 259, (a report from the Secretary of the Treasury):

" On the basis of the Steel Corporation's public reports, its net profits for the two years 1916 and 1917, ' after the payment of interest on bonds, and other allowances for all charges growing out of the installation of special war facilities,' amounted, according to Mr. Manly, to $888,931,511. The bonds of the corporation represent all the money actually invested in the concern, for the common stock is ' nothing but water.'

" Of course out of the net income the Steel Corporation had to pay its taxes to the federal government, but the hundreds of millions that remained represented earnings on ' shadow dollars.' "

tectives " were employed and efforts were made to influence the local press, pulpit and police authorities.

In Western Pennsylvania the civil rights of free speech and assembly were abrogated without just cause, both for individuals and labor organizations. Personal rights of strikers were violated by the State Constabulary and sheriff's deputies.

Federal authorities, in some cases, acted against groups of workmen on the instigation of employees of steel companies. In many places in Western Pennsylvania, community authorities and institutions were subservient to the maintenance of one corporation's anti-union policies.

11. The organizing campaign of the workers and the strike were for the purpose of forcing a conference in an industry where no means of conference existed; this specific conference to set up trade union collective bargaining, particularly to abolish the twelve-hour day and arbitrary methods of handling employees.

12. No interpretation of the movement as a plot or conspiracy fits the facts; that is, it was a mass movement, in which leadership became of secondary importance.

13. Charges of Bolshevism or of industrial radicalism in the conduct of the strike were without foundation.

14. The chief cause of the defeat of the strike was the size of the Steel Corporation, together with the strength of its active opposition and the support accorded it by employers generally, by governmental agencies and by organs of public opinion.

15. Causes of defeat, second in importance only to the fight waged by the Steel Corporation, lay in the organization and leadership, not so much of the strike itself, as of the American labor movement.

16. The immigrant steel worker was led to expect more from the twenty-four International Unions of the A. F. of L. conducting the strike than they, through indifference, selfishness or narrow habit, were willing to give.

17. Racial differences among steel workers and an immigrant tendency toward industrial unionism, which was combated by the strike leadership, contributed to the disunity of the strikers.

18. The end of the strike was marked by slowly increasing disruption of the new unions; by bitterness between the "American" and "foreign" worker and by bitterness against the employer, such as to diminish production.

The following question was definitely placed before the Commission of Inquiry: Were the strikers justified? The investigation's data seem to make impossible any other than this conclusion:

The causes of the strike lay in grievances which gave the workers just cause for complaint and for action. These unredressed grievances still exist in the steel industry.

*Recommendations:*

I. Inasmuch as—

(a) conditions in the iron and steel industry depend on the conditions holding good among the workers of the U. S. Steel Corporation, and—

(b) past experience has proved that the industrial policies of large-scale producing concerns are basically influenced by (1) public opinion expressed in governmental action, (2) labor unions, which in this case have failed, or (3) by both, and—

(c) permanent solutions for the industry can only be reached by the Steel Corporation in free cooperation with its employees, therefore—

It is recommended—

(a) that the Federal Government be requested to initiate the immediate undertaking of such settlement by bringing together both sides;

(b) that the Federal Government, by presidential order or by congressional resolution, set up a commission representing both sides and the public, similar to the Commission resulting from the coal strike; such Commission to—

1. inaugurate immediate conferences between the Steel Corporation and its employees for the elimination of the 12-hour day and the 7-day week, and for the readjustment of wage rates;
2. devise with both sides and establish an adequate plan of permanent free conference to regulate the conduct of the industry in the future;
3. continue and make nation-wide and exhaustive this inquiry into basic conditions in the industry.

II. Inasmuch as—

(a) the administration of civil law and police power in Western Pennsylvania has created many injustices which persist, and—

(b) no local influence has succeeded in redressing this condition, therefore—

It is recommended—

(a) that the Federal Government inaugurate full inquiry into the past and present state of civil liberties in Western Pennsylvania and publish the same.

III. Inasmuch as—

(a) the conduct and activities of "labor-detective" agencies do not seem to serve the best interests of the country, and—

(b) the Federal Department of Justice seems to have placed undue reliance on cooperation with corporations' secret services, therefore—

It is recommended—

(a) that the Federal Government institute investigation for the purpose of regulating labor detective agencies; and for the purpose of publishing what government departments or public moneys are utilized to cooperate with company "under-cover men."

IV. It is recommended that the proper Federal authorities be requested to make public two reports of recent investigations of conditions in the steel industry, in making which public money was spent, and to explain why these and similar reports have not hitherto been made public, and why reports which were printed have been limited to extremely small editions.

(Reference is made specifically to Mr. Ethelbert Stewart's report on civil liberties in Western Pennsylvania, made to the Secretary of Labor; to Mr. George P. West's report made to the War Labor Board; to the Testimony of the Senate Committee's strike investigation, 2 vols., printed in an edition of 1,000 only; and to Senate Document 259.)

V. It is recommended that the Industrial Relations Department of the Interchurch World Movement continue and supplement the present inquiry into the iron and steel industry with particular reference to—

1. Company unions and shop committees;
2. Social, political and industrial beliefs of the immigrant worker;
3. Present aims of production in the industry.
4. Conduct of trade unions with reference to democracy and to responsibility.

VI. It is recommended that immediate publication, in the most effective forms possible, be obtained for this report with its sub-reports.

## II.

## IGNORANCE: BOLSHEVISM

As a preliminary to the whole report, analysis of the data gathered in the inquiry warrants the following conclusions on two salient and inter-related phases of the strike:

The steel companies had no adequate means of information on the usual conditions of employment, previous to the strike, nor on the motives of employees in joining the unions during the organizing campaign; they therefore placed undue reliance on information obtained from secret and mercenary sources.

The public purveyors of information on normal steel conditions and on the causes of the strike failed to ascertain and publish the facts. Ignorance of the facts was so general that it was possible for one interpretation of the strike to obtain wide acceptance, viz. the companies' explanation that the strike was a plot of Bolshevists, supported mainly by "radicals" who were largely aliens.

Evidence on this interpretation of the strike as a Bolshevist plot failed entirely to substantiate it. On the contrary, it tended to show that this conception was without foundation in fact.

Concerning the basic facts of normal steel employment conditions, not only were the public and the companies uninformed but the strikers' leaders were also uninformed. It is not unusual for strikes, like presidential elections and wars, to be fought out on extraneous issues, with little elucidation of fundamental facts. In most such cases, however, some of the basic facts finally do come to the surface. In this strike,

so far as the public was concerned, lack of information remained so general that it was possible to set up straw-man
explanations and keep public attention diverted to knocking
them down.

It was necessary for this Commission to consider such
questions as the following:  Was there any substantial
general knowledge of the customary organization of the steel
industry, its hours, its wages, its workers and their modes
of living?  Did the government have the basic facts regarding employment in the industry, and did it make use of the
facts it had?  Did the United States Steel Corporation, in
normal times, possess adequate means of ascertaining the
truth about living conditions and the desires of its workers?
Was the Corporation subject to misinformation?  Were the
press and the pulpit in possession of the facts?  Within steel
communities, are the facts about steel workers' lives obvious
and immediately accessible to the rest of the community?

As to the allegation that the strike was plotted and led by
" Reds " or syndicalists or Bolshevists, that it was supported
mainly or entirely by alien " radicals," and that its real
objects were the overthrow of established leaders and established institutions of organized labor and perhaps the
overthrow of the established government of the country, it
was necessary to consider such questions as:  What sort
of facts were essential to determine the problem?  Who
offered this allegation and with what proof?  Why was this
allegation made?  Did the allegation seriously affect the
strike?  What were its effects on the public?

Analysis of the data collected proved that neither the
United States Steel Corporation, nor organized labor, nor
governmental agencies have considered it their normal business to ascertain the current facts regarding conditions of
employment, etc., in the steel industry and to take the public
constantly into their confidence on such facts.  The Corpora-

tion's annual report is made public, but the facts therein which deal with labor are confined to a few lines and are not illuminating.  Organized labor has never understood the business of gathering facts about any industry nor the advisability of presenting such facts to the public.  The government's bureaus for collecting such statistics as hours, wages, working conditions, costs and profits, are ridiculously inadequate, are almost invariably undercut by Congress in appropriations, and are not primarily concerned with popularizing such facts as they possess.  What might be considered as a prime business of any government, i.e. the discovery and current publication of fundamental facts of the country's basic industries was not considered the national government's business in relation to the steel industry.

In normal times, the Steel Corporation had no adequate means of learning the conditions of life and work and the desires of its employees.  Company officers admitted that they had no real way of reaching, or of keeping in touch with, the mass of workers who became involved in the strike, that is the foreign-speaking unskilled workers and the lower half of the semi-skilled, constituting up to 80 per cent. of the force in representative plants.  Even such machinery of contact as is provided in " modern employment management " systems had not been installed very long in the steel plants and was not developed beyond the point of keeping in contact at the moment of hiring and firing.  With the employment managers were usually joined one to four welfare workers of limited training who were little concerned with interpreting the difficulties and desires of the " foreign " steel worker because they were powerless to effect changes. The President of the Carnegie Steel Company declared to the Commission that there was " no real way of getting hold of the foreigner."  The head of the Corporation's Sanitation, Safety and Welfare Department, Mr. C. L. Close agreed with this statement. Neither seemed to think that this inability was due to a lack of machinery and it was apparent that steel officials generally relied on some other method for information than an openly organized system of studying the minds and needs of the workers. A suggestion that companies might foster and enlist the aid of organizations of the workers themselves for the purpose of insuring such information was commented on by company officers with surprise not to say suspicion. Mr. Gary gave the clearest testimony in confirmation of his subordinates, though that was not his immediate purpose. He told the Senate Committee that his men were "contented." He said he knew this to be the case and that he had adequate means for knowing it; that there was "no cause" for the strike and that "the men were not complaining; the workmen had found no fault; we are on the best of terms with our men and have always been, with some very slight exceptions, very inconsequential exceptions." Then he volunteered the following, (quoted in full from the Senate Testimony, Volume I, pages 161 and 162):

Senator Walsh. "How did you personally know that hundreds and thousands of your men were content and satisfied?"

Mr. Gary. "Senator, I know it because I make it my particular business all the time to know the frame of mind of our people. Not that I visit every man; I do not do that; of course, I could not do that; not that there could be something done or something said in the mills that I would not know; but, in the first place, my instructions regarding the treatment of the men are absolutely positive, given to the presidents at the presidents' meetings regularly—plenty of my remarks to the presidents have been printed and can be exhibited if necessary—and because I am inquiring into that; and we have a man at the head of our welfare department, Mr. Close, who is here, who is around among the works frequently, and all the time, more or less, trying to ascertain conditions; because public writers, unbeknown to us, have been among our works making inquiry and reporting and writing articles on the subject; and because we come in contact with the foremen and often with the men, going through the mills, Mr. Farrell and myself, and others from time to time; because we have a standing rule, and have had, that if any of our men in any department are dissatisfied in any respect they may come singly or they may come in groups, as they may choose, to the foremen and ask for adjustments, make complaints, and if necessary they may come before the president of the company, or they may come to the chairman of the Corporation. Now then, sometimes there have been complaints made. For instance, to mention a somewhat trivial circumstance, some three or four years ago—not to be exactly specific as to date—one of our presidents telephoned to the president of our Corporation, who is in general charge of operations, that a certain number of men—it may have been a thousand or it may have been two thousand men—in a certain mill had all gone out, and his report was that there was no reason for their going out——"

Senator Sterling. "When you speak of 'one of our presidents,' you mean the president of a subsidiary company?"

Mr. Gary. "Yes; the president of a subsidiary company. And he said, 'It is very easy for me to fill this mill, and I will proceed to do it.' The president of the Corporation came to me immediately and reported this. I said, 'Tell him to wait and to come to New York.' He came the next morning and he made substantially that same statement to me. I said, 'Have you taken pains to find out; has anybody spoken to you?' 'No,' he said, 'I have not received any complaint whatever.' I said, 'Are you sure no complaint has been made to anyone?' He said, 'I will find out.' I said, 'You had better do so before you decide what you are going to do or what you propose to do.' He went back; got hold of the foreman. A committee of men had come to the foreman and said that they thought three things, if I remember, were wrong—not very important, but they claimed they were wrong. And the president came back the second time and reported that; and I said, 'Well, now, if they state the facts there, isn't the company wrong?' 'Well,' he said, 'I don't consider it very important.' I said, 'That is not the question. Are you wrong in any respect? It seems to me you are wrong with respect to two of those things, and the other not. Now, you go right back to your factory and just put up a sign that, with reference to those two particular things, the practice will be changed.' "

The foregoing revelation of Corporation practice must be analyzed from the standpoint of Mr. Gary's machinery for getting information about his workmen.    Mr. Gary's system is:  1)  To give instructions to the subsidiary company presidents; as to whether the presidents carry out those instructions, he "is inquiring into that."  2.) He has one man, head of a busy and complex department, who is "more or less trying to ascertain conditions."  3.) Public writers write articles on his steel works.  4.)  Mr. Gary and Mr. Farrell sometimes go through the mills and "come in contact with the foremen and often with the men."  5.)  Mr. Gary knows his system is adequate because of "a standing rule" that anybody in the plant is privileged to come to him with complaints.  He did not cite, nor, so far as the Commission has been able to ascertain has anybody in his office cited, any example of any workman or committees of workmen coming to him.  In short, it would appear that he gets no information under "the standing rule."    Finally, he gives in full the circumstances of how he learned of the desires of one thousand, "it may have been two thousand," whose grievance was so vital to themselves that they went on strike.

That is, these one thousand, or two thousand, workmen whose complaint was just, or two-thirds just, according to Mr. Gary himself, after weeks or months of effort to obtain redress, took the desperate venture of quitting their jobs.

That they might never get the jobs back again was likely, as the president of the subsidiary company told Mr. Gary that he could easily fill their places. The livelihood of more than five thousand men, women and children (if the strikers numbered one thousand) of over ten thousand men, women and children (if the strikers numbered two thousand) was vitally involved. Without redress, and without jobs, this population would have had to move from their community, perhaps, and would certainly have had to seek new ways of earning a living except for Mr. Gary's casual intervention in deciding to ask them what they wanted.

Why it is normally impossible for steel workers to get their lesser grievances considered by officers in power is considered in another section of this report. The greater grievances, concerning hours and wages, are admittedly outside the province of the Corporation's theoretical committee system. In practice, grievances which drive workers out of the steel industry are effectually stopped from getting higher than the first representative of the company reachable by the workers,—the foreman. Is it not clear, therefore, that the Steel Corporation disposes of the work and livelihood of its 260,000 employees without learning how such disposal really affects them?

The Corporation relies upon other means of information than a system of open and cooperative machinery operating within the mills. Mr. Gary's testimony on this subject is brief: (Senate Testimony, Volume I, Page 177:)

Senator Walsh. "Have you a secret service organization among your employees at any of the subsidiary plants of the Steel Corporation?"

Mr. Gary. "Well, Senator, I cannot be very specific about that, but I am quite sure that at times some of our people have used secret service men to ascertain facts and conditions."

It was not the original intention of the Interchurch Commission to gather evidence on the widespread charges of "company spy systems," "industrial espionage," etc. Steel workers and their spokesmen asserted that such spy systems were the ever-present instruments resulting in an ever-present fear,—some workers called it "terrorization,"—evident among the rank and file of steel workers. For one thing, it would have seemed impossible to get such secret evidence. For another thing, the Commission doubted its importance. But it became apparent that some officials of some steel companies were so accustomed to look upon their secret service reports as the basis on which their, or any company's, labor policy would have to be formed that they showed no hesitancy in producing information about them from their secret files.

The Commission's investigators, asking the officers of a company in the Pittsburgh district for information concerning their machinery for ascertaining their workers' needs, encountered this: "Bring in the labor file." The labor file, this company's basis for a labor policy, consisted of the secret service reports of various detectives and of "labor agencies." Here were hundreds of misspelled reports of "under-cover men," "operatives 'X,' 'Y,' and 'Z,'" contracts for their services, official letters exchanged between companies giving lists of strikers, commonly known as "black lists." In some instances original pencilled scraps of paper contained secret denunciations of workers, which denunciations, raised to the dignity of typed documents, were then circulated to other companies and even to the Federal Department of Justice. The names of independent concerns and of subsidiary companies of the Steel Corporation appear on letterheads showing how this information or misinformation was passed along.

A detailed study of this file and of the spy system is given in another section of this report. It is sufficient to note here that no small part of the labor policy of this company was founded on the inaccurate, prejudiced and usually misspelled reports of professional spies.

In Chicago one labor detective agency had operatives at work during the strike in the South Chicago district, where a subsidiary of the Steel Corporation and independents have plants. This concern was investigated by agents of the War Department, its offices were raided by the State's Attorney and one of its responsible heads was indicted for intent to " kill and murder divers large numbers of persons " and to create riots. A published statement that these operatives had been employed in behalf of the Steel Corporation among others was put before the President of the Illinois Steel Company, the Corporation's big Chicago-Gary subsidiary, who declared it untrue. The statement was put before the head of the raided concern who declared that his operatives were working for the Illinois Steel Co.

The Commission of Inquiry had not expected to ask Mr. Gary whether the head of the United States Steel Corporation made use of such detectives' reports. However, one such report, received by Mr. Gary, was produced by him. This document dealt with the present investigation of the steel strike, the activities of the Interchurch World Movement and its Commission of Inquiry. The same curious illiteracy, characteristic of the labors of these " under-cover men," characterized the " report " on the Commission of Inquiry. Mr. Gary made this document the primary subject of discussion when conferring with a committee of Commissioners whose business with him was nothing less than a plan of mediation designed to end the whole strike.[1]

---

[1] That is, the committee men representing the Interchurch Commission visiting Mr. Gary by appointment were first asked by Mr. Gary's secretary if they had seen the secret document which he handed them. They replied that they had.

Mr. Gary's secretary expressed surprise and he wondered " where it had come from."

A Commissioner noted that " The report is anonymous." The sec-

It is undeniable that labor policies in the steel industry rest in considerable part on the reports of " under-cover men " paid directly by the steel companies or hired from concerns popularly known as " strike busters." The " operatives " make money by detecting " unionism " one day and " Bolshevism " the next. The importance of the espionage system as revealed by this evidence lies in the light it sheds on the atmosphere of war normal to the steel industry, and this atmosphere is due to the dominant policy of preventing organization among the workers, even organization for aboveboard study of the men's conditions of labor and thought. This state of latent warfare is now so customary that the highest company officers can consider it a matter of routine, consonant with their practice and dignity, to examine with judicial solemnity the reports of anonymous spies.

For the country at large, the source of information about conditions in the steel industry and the progress of the strike, was, of course, principally the press. The wide discrepancies between the facts now disclosed and most of the press reports at the time are the subject of exhaustive analysis elsewhere. The findings are that most newspapers, traditionally hesitant in reporting industrial matters, failed notably to acquaint the public with the facts, failed to take steps necessary to ascertain the facts, failed finally to publish adequately what was brought out by the brief investigation of the U. S. Senate committee.[1]

Within the steel communities themselves the facts about the organization of the steel industry are not known. Even in the case of the American workers, the conditions of their

retary agreed that "the copy which they had was also anonymous and they had no idea where it came from."

Then the whole matter of the weighty business in hand had to wait while Mr. Gary read excerpts of the " anonymous " report and cross-examined the Commissioners as to whether the persons named in the report were Bolshevists or I.W.W.'s or some other kind of radical. (The secret report is analyzed elsewhere.)

[1] A notable exception to the general rule was shown by a series of articles during the strike carried by the *New York World*.

jobs, their hours, rates of pay, methods of promotion and attitude to the companies are not common knowledge. Even in normal times it is difficult to get American skilled steel workers to discuss their jobs. These men say when pinned down, "How do I know who you are? Even in the mill I can't talk about conditions. If I talk, I may find myself transferred to a worse job or laid off. I can't afford to talk."

In the case of the "foreigner," the facts lie behind the further screen of physical and mental segregation. The unskilled foreign-language steel workers congregate in communities of their own. In the narrow valleys of the great Pittsburgh and Mahoning Valley districts, they are for the most part crammed into old houses and tenements fringing the great plants. The worker's life is to hurry from his segregated home to the plant and then hurry back and sleep. Not even on street cars is there much communication between the "foreigner" and the ordinary American citizen.

Within these bounds of physical segregation there are twenty or thirty distinct mental worlds, belonging to as many different races. What influences move those worlds is an unanswered question to most good Americans and for the most part an unasked question. To this lack of understanding and sympathy much of our popular distrust of the "foreigners" can be traced. Physically powerful men, with dark or dirty faces, with heavy brows or long mustaches, in whose former home lands strange political events are going on, these men are feared because nothing is known about them. A few years ago East Youngstown, the district's "hunkie" town, was a scene of riot and wholesale burning during a strike. But what caused that strike and what moved those "foreigners" to violent outbreak are still unknown to the good Americans who live on the hill tops.

The employment managers, welfare workers and other mill officials who try to make it their business to know at

least a little something of what is going on in the " foreigner's " head, say frankly that they cannot follow him, they
cannot speak his twenty or thirty languages nor break down
his suspicion of " bosses."

The situation, then, during the strike, and existent now,
is that the fundamental facts about the steel industry and
especially about the masses of unskilled foreign workmen
are not known and that this ignorance breeds a public fear
akin to panic.

*" Bolshevism " :*

The second preliminary phase of the report concerns the
charge, widely current, that the strike was a product of
Bolshevism. The evidence, from steel company officials,
strike committee records, local and national governmental
officers and from observations by the Commission and its investigators is completely adequate for forming a judgment.

A stranger in America reading the newspapers during the
strike and talking with steel masters both in and out of
steel communities must have concluded that the strike represented a serious outbreak of Bolshevism red hot from Russia. The chief memory that American citizens themselves
may have a few years from now may well be that the strike
was largely the work of Reds. *" ' Reds ' back of the Steel
Strike "* was a frequent headline in September. As late as
January 4, 1920, an article in *The New York Times* contained the following:

" Radical leaders planned to develop the recent steel and coal
strike into a general strike and ultimately into a revolution to
overthrow the government, according to information gathered
by federal agents in Friday night's wholesale round-up of members of the Communist parties. These data, officials said, tended
to prove that the nation-wide raids had blasted the most menacing revolutionary plot yet unearthed."

Data on the strike as a Bolshevist manifestation were analyzed with the following questions in mind:

1. Who started this explanation?
2. Why was it offered?
3. Was there Bolshevism in the strike? Was there radicalism?

The allegation was not offered by the strikers nor by the government. It was traced chiefly to two sources: first, the newspapers; and these led to the second and main source, the steel companies.

The following efforts, among others, were made to obtain from officials of the steel companies their evidence.

First, the commission addressed to Mr. Gary, after long discussions with him personally and after considering particularly his statements that men still out were " Bolsheviki," a letter which formally asked him to furnish the evidence on which he based that judgment. The Commission at the time felt confident that Mr. Gary could furnish considerable evidence and that any discussion would turn on whether or not the evidence he produced proved the case. But Mr. Gary produced nothing.

Second, Mr. H. D. Williams, President of the Carnegie Steel Company, the largest subsidiary corporation, when asked for the evidence referred the Commission to " Margolis' testimony before the Senate Committee." When told that the Margolis testimony established no connection between Bolshevism and the leaders of the strike, Mr. Williams expressed surprise. He admitted that he had not read the transcript of the testimony but was sure, however, that the newspapers had said so. Anyway, he said, there were many other things that could be produced to prove the point. Eleven subsequent calls for this evidence were made on Mr. Williams' office but without result.

Third, the Commission's desire for evidence on this point was explained to Mr. E. J. Buffington, President of the Illinois Steel Company, and he was asked for the facts on which he endorsed Mr. Gary's Bolshevist theory of the strike. He expressed wonder at the Commission's inability to find such proofs. He did produce a photograph of a poster, saying, "Look at that." The poster consisted of photographs of strike scenes, showing among other things the dead body of a union organizer, Mrs. Fanny Sellins. This poster was signed by A. F. of L. officials and was headed "Abolish Garyism." When doubt was expressed as to the conclusiveness of this exhibit as proving the Bolshevist origin of the strike, Mr. Buffington was certain that he had seen other "evidence," but he produced none.

Of the many interviewed, no steel company official presented to the Commission any evidence of Bolshevism. In declaring on December 5 that the workmen who "followed the leadership of Fitzpatrick and Foster were Bolsheviki," Mr. Gary insisted to the Commission that the strike aims were "the closed shop, soviets and the forcible distribution of property." Mr. Gary warned the Commissioners to remember that any statement that they might make about the U. S. Steel Corporation and the strike should be "gravely considered" inasmuch as "the foundations of the United States Government were involved."

Mr. Buffington, in supporting Mr. Gary's position, said: "The organizers were all subversive. They said things to make the labor forces want more than fair wages; made 'em want to share the profits."

Mr. Gary was finally asked in the course of one of these discussions if he did not really mean that "labor was getting too strong." To this he gave general assent.

In addition to the efforts above cited, the Commission carefully examined the organization of the strike, and the union literature, listened to speakers, consulted Federal and State officials, and in every way sought to get at the bottom of the Bolshevist theory. The line of inquiry included such questions as: What induced the newspapers in many states in the first week after September 22 to print on their front pages extensive extracts of a pamphlet called " Syndicalism " by Wm. Z. Foster? Why was " radicalism " charged? Were ideas of political radicalism as inextricably mixed with ideas of industrial radicalism in the actual situation as they were in the published charges? Was there industrial radicalism, that is, ulterior strike aims for something beyond orthodox trade union demands on hours, wages, conditions and organization?

The first facts persistently brought up were: Mr. William Z. Foster, Secretary-Treasurer of the National Committee for Organizing Iron and Steel Workers, and his " Red Book," the above mentioned tract on " Syndicalism." The two must be separated. The " Red Book's " actual relation to the strike is undisputed. No copy of the original book, out of print for several years, was found in possession of any striker or strike leader. A reprint, which was a fac-simile in everything except the price mark and the union label, was widely circulated from the middle of September on by officials of the steel companies. The absence of the union label indicated that the reprint was not in behalf of any labor organization. What organization bore this expense of reproducing the book was not investigated. There was no need to investigate who distributed it. Steel company officials openly supplied it to newspapers, to preachers and investigators. In McKeesport, for example, it was mailed to all the pastors in the city who were then summoned to a meeting with the Mayor, attended also by representatives of the Sheriff, the State Constabulary and the Steel Corporation. The representative of the Steel Corporation, who was the Superintendent of the local Corporation plant, came well supplied with "Red Books" and read extracts. In cities like New York and Boston, far from the strike areas, newspapers carried extracts from the book as the principal news of the beginning of the strike. The book's relation to the strike, therefore, was in no sense causative; it was injected as a means of breaking the strike.

Mr. Foster, however, was a causative factor in the strike. 'Attempts to raise the question, "Was Mr. Foster really sincere in recanting Syndicalism," inevitably raised the other question, "Was Mr. Gary really sincere in charging Bolshevism." It seemed best to leave such analysis to speculative psychologists. Instead the test of Mr. Foster's acts was applied to Mr. Foster's mind. In two other sections of the report this analysis is made, based on full examination of the private official records involved and on reports of first hand observers both of the strike and of the organizing campaign. Only the conclusions need be set down here and these are—

That the control of the movement to organize the steel industry, vested in twenty-four A. F. of L. trade unions, was such that Mr. Foster's acts were perforce in harmony with old line unionism.

That Mr. Foster "harmoniously" combated the natural tendency of sections of the rank and file toward industrial unionism.

That a mass movement involving 300,000 workers and twenty-four national unions cannot be controlled to secret, opposite ends.

The organizing plan was the same and was directed by the same two men as that of the stock yards employees in 1918. That campaign was carried through to recognition of the unions without anyone calling it Bolshevism. The plan rejected the opportunity to organize along the line commonly called the One Big Union. From the standpoint of the Industrial Workers of the World and the other One Big Unionists, no group ever had such an opportunity to establish the new kind of organization as did the National Committee for Organizing Iron and Steel Workers. I. W. W.s throughout the campaign spoke with contempt of the Committee's plan of splitting up each batch of union recruits into twenty-four separate craft unions. Despite the fact that most professed industrial revolutionaries " favor " all strikes there is evidence as to their indifference or active opposition to this one. When Mr. Foster's organization was having hard sledding in organizing Youngstown, Ohio, Eugene V. Debs visited the district and began severely criticising the whole plan in public speeches. It was necessary to send a committee to Debs before he could be induced to drop the subject. In the Pittsburgh District, I. W. W.s tried to break the strike a few days after it had been started by circularizing the mills with leaflets declaring that the old A. F. of L. plan would fail and that the A. F. of L. would not support the strike.

As to literature: the official strike pronouncements and leaflets were confined to orthodox texts. Investigators saw one bunch of Communist leaflets but these had been confiscated by strike leaders who had thrown the distributor out of a hall into which he had wormed his way. Mr. Foster refused to allow in an official strike bulletin even the mild advice that laboring men should join a labor party, until the chairman of the National Committee, John Fitzpatrick himself, ordered it put in. One of the leaflets ended with the supposedly poetical quotation: " Forward to bleed and die! " The Committee's translator rendered this into Polish to read, " Forward to wade through blood! " The Polish leaflets were returned by local Polish organizers with this objection,—" My people are all good Catholics. They won't stand for advice like that."

As to national organizers: there were socialists among them but the most were old organization standard bearers of the A. F. of L. Moreover in the Pennsylvania district the meetings were few, police were on the platform and the power of the organizers was greatly lessened. Most organizers were overworked and preoccupied with details. These A. F. of L. veterans could not get over their surprise at being denounced as Bolshevists.

As to local leaders: these generally followed the ideas and methods of the National Committee but were less considerate of A. F. of L. doctrine and more influenced by the feeling of the rank and file. Finding that organization by shops, departments and plants was often the most natural to their inexperienced fellow-workers, they followed that plan even though the result was industrial unionism in miniature. They had no labor reputations to preserve against charges of Bolshevism. They used as assistants the boldest and most energetic spirits and these were frequently readers of the only sort of labor papers customarily circulating among unorganized workers, that is, socialist and I. W. W. papers. The local leaders' talk ran more freely to downright terms and to soaring speculation about " sharing in industrial control." Their sole object was to win the strike. They expected to have " public opinion " against them anyway and so they cared less about exhibiting to the public a conventionally conservative front. They looked to their followers, men speaking thirty different dialects, and did not mind if some of the followers imbibed ambitious ideas about " ending the rule of the bosses." But it took very few repetitions of these ambitions, in broken English, to the mill bosses to spread the fear that the " foreigners " had revolutionary intentions.

The investigators searching for political revolutionaries

among the leaders or even the great rank and file became convinced, from the attitude taken by local, state, federal and army officials, that if such revolutionaries existed the authorities would surely find them.

No leaders of the strike were convicted of " radicalism " in court. Hundreds of strikers were rounded up in " radical raids," but none tried and convicted. In McKeesport in one raid 79 workmen were taken, three were detained and one on final examination was held by the Federal authorities. Federal officers testified that the denunciations which had led to these arrests were made by plant detectives or " under-cover men " of the steel companies, many of them sworn in as sheriff's deputies during the strike. In the Pittsburgh District raids and arrests for Bolshevism were made on the sole complaint of company " under-cover men." Meetings were broken up but most of those arrested were released. The testimony of Federal authorities in two districts in December was that after the raiding and arresting at the instigation of company " under-cover men," no striker had been held by the Federal authorities on any charge of radical agitation in the strike.

In the Gary district in October out of 16,000 strikers, seven immigrants were turned over for deportation by the military officers whose agents had been working in Gary since May, 1919. In February, 1920, these seven had still not been ordered deported. None of these was arrested on charges of radical agitation during the strike but for being members of organizations, such as the I. W. W. and various Russian societies or for professing Communist beliefs. That is, the arrests might have been made, so far as the charges were concerned, at any time irrespective of the strike. In view of the undoubted efforts by various organizations to spread political or industrial revolutionary teachings in America, it seemed probable that some of the workers, if not the leaders, among 300,000 strikers would utilize the strike as a platform for organizing agitation of their views. Despite this, no records of conviction through legal process on charges of such agitation were discovered by investigators. (The charges on which many hundreds of arrests were made are considered elsewhere.)

Were there any radicals in the sense of rebels against their present way of life? The steel industry was full of them. They wanted big changes. But the changes were all related definitely to the right to organize, the twelve-hour day, the seven day week, the foremen's ways, the company's methods, or some other definite thing which they were sick of. It is possible that the workers throughout the whole steel industry might much more easily have been organized on a radical appeal. But the Strike Committee were opposed in principle to any such appeal. After the first three months of the strike when the nerves of strikers and leaders were worn by the struggle, Mr. Foster was constantly complaining of fighting the "radicals," meaning those who wanted to have a general strike called or the whole strike called off in order to be called on again and again and again. But that kind of "radical" still was concerned only with steel matters, not with social or political programs.

The upshot of the matter is this: the methods of organization used in the steel strike were old fashioned and became ostentatiously so as the organizers recognized the radical possibilities of the strike and conscientiously believed that anything other than tried trade unionism would be bad for the steel workers in their newly organized state. The cry of Bolshevism was not only a fraud on the public; it was a dangerous thing because it advertised to the mass of immigrant steel workers, who went down to defeat under old flags and old slogans, an idea and untried methods under which they might be tempted to make another battle. It roused in the minds of hundreds of thousands who know best that they are not Bolsheviki a distrust, which abides, and a suspicion of government agencies and of American public opinion which seemed to lend themselves to a campaign of misrepresentation.

The evidence justifies the following observation of general significance: Not one new development of major importance was discovered in this strike. That is, in the light of industrial history there was nothing in the strike which deserves to be called industrially new, or revolutionary.

It was an old-fashioned strike, preceded by a slightly new mechanical quirk in organizing. It ran on rather unusually old-fashioned lines, especially in comparison with such upheavals as the coal strike, the printers' strike, the clothing strikes of recent years and the recent aims of railroad labor organizations. The steel strike had old style methods and aims, it was attended by the usual futile governmental attempt to avert and futile Senatorial effort to investigate. By the end of the year it was evident that the strikers were getting an old-fashioned licking. There was the usual crippling of industry, threatening to hang over into the months after the strike was called off.

As the strike ended there was in steel master circles the usual after-strike feeling " that something would have to be done." The word was " the Corporation is going to do something." The Corporation in January raised wages 10 per cent. " Independent " small concerns began trying to put in the eight-hour day. The feeling was general that the eight-hour day and collective bargaining could not be staved off forever. Corporation subsidiaries announced more extensive welfare work, company stores, etc. The latter weeks of the strike saw Mr. Gary expressing to public-spirited inquirers his open-minded desire " to consider any well thought out plan which anyone can suggest " for bettering conditions in the steel mills. (Another section of this report considers what soundness there may be in any attitude of looking outside the industry for " any well thought out plan.")

That the whole strike seemed extraordinarily old-fashioned to observers in England is evident from even a hasty examination of such conservative papers as the London *Times* (October 28, 1919):

" The steel workers' strike, which is the rock upon which the Industrial Conference split, turns on the question of recognizing unions, *an issue which has gone into the limbo of almost forgotten things here,* as between employers and employed. . . . The employers in America have evidently something to learn in these matters. They have been apt to compare with some complacency their own relations with labor to those existing in this country and to attribute their comparative immunity from labor troubles to the superior atmosphere of the United States or to their own superior management. It is really due to the simple fact that the Labor Movement in the United States is historically a good many years behind our own. But it will infallibly tread the same broad course with certain differences determined by local conditions, and to resist the inevitable is a great mistake. There are many different elements present in the States, and a far greater tendency to violence is one of them."

Not only the issues but the attendant circumstances of the steel strike seem antique. A hundred cases could be cited. The famous " Dorchester Laborers' case " which happened in 1833, was also a first attempt at organizing common labor, that time on the farm. Farm hands at Tolpuddle, a tiny English village, faced with a cut in wages from 8 shillings to 6 shillings a week went to the magistrate who interpreted to them the noted " law of supply and demand." " We were told," writes their leader, the Methodist lay preacher, Loveless, " that we must work for what our employers saw fit to give as there was no law to compel masters to give a fixed sum." Then the farm hands heard of trade societies in the nearby towns and they were visited by two delegates or " outside agitators," who formed a Friendly Society among them and " instructed them how to proceed." Among the instructions were the directions for a secret oath. The union's constitution read: " That the object of this society can never be promoted by any act of violence, but on the contrary, all such proceedings must tend to injure and destroy the society itself." Within four months, six of the leading members were arrested as " evil disposed persons " and thrown into jail.

Since the law against unionization had been repealed in 1824 it was necessary to discover some other under which these men could be tried. An old statute intended for the suppression of seditious societies was specially invoked and the six persons, after a brief trial, were sentenced to seven years' transportation to Botany Bay, for the crime of having administered an oath.

This law, Daniel O'Connell said, " has only been raked up to inflict an enormous punishment on unfortunate men who were wholly ignorant of its existence and innocent of any moral offence." But the London Times of that age declared that " The real gravamen of their guilt was their forming a dangerous union to force up, by various modes of intimidation and restraint, the rate of laborers' wages." Other spokesmen of public opinion agreed on the need for rigorous action against " that criminal and fearful spirit of combination." A wave of panic swept the country; Lord Howick tried to prove in Parliament that these laborers, who worked all day, knew they were doing wrong for " did they not hold their meetings at night? " The first great procession of industrial protest ever formed in England marched through London to present a petition which the government refused to receive.

In western Pennsylvania in 1919 steel workers were tried

and fined in cases where the major allegation was "smiling at the State police."

In his testimony before the Senate Mr. Gary, discussing the cause of the strike, specifies "intimidation" on pp. 151, 153, 164, 174, 201, et al.

In the course of the strike deputations of workers sought the government with petitions. Attorney General Palmer, they considered, gave them the government's only answer in his letter, published on November 26, commending a patriotic society's efforts to run labor "agitators" out of Pennsylvania. "It is a pity," the Attorney General wrote, "that more patriotic organizations do not take action similar to that of your order."

Altogether, analysis of all data seems to make it more profitable to consider the steel strike of 1919 in the light of one hundred years' industrial history than in the glare of baseless excitement over Bolshevism.

# III

## THE TWELVE-HOUR DAY IN A NO-CONFERENCE INDUSTRY

ANALYSIS of the data gathered in this inquiry proves that a prime fact in the organization of the steel industry and a prime fact in explaining the strike may be formulated as follows:

Approximately half of the employees in iron and steel manufacturing plants are subjected to the schedule known as the twelve-hour day (that is a working day from 11 to 14 hours long).

Less than one-quarter of the industry's employees can work under 60 hours a week " although in most industries 60 hours was regarded as the maximum working week " [1] ten years ago.

In the past decade the U. S. Steel Corporation has increased the percentage of its employees subject to the twelve-hour day.

The mass of unskilled and semi-skilled workmen, mostly " foreigners," in the twelve-hour day class were the backbone of the strike.

The relation of a prevailing schedule of excessive hours to the facts that no means of conference affecting hours and wages, or collective bargaining exist in the plants of the Steel Corporation, and that the Corporation's workmen hitherto

---

[1] " Conditions of Employment in Iron and Steel Industry," Senate Document 110, Vol. I, p. xlii (1910). At that time 14.39 per cent. of all steel employees worked less than 60 hours.

were unorganized, is analyzed in Section V of this Report, on "Control in a No-Conference Industry."

What is true of the Corporation's hours and wages is mainly true of the industry of which it constitutes the dominating half.

Consideration of hours is inseparable from wages; the next section determines what proportion of the twelve-hour day men fall in the following class:

The high percentage of steel workers whose earnings, despite their long hours, fall from 5 to 25 per cent. *below* the lowest level which Government experts have been willing to call an "American standard of living" for an average family.

It must be clearly noted that the twelve-hour day schedules are compulsory. The Steel Corporation's "basic eight-hour day" is a method of paying wages and in no way concerns hours. The twelve-hour day workman cannot knock off at the end of eight hours, if he wants to retain his employment. Neither can he escape the eighteen-hour or twenty-four hour "turn," usually every fortnight, which goes with most of the twelve-hour day schedules. He can "take it or leave it" but he cannot bargain over his job's hours.

The present analysis deals with the length of hours in the industry and the nature of the long-day jobs; whether the hours are necessary; what excuses for such schedules are made by the Corporation; what validity attaches to these excuses; what amount of seven-day work persists; and what the twelve-hour day means to the worker and to the community.

Data considered were drawn from the U. S. Steel Corporation, "independent" concerns, Federal bureau reports, diaries by steel workers before the strike, records of independent investigators, the testimony before the Senate strike investigating committee, hearings before this Commission and interviews with hundreds of strikers and non-strikers.

Literature on the subject of the steel industry's hours, especially on the twelve-hour day enforced by the U. S. Steel Corporation, has accumulated since 1907; each year of these records is punctuated with plans, promises or expectations that the Corporation was about to abolish such hours. Ten years ago the practice was referred to as " notorious "; the literature includes sardonic references even by steel masters. For example, W. B. Dickson, Chairman and Vice President of the Cambria-Midvale Co., and former director of the U. S. Steel Corporation, in an address in 1919 to a scientific body, spoke of the spectacle of Mr. Gary as chairman of a committee to relieve unemployment (in 1916 in New York), when the " large proportion of his men were working twelve hours a day and are still doing so."

General conclusions to be drawn from this literature are,—

> that the development of large-scale production enterprises under absentee financial control tends inevitably to sacrifice the labor force in favor of utilizing, to the maximum, the costly machines; that is, trust management lengthens hours, unless combated by—
> (a) public opinion (generally, in legislation), or
> (b) organization of the workmen (generally, in unions) :—
> that in the steel industry the Corporation, by resisting public opinion and by preventing organization among its workmen, tends persistently to lengthen the hours of labor.

Examination of government statistics assembled in this Inquiry proves that hours in the steel industry have actually lengthened since 1910 and that now over 400,000 steel workers, or a population of about two million men, women and children are more or less directly affected by this unrestricted tendency toward lengthened hours.

In the following discussion, therefore, the frequent quotation of Mr. Gary—necessary because he was almost the sole spokesman of the industry during the strike and is the only authorized source of statistics for the Steel Corporation—must not be misinterpreted to imply that Mr. Gary could be personally and solely responsible for the labor hours of which he testifies. Industrial history would seem to indicate that despite the " good deal of authority and power " which Mr. Gary [1] says he possesses, the effectiveness of personal wills, *once they have committed an industry to a labor policy such as the Corporation's,* greatly diminishes, as regards hours and several other matters.

However, the Corporation ended the strike without making any promises on the twelve-hour day and the Corporation's statements on " eliminating " the seven-day week were found to be inaccurate.

The term " twelve-hour day " is precise only where the day's work at the blast furnace, open hearth and other more or less continuous processes, is actually divided into two shifts of twelve hours each. But in many plants it is divided into an 11-hour day shift and a 13-hour night shift, or a 10-hour day and 14-hour night. Usually the shifts alternate weekly and men must work the " long turn " of 18 hours or 24 hours, —a solid day at " heavy " labor. In some plants the 36-hour turn is still not unknown. (The 7-day week of 12-hour turns will be considered later.)

Consideration of the number on the 12-hour day may begin with Mr. Gary's figure of 69,000 ; and might stop there since this means that the daily hours and lives of over 350,000 men, women and children are directly dominated and " arbi-

[1] Senate Testimony, Vol. I, p. 216.

trarily "[1] ordered by the Corporation's 12-hour day. The total, however, assignable to this class seems to be larger.

Mr. Gary testified (Senate Testimony, Vol. I, p. 157):

"Twenty-six and a half per cent. of all employees work the twelve-hour turn and the number is 69,284."

"All employees," however, includes nearly 80,000 of the Corporation's metal miners, coal miners, railroaders, ship crews, dockers, etc., not concerned in the strike or in the 12-hour day. Mr. Gary furnished data to the Commission, however, enabling correction of the misleading "twenty-six and a half per cent."; the total of all Corporation employees in "the manufacturing plants," that is, in the strike areas, is 191,000. Mr. Gary's "69,284" is 36 per cent. of 191,000. The 36 per cent. of men working 12 hours or over fails to account for a large number working 11 hours or even 10 hours, and, on alternate weeks, 13- and 14-hour turns; that is, a large number properly to be classed as 12-hour men. The only attempt at exact analysis of hours furnished by a Corporation plant to the Senate Investigating Committee was the following given by Superintendent Oursler of the typical Homestead works (Senate Testimony, Vol. II, p. 482):

"21.2 per cent. working eight hours; 25.9 per cent. working ten hours; 16.4 per cent. working eleven hours; 36 per cent. working twelve hours."

The "16.4 per cent. working 11 hours" is made up of day shift "12-hour men" whose hours on night turn will be 13;[2] that is, a proper classification is 36 per cent. plus 16.4 per cent. or 52.4 per cent. on the 12-hour turn at Homestead.

---

[1] "Arbitrarily" controlled is Mr. Gary's term in relation to fixing wages. Senate Testimony, Vol. I, p. 226; it also applies to hours.

[2] Mr. Gary's explanation, letter of Feb. 13: "16 per cent. of the total employees at Homestead work 11-hour and 13-hour turns alternately weekly." See next footnote, quoting letters.

This does not equal the verbal estimate of the President of the Carnegie Co. (of which the Homestead works is a part), made to the Commission of Inquiry in November, 1919, whose estimate was 60 per cent. of his 55,000 employees on the 12-hour turn.

Moreover the Homestead figures seem to be compiled on the same method of classification as Mr. Gary's for the total of the Corporation's manufacturing plants: the Homestead 36 per cent. agrees exactly with Mr. Gary's 36 per cent.; the Homestead 21.2 per cent. on " the 8-hour day " agrees with Mr. Gary's 22 per cent. on " the 8-hour day," as furnished to the Commission. The proper classification, indicated for the Corporation's manufacturing plants, is thus 52.4 per cent. on " the 12-hour " turns.

Hours in the " independent " plants comprising the other half of the industry are approximately the same as the Corporation's (with a few notable exceptions such as the Pueblo works of the Colorado Fuel and Iron Co., which are on a three-shift 8-hour basis, and Pacific Coast plants which are on an 8-hour basis). The only exact figures obtained for an " independent " plant were for a department in the Youngstown Sheet and Tube as follows:

On 8 hours................ 10 per cent.
On 10 hours................ 35 per cent.
On 12 hours................ 55 per cent.

The Corporation's figures which were submitted by Mr. Gary as estimates, not as exact tabulations[1] (admittedly diffi-

---

[1] The Steel Corporation's lack of knowledge of how its decrees affect its workmen extends to its statistics of hours. Mr. Gary's letters to this Commission, again and again replying that "we have no compiled statistics " showing the exact data requested, indicate that the task of determining precisely the trend of steel hours is left to outside agencies, such as the U. S. Bureau of Labor Statistics. Even the apparently absolutely precise figures supplied by the Homestead Superintendent, cited above, fail to total up precisely 100 per cent. Mr. Gary's explanation of Mr. Oursler's testimony, in a letter to this Commission dated Feb. 13,

cult to compile owing to the widely differing methods of time-keeping in the Corporation's 300 plants) are borne out by more comprehensive statistics from more impartial sources. The chief of these sources is the U. S. Bureau of Labor Statistics whose figures are taken from the company pay rolls of representative plants all over the country.

Government statistics are reckoned on the basis of hours per week; roughly interpreted these mean that hours averaging 70 to 72 weekly mean 6 days of 12 hours each; hours averaging 80 to 84 weekly mean 7 days of 12 hours each; this is irrespective of how the shifts are actually divided in various plants, of 12, 11, 10½ or 10 hours, alternating weekly with 12, 13, 13½ or 14 hours. Taking the statistics for the center of the industry, the Pittsburgh District, by departments of plants, for the last quarter of 1918 and the first quarter of 1919, as compiled by the Bureau of Labor Statistics (October, 1919, Monthly Review), we have for the largest department in the industry:

1920, contains the following interesting comment: "The percentage Mr. Oursler quoted of 16 per cent. for employees working 11 hours is correct although his statement, to be exactly right, should have read '16 per cent. of the total employees at Homestead work 11-hour and 13-hour turns alternating weekly.'" So far so good, but Mr. Gary went on: "The percentage given of 36 per cent. is not correct if the percentage was intended to indicate those who work straight 12-hour turns. The number of these straight 12-hour turn men is 26 per cent. of the total. Thus at Homestead 26 per cent. of the total men work straight 12-hour turns, 16 per cent. 11 and 13-hour turns, alternating as explained and the balance of the men work 10 hours or less."

Now, statistically analyzed, Mr. Gary's letter comes to this: Supplying his "26 per cent." of "straight 12-hour men" (whatever that may mean) for Mr. Oursler's 36 per cent. and totaling all up gives only 89.5 per cent. and fails to account for the remaining 10.5 per cent. at Homestead. His letter indicates plainly that the two classifications should be lumped, that is, 16 per cent. plus "26 per cent.," or 42 per cent.; the remaining 10 per cent., of course, is in Mr. Oursler's figures, making 52.4 per cent. as the true total of 12-hour men.

Mr. Gary's letter of Jan. 30 to the Commission contains estimates even harder to reconcile with his other estimates. This letter gives the "standard daily service or turn" as "for about 70,000—10 hours; for about 68,000—11, 12, 13 hours." This attempts to lump the 13-hour men under the 68,000 but Mr. Gary gave the Senate Committee (Vol. II, p. 157) "69,284" on "the 12-hour turn," with no mention of the

Stockers, 83.6; larrymen, 82.6; larrymen's helpers, 82.3; skip operators, 81.6; blowers, 81.7; blowing engineers, 81.7; keepers, 81.9; keepers' helpers, 81.8; pig machine men, 83; cindermen, 81.8; laborers, 82. Average, 82.1.

That is, the whole department, the largest in the industry is on the 12-hour basis, 7 days a week, a mathematical average for all workers in the department being 11.7 hours daily.

Open hearth furnaces, the next largest producing department, hours per week by occupations are:

Stockers, 78.8; stock cranemen, 76.6; charging machine men, 76.8; melters' helpers, first, 78.9; melters' helpers, second, 76.1; melters' helpers, third, 76; stopper setters, 75.8; steel pourers, 75.7; mold cappers, 77; ladle cranemen, 76.1; ingot strippers, 70.5; laborers, 78.5. Average, 76.4.

That is, with one exception, all occupations are above 72 hours, or the 12-hour day, on a 6-day week basis, and the

thousands of 12-hour men whose hours on alternate weeks are *14;* that is, 10 hours by day for one week, and 14 hours by night for the next week. It would be a highly misleading classification to lump under the 10-hour class, for example, 15,000 men actually working 10 hours one week but subject to 14 hours the next.

At the same time that Mr. Gary was writing to the Commission, he made the following admission, as quoted in the statement made by Dr. Devine of the Federal Council of Churches to the presidents of the Corporation's plants: "the proportion (of 12-hour men) would be 50 or 60 per cent. Judge Gary said that this might be correct."

The Corporation's entire statistical reckonings, as furnished to the public, are on the wrong basis. The hundreds of different kinds of steel jobs vary so in hours-requirements that, *for its own benefit,* the Corporation can get accurate estimates only by dropping the vague "alternating turns" classification and by adopting the long-established government bureau classification of "hours per week." The government's "72 hours per week," for example, plainly indicates 6 daily 12-hour "turns" whether the turns are actually divided into 12 and 12, 11 and 13, 10 and 14, or any other shifts; likewise "82 or 84 hours weekly" indicates the 7-day week of 12-hour turns, no matter how divided. As against this system the total "69,284" on "the 12-hour turn" sounds very exact but means little without additional information as to (a) the length of the period for which the figure is given; (b) the number outside this 69,284 working 10 or 11 hours but subject bi-weekly to 13 and 14.

78.5 weekly hour average of laborers (who constitute 46 per cent. of the whole) is nearer the 12-hour day, *7-day week* average.

Take the same departments, from the latest figures for 1919 in the Bureau of Labor Statistics, giving the numbers employed instead of percentages and affording comparison of other districts with the Pittsburgh District.

## HOURS

*Blast Furnaces*

| No. establishments | No. of employees | Average full time hours | Schedule of 12-hour day | | | | | | | | |
|---|---|---|---|---|---|---|---|---|---|---|---|
| | | | 56 | 60 | 60-66 | 66-72 | 72 | 72-78 | 78 | 78-84 | 84 |
| 24 | 6315 | 78.8 | 456 | 178 | 29 | 364 | 483 | 38 | 702 | 16 | 4049 |

All under 72 hours per week are from Great Lakes and Middle West and Southern Districts (except one laborer at 60 hours, and 41 laborers at 66-72 hours, in Pittsburgh District). With this exception, Pittsburgh blast furnace workers are all twelve-hour day and three-quarters are seven-day week.

*Open Hearth Furnaces*

| No. establishments | No. of employees | Average full time hours | Schedule of 12-hour day | | | | | | | | |
|---|---|---|---|---|---|---|---|---|---|---|---|
| | | | 56 | 60 | 60-66 | 66 | 66-72 | 72 | 73-78 | 78 | 84 |
| 19 | 4702 | 73.8 | 751 | 80 | 10 | 38 | 39 | 1010 | 24 | 1913 | 337 |

In this table the only men 60 hours or under, *in the Pittsburgh District,* are five ingot strippers at 56 and one laborer at 60. Practically everything 60 and under is Great Lakes and Middle West and Pacific Coast Districts (which include a number of three-shift, eight-hour day plants).

The only available late figures for a rolling mill department exhibit 78 per cent. of the employees on the 12-hour
day, almost altogether with the 6-day week.

*Rail Mills*

| No. estab-lishments | No. of employees | Hours | | | | |
|---|---|---|---|---|---|---|
| | | 48 | 50-60 | 60 | 72 | 84 |
| 5 | 1170 | 237 | 3 | 18 | 900 | 12 |

None under 60 in the Pittsburgh District. All 60-hour and
84-hour men were laborers in this district. The 48-hour men
were from one mill in the Great Lakes and Middle West District.

What do these figures for principal departments mean in
relation to the Corporation's statistics (keeping in mind that
half the industry is in the Pittsburgh District and that the
influence of Corporation practice is less hampered in this
District)?  They mean altogether—

> that the large continuous-process producing depart-
> ments,—the pace setters of the industry—were being
> run largely on a 12-hour day basis and largely 7 days
> a week;

> that the resultant hours approximated 12 hours daily
> for about half the employees;

> that to these must be added about a quarter more, mak-
> ing three-quarters of all employees whose hours per week
> were 60 *or over,* that is, beyond the generally accepted
> maximum for most other industries.

These long hours appeared, in the course of the Commission's inquiry, to have a more causative bearing on the strike than " Bolshevism." Of the hundreds of strikers and non-strikers interviewed in this inquiry, few could put together two sentences on " soviets " but almost all discoursed or, more accurately, cursed " long hours."

Comparisons of wider-sweeping government statistics, also based on company pay-rolls, only confirm conclusions. The average of hours for the entire industry, including great numbers of foundries and fabricating plants whose hours average less than those of the plants against which the strike was aimed, was 68.7 hours per week or over 11⅖ hours per day on a 6-day mathematical average. (U. S. Bureau of Labor Statistics. Monthly Review, Sept., 1919.)

Ten years ago the Labor Commissioner, at the order of Congress, made the exhaustive survey of the industry (Senate Document 110, four vols.) which formed the standard on which to make comparisons. In May, 1910, the percentage of employees working 72 hours and over per week, i.e. at least 12 hours a day, was 42.58 per cent. (*ibid.,* Vol. I, p. xlii). How much the 1919 percentages of 12-hour men may have increased over that 42 per cent. cannot be exactly determined. The average of weekly hours for the industry in 1910 was 67.6; for 1919 it was 1.1 hours higher. The average weekly hours for the Pittsburgh District in 1910 and 1919 for three departments for which 1919 statistics were available were:

| Year | Blast Furnaces | Open Hearth | Plate Mills |
|------|----------------|-------------|-------------|
| 1910 | 78.7 | 75.3 | 67.3 |
| 1919 | 82.1 | 76.4 | 71.1 |

These increases were from 1 to nearly 4 hours weekly. They are insufficient to prove, but they do suggest, that if the government had ordered another exhaustive survey of the iron and steel industry in the months immediately preceding the strike, it would have found conditions materially worse than they were in 1910 when strikes due to lengthening hours started the government survey.

The requirements of the war, which permitted the steel companies free rein as regards hours, ceased with the armistice and according to steel company officials war conditions were largely eliminated [1] in the spring of 1919. By the summer of 1919 then there could be no legitimate excuse for war conditions; yet it was in the months of July, August and early September, 1919, that the steel industry was speeded up in every direction; and for these critical months the government statistical bureaus have published no figures.

These, then, were the steel hours constituting one of the " relics of barbarism " referred to by an official of a steel company, who told an independent investigator [2] that his sympathies in the strike were " entirely with Judge Gary " but whose stand on hours was set forth in a letter as follows:

" At the greatest personal sacrifice, both in friendship and in money, for the past twenty-five years I have waged unceasing warfare against the Steel Corporation on the question of the seven-day week, the twelve-hour day and the autocratic methods of dealing with workmen."

These were the hours which must be compared with hours in other industries of the country. The steel workers' 68.7 hours a week must be compared with the street railwaymen's 56.4 in another " continuous industry " and the nearest competitor to steel hours in the list of principal industries compiled by the Bureau of Applied Economics, Washington, D. C.; [3] with the anthracite coal miners' 52-hour weekly

[1] "With the close of the war . . . the 7-day service has been largely eliminated. At the present time there is comparatively little of it." Letter of Mr. Gary to Commission, Jan. 30, 1920.
[2] R. S. Baker in N. Y. Evening Post, Dec. 31, 1919.
[3] See Sub-Report for charts and details.

schedule and the bituminous coal miners' 52.9-hour weekly schedule; with the standard 48 hours weekly of the United States Arsenals, the United States Navy Yards, the railroad shop men, railroad freight firemen, the ship yards; comparison is impossible with the 44 hours weekly of the building trades, the 30 hours average for passenger firemen on the railroads.

These were the hours which must be compared with steel hours in England [1] where the twelve-hour day had largely disappeared before 1914 and where the elimination of the twelve-hour day was directly retarded by the competition of the American plants' longer schedules.

These were the hours which must be compared with what government sanction and public opinion had for manys years considered a standard work week,—48 hours; the steel week averaged more than 20 hours longer. For thousands of steel workers the " normal " work week was nearly twice as long as the 44-hour standard customary in many industries.

These were the hours for 1919 which must be compared with the industry's own hours for 1914 and 1910. Five years ago the steel week was 2.4 hours shorter; 10 years ago 1.1 hours shorter. Steel hours have lengthened in a decade when other industries were shortening hours. This in spite of Mr. Gary's statement before the Senate Committee: " The Chairman of the Committee will bear in mind that we have been reducing these hours from year to year, going back many years, as rapidly as we could " (Senate Testimony, Vol. I, p. 202). The emphasis of the analyst must be laid on the " as we could." Industrial history, as noted before, indicates that hours inevitably tend to lengthen under absentee corporation control, unless restricted by public opinion or by labor organization. Competition, foreign markets, " the

[1] General average of steel hours in England, July, 1919, 47-48 hours weekly.

war," each in turn, is an actual cause for lengthening hours, or an excuse for it long after the cause is gone. Personal will alone,—or " as we could,"—simply has not worked reform. Whoever ought to do the reforming, it is a matter of record that in England the abolition of the twelve-hour schedule was initiated and pressed by trade unions. So far as the twelve-hour day can be laid to choice, the responsibility is flatly put by " independent " steel companies on the Steel Corporation.

The twelve-hour day is not a metallurgical necessity; steel masters are not caught in the grip of their gigantic machinery. Thirty years ago train wrecks burned up a lot of passengers because of the " deadly car stove "; and the solidest, most responsible railroad presidents assured the legislatures that coal stoves were an unescapable necessity, that cars could not be heated by steam from the engine. Do steel masters fail to end the twelve-hour day because they cannot? The fact that the eight-hour day has replaced the twelve-hour day in England, on the Pacific Coast, in the Pueblo plant of the Colorado Fuel and Iron Co., and in some " independent " plants near Chicago and Pittsburgh, proves that it is not a matter of necessity. Metallurgists agree that production is better,—by a small percentage, but better,—on the three-shift eight-hour day. Steel engineers do not dispute that three shifts mean more steel and better steel. Only one process is absolutely " continuous," requiring, on the eight-hour basis, three shifts. The final findings of the 1910 survey of the industry, which are true today, read (Senate Document 110, Vol. I, p. lxii) :

" The blast-furnace department is the only one of the fourteen departments where there is any metallurgical necessity for continuous operation day and night throughout seven days per week. . . . Throughout the iron and steel industry . . . the employees were expected to work seven days wherever the de-

partment in which they were working was running seven days
and the occupation in which they were engaged required continuous work. . . .

"The large proportion of Bessemer converters, open hearth
furnaces and rolling mills *working seven days* or turns was due
to the fact that these departments were in continuous operation
in some plants, although no real necessity for this condition existed, only a desire to increase the output of the plant."

Only two excuses were offered to the Commission for the
twelve-hour day: labor shortage and workmen's preference.
On analysis we shall see that both are baseless and that the
true causes concern much more the helplessness of disorgan-
ized immigrant labor. First, it is advisable to analyze steel
production sufficiently to understand the kinds of jobs these
are which must be followed twelve hours a day.

It is an epigram of the industry that "steel is a man
killer." Steel workers are chiefly attendants of gigantic
machines. The steel business tends to become, in the owners'
eyes, mainly the machines. Steel jobs are not easily characterized by chilly scientific terms. Blast furnaces over a
hundred feet high, blast "stoves" a hundred feet high, coke
ovens miles long, volcanic bessemer converters, furnaces with
hundreds of tons of molten steel in their bellies, trains of hot
blooms, miles of rolls end to end hurtling white hot rails
along,—these masters are attended by sweating servants
whose job is to get close enough to work but to keep clear
enough to save limb and life. It is concededly not an ideal
industry for men fatigued by long hours.

To comprehend precisely what the twelve-hour day meant,
the Inquiry gathered data from steel mill officials and from
the workers themselves. Mr. Gary's testimony was:

"It is not an admitted fact that more than eight hours is
too much for a man to labor per day. . . . I had my own ex-

perience in that regard (on a farm) ; and all our officers worked up from the ranks. They came up from day laborers. They were all perfectly satisfied with their time of service; they all desired to work longer hours . . . the employees generally do not want eight hours. . . . I do not want you to think that for a moment." (Senate Testimony, Vol. I, p. 180.)

Mr. H. D. Williams, president of the Carnegie Steel Company, said that he had worked fourteen hours a day and did not feel he was any the worse for it.

Mr. W. B. Schiller, president of the National Tube Company, said that he had worked the twelve-hour day when young and that it never did him any harm.

Mr. E. J. Buffington, president of the Illinois Steel Company, said that he had worked the twelve-hour day when a young man and he rather thought it did him good.

This official attitude is important despite the fact that it is the testimony of experience undergone twenty-five to forty years before, the severity of early work being tempered and mellowed in recollection by decades in comfortable office chairs. Corporation officials do regard the twelve-hour day as a young man's " experience," to be left early. For the workers who do not rise to be a steel corporation's subsidiary president but who are held for years to the twelve-hour day a phrase has been coined which is well understood by them: " Old age at forty." Especially they understood it when a corporation plant made the rule of hiring no man over forty years of age.

First, what exactly is the schedule of the twelve-hour worker ? Here is the transcript of the diary of an American worker, the observations of a keen man on how his fellows regard the job, the exact record of his own job and hours made in the spring of 1919, before the strike or this Inquiry, and selected here because no charge of exaggeration could be made concerning it. It begins:

" Calendar of one day from the life of a Carnegie steel work-man at Homestead on the open hearth, common labor:

" 5:30 to 12 (midnight)—Six and one-half hours of shovel-ing, throwing and carrying bricks and cinder out of bottom of old furnace. Very hot.

" 12:30—Back to the shovel and cinder, within few feet of pneumatic shovel drilling slag, for three and one-half hours.

" 4 o'clock—Sleeping is pretty general, including boss.

" 5 o'clock—Everybody quits, sleeps, sings, swears, sighs for 6 o'clock.

" 6 o'clock—Start home.

" 6:45 o'clock—Bathed, breakfast.

" 7:45 o'clock—Asleep.

" 4 P. M.—Wake up, put on dirty clothes, go to boarding house, eat supper, get pack of lunch.

" 5:30 P. M.—Report for work."

This is the record of the night shift; a record of inevitable waste, inefficiency and protest against " arbitrary " hours. Next week this laborer will work the day shift. What is his schedule per week? Quoting again from the diary:

" Hours on night shift begin at 5:30; work for twelve hours through the night except Saturday, when it is seventeen hours, until 12 Sunday noon, with one hour out for breakfast; the fol-lowing Monday ten hours; total from 5:30 Monday to 5:30 Monday 87 *hours, the normal week.*

" The Carnegie Steel worker works 87 hours out of the 168 hours in the week. Of the remaining 81 he sleeps seven hours per day; total of 49 hours. He eats in another fourteen; walks or travels in the street car four hours; dresses, shaves, tends furnace, undresses, etc., seven hours. His one reaction is ' What the Hell!'—the universal text accompanying the twelve-hour day."

What kinds of job are these twelve-hour turns? Here are the observations of his own successive jobs by a second worker, also an American, also written before the strike

began, in the summer of 1919 in an " independent " plant in
the Pittsburgh district.   (Both these workers were distinctly
critical of labor organizers.)

*" Job of labor in the clean-up gang in pit of open hearth*
*furnaces:*
" The pit is the half-open space where furnaces are tapped
into ladles (pocket shaped, ten feet high, swung by overhead
cranes) and ' poured ' into ingot molds.   As the hot metal comes
from the tap-hole much spills and when partially cool must
be broken with picks and cleaned out, and ' slag ' and ' scrap '
separated into different cars.

" The job is: clean up cinder when ladle is dumped; break
clay covers from valve pipes, pile pipes at side of pit, repile
pipes on flat car.   After pipes have been moved to blacksmith,
affix chains for swinging them to blacksmith's door, repile in
shop.   Get straightened pipes back to pit by same series of
steps; same going and returning for broken chains.   Affix hooks
to ladles when crane shoves ladle in your face.   Clean out all
hot cinder and scrap under all furnaces, take cinder by hand
or barrel to cinder boxes.   Clean hot overflow metal or slag
from tracks.   Very hot work.   Tools used, pick, shovel, fork,
crowbar, sledge-hammer, chains, barrel.   Heavy work, but considered here as one of the ' easier jobs.'   Hours: 14 hours on
night turn, 10 hours on day turn; long turn of 24 hours every
two weeks.

*" Job of third-helper, open hearth furnace:*
" With other helpers he makes ' back wall,' which means
throwing heavy dolomite with a shovel across blazing furnaces
to the back wall, to protect it for the next bath of hot steel.
Every third-helper makes the back wall on his own furnace
and on his neighbor's, sometimes making three or four a shift.
You march past the door of the furnace, which is opened in your
face for a moment.   Heat about 180° at the distance from which
the shovelful is thrown in; each shoveler wears smoked goggles and protects his face with his arm as he throws.   After a
back wall it is necessary to rest at least 15 minutes.

"Second and first helpers work 'hook and spoon' to spread dolomite for the front wall. Very easy for a new man to get badly burned in approaching furnace to fill his spoon.

"When front wall and back wall are both made there is usually a long 'spell' unless the adjoining furnace needs attention. A man may have four or five hours to himself out of the fourteen-hour shift or he may work hard the whole turn. *He may have two or three such easy days or he may have a week of the most continuous and exhausting kind.*

"After making the front and back walls the third-helper wheels mud to the tap-hole for lining on the spout; it takes 40 minutes to one hour; temperature around spout about 110°.

"Scrap, in chunks from small bits to thousand-pound blocks, fall from charging boxes when furnace is being charged and must be cleaned up by second and third-helpers.

"The third-helper fills ·large bags with coal to throw into the ladle at tap time; easy to burn your face off.

"Helps drill a 'bad' hole at tap time, work of the most exhausting kind; also must shovel dolomite into ladle of molten steel. This is the hottest job and certainly the most exposed to minor burns. Temperatures around 180°, but it takes only four or five minutes. Nearly every tap time leaves three or four small burns on neck, face, hands or legs. It is usually necessary to extinguish little fires in your clothing. Altogether not so bad as heavier lifting parts of the furnace job which are most hateful, together with the monotonous exposures.

"*On the blast furnaces. Job of the stove gang:*

"Six to ten men in a gang keep the blast furnace stoves cleaned (a stove is an oven for heating the blast and is as big as the blast furnace itself, full of a gigantic brick checker work); as stove cools, gang cleans out hardened cinder in combustion chamber with pick and shovel. Men go inside the stove. Ten minutes to one hour is the length of time inside, according to degree to which the stove has been allowed to cool. Before going in the man puts on wooden sandals, a jacket which fits the neck closely and heavy cap with ear flaps; also goggles.

Cleaning out the flue dust not so hot, but men breathe dust-saturated air.

" Hardest job is ' poking her out,' ramming out the flue dust in checker work at top of stove. Large pieces of canvas tied over feet and legs to keep heat from coming up the legs; two pairs of gloves needed; handkerchiefs cover all head except the eyes. Three minutes to ten minutes at a turn are the limit for work in the chamber at top of stove; very hard to breathe. Average man can do four holes each trip.

" *Easy days with couple of hours' sleep are sandwiched in between hard ones, after which the men leave the mill exhausted. Hours: 12 hours a day.*

" *Job of stove-tender helper:*

" Learners' job following stove tender; manipulates large, clumsy valves; operations, if performed in wrong order, stove tender will break his stove and kill himself. Unless tremendous pressure is first ' blown off ' the opening of another valve will blow the opener into bits. Hours: day shift, 10 hours; night, 13 hours."

These workers' records were made before the strike began and are open to no possible charge of bias. They record in exact form what many " hunkies " tried to tell investigators. As actual experience—as opposed to theory—they may be contrasted with this excerpt from Mr. Gary's testimony before the Senators (Senate Testimony, Vol. I, p. 160):

Mr. Gary. " Nowadays none of these men, with very few exceptions, perform manual labor as I used to perform it, on the farm, neither in hours, nor in actual physical exertion. It is practically all done everywhere by machinery and the boy who opens the door I think touches a button and opens the door. And this work of adjusting the heavy iron ingots is done by the pulling of a lever. It is largely machinery, almost altogether machinery. That is not saying there is no work in that, because of course there is, and I would not belittle it, of course.

It is hard work to work hard whatever one does, and to the extent one does work hard he, of course, is doing hard work."

Mr. Gary submitted to the Senate Committee "photographs of open hearth laborers at leisure" and asserted that they worked but half the time. This hardly accords with the open hearth laborer himself who worked that twelve-hour day every day in the week and whose daily job includes such as the following, and this is described as "not the worst of his daily grind" (from Carnegie Steel worker's diary):

"You lift a large sack of coal to your shoulders, run towards the white hot steel in a 100-ton ladle, must get close enough without burning your face off to hurl the sack, using every ounce of strength, into the ladle and run, as flames leap to roof and the heat blasts everything to the roof. Then you rush out to the ladle and madly shovel manganese into it, as hot a job as can be imagined."

Nor are the above at all the extreme hours of the plant. In the millwright department of the Carnegie Steel Company everyone in the department works fourteen working days out of every fourteen calendar days, on the thirteen-hour night turn, including the twenty-four-hour turn within the fourteen days. Here is the actual schedule of the above quoted worker when employed in the millwright department of the Carnegie Steel Company last spring:

"Five nights at 13 hours, regularly............... 65 hours
Saturday night, regular..................... 15 hours
Sunday double turn, regular every other week.... 24 hours
                                                 ———
    Total .................................... 104 hours

"Add to this half an hour each night for dinner means three hours more, or 107 hours under the plant roof in the 168 hours in the week."

That conditions in Corporation plants are not worse than in " independents " is shown by this from the records of an investigator for the Commission (Youngstown, Oct. 27, 1919):

" Timekeeper in the sheet mill department of a large ' independent' stated: that among the men whose time he kept there were about 45 rollers who worked eight hours, 110 laborers who worked ten hours and 190 who were on the twelve-hour basis, seven days a week. They changed every week from day to night turn, making a 24-hour shift. These latter included electricians, mill hands, engineers, pipefitters, cranemen, loaders, loader-helpers, and gasmen. In the sheet galvanizing department the men worked a twelve-hour day with no rest spells and no lunch hour. Their rates were 42, 42½, and 44 cents. So many men gave out under the strain and had to be fired for not being able to do the work that checks for these men gave out in the time department, and the timekeeper begged the foreman not to discharge so many. There were about 100 men in the department, and from 35 to 50 were hired and fired each month."

None can dispute the demoralizing effects on family life and community life of the inhuman twelve-hour day. As a matter of arithmetic twelve-hour day workers, even if the jobs were as leisurely as Mr. Gary says they are, have absolutely no time for family, for town, for church or for self-schooling, for any of the activities that begin to make full citizenship; they have not the time, let alone the energy, even for recreation.

At Johnstown a member of the Commission was approached by a man of middle age who said that he was determined never to go back to work until the question of hours was settled. He gave as his reason the fact that his little daughter had died within the last few months; he said he had never known the child because he was at work whenever she was awake, or else he was asleep, during the day time. He was determined that he would know the other children and for that reason felt that it was imperative that he should have the eight-hour day.

This man was an American, getting good wages and embittered, not by " outside agitators " but by the facts of his life as he found them.

When the Commissioners spoke to President Williams of the Carnegie Company about this, he smiled and said that it was very evident that the man's case was an exceptional one and not to be taken as typical. He did not go on to explain how such a man who worked from eleven to thirteen or fourteen hours a day or a night could secure time in which to be a normal father to a family of children.

Insufficient evidence was gathered by the Commission to pass any judgment on one phase of the twelve-hour day—the resultant rate of accidents. The accident rate in the steel industry is, of course, still high. After the various criticisms of its policies thirteen years ago, and after engineers had proved to the companies the loss entailed by accidents and especially after compensation laws threatened to make accidents pretty costly to the companies, the steel companies began installing safety devices; the Steel Corporation set up a Safety Department which has been the recipient of many medals. Only statistics can determine to what extent the safety campaign is adequate. Statistically steel still ranks with mining for fatal accidents. The 1918 report of compensable accidents for the state of Pennsylvania gives the four largest hazardous industries as follows:

| | Number | Percent of Total |
|---|---|---|
| Mines and quarries.......... | 23,161 | 33.12 |
| *Metals and metal products*... | 22,222 | 31.78 |
| Public service .............. | 4,985 | 7.13 |
| Building and contracting.... | 4,184 | 5.98 |

It was surprising, in view of the reputation which the Steel Corporation had been accorded for safety, to find so large a number of strikers complaining about hazards. They described with specificness menaces to limb or life, concerning which they had complained to foremen and superintendents month in and month out without avail. Without adequate statistics it was impossible to weigh the value of these complaints just as it was inadvisable to pay great heed to the number of crooked-legged men always seen in the streets of a steel mill town.

Here is a specimen of such complaints, this from a worker's testimony before the Senate Committee (Vol. II, pp. 728-9):

Mr. Colson—I worked in the mill in 1913, in the nail mill. I drew 17½ cents an hour. I enlisted in the army during the trouble in Mexico and from there I was sent to West Point Military Academy with a detachment of Engineers, and from there to Washington, D. C., with the First Battalion of Engineers. From there I went to France and I was one of the first fifty men that got off the boat—one of the first men in France.

The Chairman—What mill are you in?

Mr. Colson—The bloom mill at the steel works at Donora, Pa.; and, so far as safety conditions up there are concerned, a man has no chance, because if he ever slips, his hands are greasy and the steps are greasy, and there is no rail, and there is no chance for your life, unless you jump out of the window and kill yourself.

Senator Sterling—Did you ever know of anybody slipping there?

Mr. Colson—Yes, sir; there was one man who slipped and fell off and I got his job. I took his place as millwright helper.

Chairman—Why did you go on strike?

Mr. Colson—I went out with them, because I did not get

satisfaction from the company in no way.  I had to get down on my hands and knees and ask for a job.

Senator McKellar—What job did you have before you enlisted in the Regular Army?

Mr. Colson—I was in the tool room; and they said, ' When you come back we will give you a good job.'

Senator McKellar—And when you came back you got 44 cents an hour?

Mr. Colson—And longer hours, sir.

The Chairman—How long did you work?

Mr. Colson—Thirteen hours during the night and 11 hours during the day.

Ten years ago the Steel Corporation and all steel companies were under fire because of Sunday work, the seven-day week, the possible 365-day year, chiefly the work on the largest single department of a steel plant, the blast furnace. During the strike the Steel Corporation flatly asserted that that condition had been reformed before the war and that although the seven-day week was resumed during the war, it was quite done away with by 1919.  The president of the Carnegie Steel Company and of the Illinois Steel Company, Corporation subsidiaries,[1] assured this Commission that " seven-day work is all done away with," or where it persists, as it must in the blast furnace department, that " the seven-day week work is a thing of the past "; that is, that blast furnace employees got one day off in seven.

Mr. Gary testified before the Senate Committee (Vol. I, p. 179) : " We decided to eliminate the seven-day week if we possibly could and we practically eliminated it.  At times and places there were strikes, because the compensation was decreased."

---

[1] President Schiller of the National Tube Co. said that the 7-day week was " indefensible," that his company had none of it but that " most other companies' blast furnaces were still on a 7-day basis."

On January 30, 1920, in a letter to the Commission, Mr. Gary said:

"We have no compiled statistics in respect of employment at blast furnaces which you ask for.

"As to the seven-day week, however, beg to state that prior to the war *it had been eliminated* entirely except as to maintenance and repair crews on infrequent occasions. During the war, at the urgent request by government officials for larger production, there was considerable continuous seven-day service in some of the departments. With the close of the war this attitude was changed and the seven-day service has been very largely eliminated. At the present time there is comparatively little of it. We expect to entirely avoid it very shortly."

Concerning the eighteen-, twenty-four- or thirty-six-hour shifts customary with the twelve-hour day, especially at blast furnaces, Mr. Gary could find for the Senate Committee only "82 employees working a continuous twenty-four hours once each month," and "344 working continuous eighteen hours twice each month." (Vol. I, p. 202.)

Analysis of all data before the Commission proved that conditions regarding the seven-day week work are radically different from the impression conveyed by Mr. Gary.

Moreover the evidence showed this fact: that the conditions concerning seven-day week work complained of and proved in 1910 still exist in the steel industry. The thing in the situation which needs explaining is not so much *whether* these evil and unnecessary conditions exist today as *why* they exist, especially in the face of the Steel Corporation's asserted desire to better them.

The Commission of Inquiry composed as it was of churchmen, liable to a biased interest in the observance of Sunday, for that very reason attempted to confine its studies to industrially important facts. *Sunday violation by seven-day work is a minor consideration compared to the violation of American life worked by the twelve-hour day even for only six days a week throughout an industry.* The seven-day week on blast furnaces and the avoidable Sunday work will go when the twelve-hour day is eliminated as the industry's basis. The Commission tried not to be unduly swayed by the testimony of local preachers and priests over the havoc wrought in their congregations by the seven-day week worked by members of their congregations. For example, part of the interrogation of the Rev. Charles V. Molnar, pastor, Slovak Lutheran Church at Braddock, Pa., by the Commission reads:

" My people are on strike. They work mostly in the Edgar Thompson Works. Some are working in Rankin, and have some members in Homestead and Duquesne, but most of the congregation are in Braddock."

Question—" Are practically all of your members on the twelve-hour day? "

Answer—" Yes, some of our men have been working longer than twelve hours."

Question—" Is there much Sunday work? "

Answer—" Very much; that is what we suffer from. The men would be very glad to be excused from Sunday work, but it seems impossible to accomplish anything."

The testimony of a Roman Catholic priest before the Senate Committee was even more emphatic. When asked about " the number of times that persons have omitted to go to church " (Senate Testimony, Vol. II, p. 544):

Father Kazinci—Well, these are from the furnaces in the Braddock mills. There are nine furnaces there, and furnaces H and A allow the men to go to church every second Sunday. The balance of the nine furnaces do not allow their men at all to go to church. Some get a Sunday off, perhaps, once in six months; but it is not taking care of their souls.

The Chairman—Do many members of your church congregation work on Sunday?

Father Kazinci—Most of them work on Sunday; and they do not see the inside of a church more than once in six months, because they are forced to work on Sunday.

What are the simple statistical facts concerning the "elimination" of seven-day work and the "reduction" of hours which according to Mr. Gary have been the object of such earnest effort by the Corporation?

Beginning by re-stating the comparison of hours in 1910 when private institutions and governmental agencies began the "great drive" against such hours, with hours in 1919, we have (Figures from Senate Document 110 and October Monthly Review, U. S. Bureau of Labor Statistics):

Average steel week, 1910............... 67.6 hours
Average steel week, 1919............... 68.7 hours

That is, ten years of "reduction" has *increased* the number of hours. In this time several "independent" concerns, such as the Pueblo plant and all the Pacific Coast plants have adopted the eight-hour day; the Corporation's hours have helped overbalance this "deficit" for the total increase.

Take the figures for 1914 and 1919:

|  | 1914 | 1919 |
|---|---|---|
| Common labor—hours per week.... | 70.3 | 74. |
| Skilled and semi-skilled—hours per week .......................... | 57. | 66. |
| All employees—hours per week..... | 66.3 | 68.7 |

In each classification the length of the week has *increased*.

Take the seventy-nine separate occupations in the steel industry for which statistics are given by the U. S. Bureau of Labor Statistics and compare 1914 and 1919. In eighteen classes hours have decreased; in four remained stationary; *in fifty-seven of the seventy-nine classes hours per week have increased,* from a few minutes up to *fourteen hours per week.*

Blast furnace and open hearth laborers constitute the great bulk of the seven-day week workers. For all districts the figures are:

|                                | 1914 | 1919 |
|--------------------------------|------|------|
| Blast furnace, common labor    | 70.8 | 78.9 |
| Open hearth, common labor      | 69.5 | 72.7 |

In one case an *increase* of eight hours per week or more than an hour per day since 1914; in the other an *increase* of three hours.

In the *Pittsburgh District,* thus eliminating the principal eight-hour independents and confining the comparison more to Steel Corporation conditions, the figures are:

|                                | 1914 | 1919 |
|--------------------------------|------|------|
| Blast furnace, common labor    | 73.1 | 82.  |
| Open hearth, common labor      | 71.3 | 78.5 |

Increases of nearly nine hours in one class and over seven in the other. Statistics from Bureau of Labor Statistics Bulletin 218 (Oct., 1917) reveal what actual successes were accomplished by the Corporation in "eliminating" seven-day work. Seven-day workers in blast furnaces were: (p. 17) 1911, 89 per cent.; 1912, 82 per cent.; 1913, 80 per cent.; 1914, 58 per cent.; 1915, 59 per cent. Open hearths, during the same period, "about equally divided among the seven-day, the seven-day and six-day alternately and the six-day groups." Even before the war seven-day "eliminating" waited on what "steel demand" decided. The best year's figures show that the Corporation never achieved even a half-reform.

For 1919, after the war, the latest figures for blast furnaces, referred to earlier in this report, mean not even a real attempt to reform. The figures were drawn from the twenty-four representative establishments' pay-rolls and of the employees in the blast furnace department, totalling 6,315, exactly 4,049 were on the flat eighty-four-hour week, i.e. seven-day week. An additional 756 were on twelve hours, six days a week, *plus Sunday work ranging up to eleven hours.* The Pittsburgh section of the twenty-four plants had on schedules *below* seventy-two hours only the following: 1 laborer at 60 hours and 41 laborers at 66 to 72 hours. All the rest of these Pittsburgh blast furnace workers in twenty-four representative plants were on the twelve-hour day and all but 485 of the 5,290 were on this twelve-hour-day seven days a week.

In the open hearth, where there was no metallurgical excuse for seven-day work, conditions were similar. In nineteen representative establishments whose open hearth employes total 4,702, 2,750 were on the six and one-half or the flat seven-day week, all on the twelve-hour schedule.

It is in the face of such facts, buried in statistics usually unread by the public, that Steel Corporation officials from Mr. Gary down assured the Commission that "seven-day work was a thing of the past."

Such statements were maddening to the strikers. A Homestead worker whose evidence happened to be in the shape of the notebook in which he had recorded all his hours and "turns" for eight months and twenty days previous to the strike, went to the Senate Committee hearing in Pittsburgh to read what the notebook showed. It showed:

| | |
|---|---:|
| Hours worked | 2,930 |
| Number of 24-hour turns | 18 |
| Number of days off | 17 |

That is, he worked the twelve-hour day in ten and one-half-hour shifts by day and thirteen hours by night for thirty-seven weeks, with the twenty-four-hour shift every fortnight and one day off every fortnight. These were the hours of his department in a Corporation mill; the schedule of that department allowed its employees seventeen days off out of 244.

He did not testify. He explained to an investigator that he saw what he feared were Corporation " spotters " in the room. He owned his home in Homestead and he said he could not afford to testify and run the risk of being blacklisted.

Mr. Gary began his account of " elimination " to the Senate Committee with the telegram sent by him to the presidents of all constituent companies on March 18, 1910, reading as follows:

" Mr. Corey, Mr. Dickson and I have lately given much serious thought to the subject matter of resolution passed by the Finance Committee April 23, 1907, concerning Sunday or seventh-day labor. . . . The object of this telegram is to say that all of us expect and insist that hereafter the spirit of the resolution will be observed and carried into effect. There should and must be no unnecessary deviation without first taking up the question with our Finance Committee. . . . I emphasize the fact that there should be at least twenty-four continuous hours interval during each week in the production of ingots.                    E. H. Gary."

This " peremptory order," putting into effect a resolution passed three years before, was sent the day after the Federal Labor Commission began an investigation of seven-day work in the Bethlehem plant on an order from Congress; which investigation was later extended to Corporation plants and the whole industry.

Following this telegram, Mr. Gary told the Senate Committee, " We practically eliminated it," and he asserted that the Corporation had now sufficiently recovered from the emergencies of war practically to re-eliminate seven-day work. To what extent the Steel Corporation lived up to this peremptory order even in peace time can be estimated. In 1916 the Lackawanna Steel Company in its petition for exemption from the one day rest law of New York State showed plainly what Professor Commons (who quotes it in the American Labor Legislation Review, March, 1917) calls " the futility of depending on even the most prosperous of the tariff's beneficiaries ":

" We are advised that the chairman of the United States Steel Corporation several years ago, while labor conditions were entirely different from those obtaining at the present time, gave instructions quite peremptory in character to all the subsidiaries of that company requiring them to follow out the one day of rest principle and warning them that any deviation from the published instructions would result in dismissal from office. We have, therefore, directed our investigations to these subsidiaries and state, without fear of successful contradiction, that *the corporation is now disregarding the one day of rest in seven principle* which it so strongly advocated several years ago and which it in the past, in good faith, earnestly strove to put into practice. It, too, has felt the shortage of men, and owing to the great and pressing demand for its product no longer observes the practice which its chairman promulgated. Having taken so firm a position, it is not strange that it is difficult to get heads of subsidiaries to admit that the published rule has become a dead letter. When labor conditions become normal the corporation will doubtless return to an observance of the rule. So far as we can ascertain, the rule was only observed by the corporation during the years when the employees of this company had far more time off than the one day of rest statute requires."

There is then some basis for estimating the probable efficacy of what Mr. Gary told the Senate Committee (Vol. I,

p. 180) when he assured the Senators that he believed in the eight-hour day and that he believed, " there are a good many employees, I do not say the majority or anything like the majority, but there are a good many employees who believe the same thing." Mr. Gary asserted that the Corporation was " very carefully considering that question." He added: " If we can make it practicable to develop the eight-hour shift throughout our works universally and the men are willing to accept that basis we would be very glad to adopt it for the reason, if for no other, that we think there is a strong public sentiment in favor of it and I would not want to be put on record here or any other place as against the eight-hour day if the men themselves want it."

The Steel Corporation offered but two excuses for the twelve-hour day to the Commission.

The first was the shortage of labor. President Williams of the Carnegie Steel Company said it would take 50 per cent. or 26,000 more workers to put in three shifts on the eight-hour day in the Carnegie Steel Company (which employs 55,000 men). He asked: " And if we could get the labor, where could we house it? It would take 20,000 more houses." Steel masters in general agreed with this viewpoint except that Mr. Gary wrote the Commission that only 16⅔ per cent. more men would be required.

On the other hand it was admitted, even by the steel masters themselves, that one of the reasons why the industry faced a shortage of labor was " because you can't get Americans to work the twelve-hour day." The labor shortage in the industry is a problem, according to the opinion of the steel masters or of their employment managers, of getting Slavic, Greek, Italian and Turk labor which will work the twelve-hour day, or even of admitting Chinese coolie labor into the country. It was admitted that Americans dislike the slavish character of common labor steel jobs as being " hunkie jobs."

Despite this, inasmuch as the steel mills were once entirely manned by Americans, it was admitted that a great many men would come back to the industry if the twelve-hour day were eliminated.

But the decisive factor, setting aside all consideration of the moral questions involved in the twelve-hour day and in suggestions of flooding the steel industry with Balkan immigrants or coolie labor, lies in this consideration which, according to engineers, disposes of the labor shortage argument against the eight-hour day; the steel requirements of the country could be met by utilizing all the first-class machinery, scrapping the rest and distributing the work throughout the available labor supply and throughout the year on a three-shift eight-hour day basis.

Engineers' findings are: that the steel industry being run for the making of profit and not primarily for the making of steel as the country needs it, favors (a) spells of idleness during which the country and the steel workers pay for the maintenance of idle machinery, and later (b) spurts of long hour, high speed labor.

Here is an analysis of steel production, made in 1919 by W. N. Polakov, who compiled coal production studies for the Council of National Defense during the war:

"It is a well-known fact that during 1914 the mills were running considerably below their capacity because of an industrial crisis manifested in a general business depression. Production of pig-iron during the two preceding years averaged thirty million tons, even at that time, however, utilizing less than 75 per cent. of the productive capacity of equipment; full productive *capacity* of blast furnaces in 1914 was 44,405,000 tons per year. The fact that only 23,300,000 tons were *produced* in 1914 left nearly half of the equipment idle. A consumer of iron should not be asked to pay for the use of furnaces in which his iron was not made any more than the tenant to pay rent of the vacant apartments of his landlord. Yet exactly the same thing was being done when the overhead charges, rent, etc., amounting to $104,052,085, were distributed on only 23,000,000 tons, while they should have been spread over 44,000,000 tons. The consumer was asked to pay rent at a rate of $4.47 per ton instead of only $2.17. The country, therefore, had to pay $2.30 more for each ton of pig-iron than it was worth and than it would have cost if production had not been curtailed by the companies. Total over-charges, therefore, appear to be about $53,552,084.

"Similarly, the capacity of steel mills was sufficient to produce 45,000,000 tons while only about 23,500,000 tons were made. Were the overhead expenses, rent, etc., of only that portion of plant and equipment that was actually used in the production of steel charged to consumer, the overhead per ton would have been not $9.95, but only $5.17, and the country would not have had to pay $112,350,000 to the steel makers for the equipment the country and the people received no benefit from. In other words, the expense of idle plant equipment was charged to consumers of both iron and steel, and this item alone cost the country $175,009,084."

The second excuse offered for the twelve-hour day was this: that the workers prefer the twelve-hour day.

This was urged by the Corporation's subsidiary presidents before this Commission just as solemnly as Mr. Gary urged it before the United States Senate.

Mr. Gary said "Let me tell you, the question of hours has been largely a question of wishes, of desire on the part of the employees themselves."

Steel presidents assured this Commission that in a few plants where the three-shift day was inaugurated the plants lost their men "because the foreigner wants to work the twelve-hour day, he wants to make as much money as he possibly can." They united in telling the Commission that "if the Corporation put in the eight-hour day, the 'inde-

pendents' would steal all our men, because they want to work
the twelve-hour day."

They stated, what there is little reason to doubt, that sometimes when they tried to put in a rule of one day's rest in
seven, blast furnace laborers would desert to a seven-day job
or go to a neighboring plant and work for that extra day when
they were supposed to be " off."

This whole argument is based on what Mr. Gary called
" compensation." Mr. Gary himself said, " Of course if we
should immediately limit hours to eight and pay for the
eight hours the same the men are now getting for ten or
twelve hours every employee would favor it." (Senate Testimony, Vol. I, p. 180.)

There seems to be not the slightest disposition on the part
of the Corporation in tackling the twelve-hour day evil to go
at their problem from this standpoint: " What is a wage
necessary for an American standard of living? Let us pay
at least that minimum for an eight-hour day." Many pages
of the Steel Corporation's testimony and hours of discussion
by presidents and plant superintendents would vanish if the
Steel Corporation would consent to such a basis of consideration of its problems. Of course there are " hunkies " who
will work just as long as possible for all the money they can
get; these are chiefly the immigrants who want to hurry back
to Europe to live in comparative leisure for the rest of their
days. Are these men to be favored at the expense of the
immigrant who has become an American, who wants to stay
here with his family, who is growing up to American speech
and ways and who wants to keep himself and his money here
forever? This latter is the immigrant who struck by the
tens of thousands against the twelve-hour day; but he looks,
to Mr. Gary, the same as the un-American worker. Mr.
Gary told the Senate Committee (Senate Testimony, Vol. I,
p. 183): " Some of the men prefer to secure their own places

of residence and save their money and take it home—take it abroad. Of course this is not objectionable from our standpoint at all." But is it not emphatically objectionable from the standpoint of American citizenship?

Mr. Gary propounded his question of pay, what he called twelve hours wages for eight hours work, as if it could not be taken seriously by practical men. It is taken seriously by his entire common labor force. Witnesses before the Senate Committee and scores interviewed in this Inquiry took the stands set forth in the following paragraph from the diary of the Carnegie Steel worker at Homestead in the spring of 1919:

" A rumor of the coming eight-hour day is commented on as follows: Negro laborer says he doesn't see how he can get along with only eight hours as long as family groceries stay up so high. One of the best first-helpers, pay check $175 to $200 every fifteen days, mainly tonnage, says it would be fine; it would cost money, but it would give him a chance to get the good of being alive."

There in a nutshell are the answers given by the two main parts of the labor force. The upper third, consisting of the ‿killed workers and upper half of the semi-skilled, would willingly accept a compromise cut in wages for the sake of the eight-hour day. The other and greater half, especially the common labor section, feel they must have their present pay when they get the eight-hour day. That the Corporation recognized some reasonableness in this stand was evidenced when Mr. Gary announced a 10 per cent. raise for all common labor three weeks after the strike was called off.

This Inquiry hesitated to raise the issue as to whether or not the rates of pay for the Steel Corporation's common labor are purposely kept low in order to force men to submit to the inhuman twelve-hour day.

Progressive steel masters have fought the Corporation's twelve-hour day for years. They instance what is well known, that the actual work delivered toward the end of the twelve-hour shift, much less the eighteen, twenty-four, or thirty-six hour shift, is nothing compared to the wear and tear on the workman delivering the labor. The following quotation from the diary of the Carnegie steel worker is pertinent:

"The twelve-hour day for common labor is impossible. To deliver heavy muscular effort for twelve hours cannot be done. The last six hours is done with a 35 per cent. load. After midnight it is a contest to see who keeps out of the boss's way and does the least work."

In sum, the twelve-hour day is the most iniquitous of the by-products of the Corporation's labor policy; which is to get cheap labor and keep it cheap. The Corporation baits floating labor with the wage possibilities of excessive hours, does nothing to combat the drainage of money out of the country by the smaller fraction of the incorrigibly un-American immigrant; and for the greater bulk of immigrants who want to be Americans it imposes un-American hours. In the light of thirteen years' history of "eliminating" the seven-day week, the conclusion seems unescapable: that the Steel Corporation moves to reform only when it has to. It must be added that if the twelve-hour day is bad for the country, the government is to blame and as long as it fails to tackle the twelve-hour day it imposes upon the trade unions alone the humane task of moving the Steel Corporation in the direction of reform.

Moreover, the conclusion is unescapable that a real cause of the persistence of the twelve-hour day and the seven-hour week is the defenselessness of the unorganized immigrant worker. Again the government, as much as the Steel Corporation, is to blame and again the Corporation and the government have seen fit to leave the field of reform to the trade unions.

In the twenty-eight pages of the Senate Committee's Report on the steel strike much space is devoted to the need for Americanization. Only a few lines were devoted to the twelve-hour day. But Americanization is a farce, night schools are worthless, Carnegie libraries on the hilltops are a jest, churches and welfare institutions are ironic while the steel worker is held to the twelve-hour day or the fourteen-hour night. Not only has he no energy left, he has literally no time left after working such schedules. He has not even time for his own family.

The facts have long been known. The National Association of Corporation Schools, the chief employers' organization for furthering workers' education, at its 1919 session heard A. H. Wyman of the Carnegie Steel Company of Pittsburgh cite the reasons given by immigrant workers for dropping out of the nightly English classes for foreigners in the South Chicago public schools:

Fatigue from long hours............................ 27
Change of jobs, unable to get to school by 7 P. M...... 36
Change from day to night work..................... 37
Overtime work ................................... 69

Total ........................................ 169

That is, nearly fifty per cent. of the startlingly small group of 341 enrolled out of the tens of thousands in the district dropped out for reasons connected with hours. Mr. Wyman did not mention the relation of steel workers' hours to the defeat of the South Chicago Americanization educational campaign; neither did anybody else in the audience mention it.[1]

The Committee of Senators investigating the strike heard

[1] Report National Association of Corporation Schools, 1919, p. 492.

testimony directly related to this matter of Americanization of which the following is typical (Vol. II, p. 602):

A. Pido—Twenty-three years old, an immigrant striker, on the stand.

The Chairman—What is the reason you struck this time?

Mr. Pido—I strike on eight hours a day and better conditions.

Senator McKellar—What sort of conditions do you want better?

Mr. Pido—This better; I think that a man ought to work eight hours today and have eight hours sleep and eight hours that he can go to school and learn something; and I think that an education is much better than any money. I have been going to night school in Clairton for a while.

The Chairman—Did a good many of the men go to night school?

Mr. Pido—They don't have any chance. They work 12 hours a day, and they do not have any chance.

The Chairman—How long did you go to night school?

Mr. Pido—I went about twenty nights altogether.

The Chairman—Is that all of the schooling that you have ever had?

Mr. Pido—I did not have any chance.

The Chairman—How many men went to the night school?

Mr. Pido—Not very much. There were about twenty-three altogether.

The Chairman—Do you think they would go to night school if they had an opportunity?

Mr. Pido—I think they would if they had a chance to go, but the way they are now they have no chance to go to school.

Another witness, a Slovak priest in Braddock, testified as follows:

Father Kazinci: "We have an Americanization course in project taking place, and they have been instructed to go and attend those night schools. They are not a very great success, for the simple reason that the men are overworked, working from 10 to 13 hours a day; and they do not feel like going to the schools and depriving their families of their own company and society even after those hours, those long hours. Sundays, they have none, for most of them go off to work.

"The men are worked from 10 to 13 hours a day. The conditions under which they are living are bad for America. The housing conditions are terrible. The work conditions, the hours of work, are absolutely impossible, and I think that it tends to make the men become disgusted with the country, and they will say, 'Well, let us go back to the old country; perhaps it is going to be better than it is for us here.' There is no hope for them bettering their condition, for they work from the time the whistle begins to blow in the morning until they are whistled out at 6 o'clock in the evening." (Vol. II, p. 544-6.)

Americanization of the steel workers cannot take place while the 12-hour day persists. Human beings un-Americanized by the 12-hour day in such scores of thousands are a stiff price paid by America for the profits of steel companies.

Recommendations along the following lines seem unescapable:

That the 12-hour day is a barbarism without valid excuse, penalizing the workers and the country.

That the church and every other American institution has a.duty to perform to the immigrant worker and that this duty cannot be fulfilled until the 12-hour day is abolished.

That effective elimination of the 12-hour day must and can be initiated and worked out only by (a) the U. S. Steel Corporation in free cooperation with its workers, and (b) by the Federal Government.

# IV

## WAGES IN A NO-CONFERENCE INDUSTRY

ANALYSIS of the wages paid in the iron and steel industry, together with comparisons with wages in other industries and with two recognized standards of living, results in the following conclusions directly bearing on the causes of the strike:

The annual earnings of over one-third of all productive iron and steel workers were, and had been for years, below the level set by government experts as the minimum of *subsistence* standard for families of five.

The annual earnings of 72% of all workers were, and had been for years below the level set by government experts as the *minimum of comfort* level for families of five.

*This second standard* being the lowest which scientists are willing to term an " American standard of living," it follows that nearly *three-quarters of the steel workers could not earn enough for an American standard of living.*

The bulk of *unskilled* steel labor, with exceptions hereafter noted, earned less than enough for the average family's *minimum subsistence.*

The bulk of *semi-skilled* steel workers earned less than enough for the average family's *minimum comfort.*

*Skilled* steel labor is paid wages disproportionate to the earnings of the other two-thirds, thus binding the skilled class to the companies and creating divisions between it and the rest of the force.

41.6 per cent. of the payroll goes to the skilled, who number but 30.4 per cent. of the whole.

30.6 per cent. of the payroll goes to the semi-skilled, who number 31.5 per cent. of the whole.

27.8 per cent. of the payroll goes to the unskilled, who, however, are 38.1 per cent. of the whole.[1]

One-half of the three-quarters earning less than an American living wage reached even their wage levels *only because of the twelve-hour day* with its "14-hour earnings."

Wage rates in the iron and steel industry are determined by the rates of the U. S. Steel Corporation. The Steel Corporation sets its wage rates, the same as its hour schedules, *without conference* (or collective bargaining) with its employees; it decrees them *arbitrarily*.

Mr. Gary testified before the Senate Committee:

"I have forgotten how many times we increased wages during the war, but repeatedly, voluntarily—*arbitrarily,* but arbitrarily in favor of the workmen." (Senate Testimony, Vol I, p. 226.)

The Commission's data on wages were furnished primarily by the U. S. Steel Corporation. The Corporation's Annual Reports, together with more recent statistics supplied by Mr. Gary are here analyzed through the media of the standard government survey of the industry, (Senate Document 110, 4 vols.), the analyses of the U. S. Bureau of Labor Statistics; and are checked by data accumulated by the Commission's investigators. Comparison is made with budgets of expenditures supplied by workers' families in the Pittsburgh District and with wage rates paid in similar industries.

In relation to the strike these wage analyses warrant the following conclusion:

[1] Figures derived from analysis of the wage tables in Senate Document 110. The proportion between the different classes of workers and other general conditions have not changed vitally since then (1910). The percentages have been carried out to the decimal point, although, of course, they represent no such precise division in fact.

Besides the skilled workers who struck principally against arbitrary (or autocratic) control and besides the mass which struck mainly against the 12-hour day, a large proportion of the unskilled and semi-skilled struck also against wages which, statistics indicate, were actually inadequate to maintain an American standard of living.

In regard to the Steel Corporation's financial *ability* to pay higher wages than it does the following facts were noted:

The Corporation increased its total undivided surplus from $135,204,471.90 in 1914 to $493,048,201.93 in 1919, that is, to a figure larger than its total wages and salary budget for 1919.

Increases in wages during the war in no case were at a sacrifice of stockholders' dividends.

Net earnings per ton of steel in 1918 were $14.39, that is, higher than the average since 1910, ($13.03). Net earnings per ton of steel in 1917 were $19.76.

These conclusions being true, some explanation should be made of what would then seem to be a popular illusion,—that steel is a highly paid industry. The most recent cause of this illusion is, perhaps, Mr. Gary's testimony on wages before the Senate Committee. Mr. Gary began his wage list with "rollers, $32.56 per day" (Senate Testimony, Vol. I p. 156). Although it became quickly apparent (ibid. p. 159)[1] that there was only one roller in the steel business making that $32.56 per day, nevertheless, the public at large seems to have accepted Mr. Gary's flat statement that "the Corporation has been in the van all the time"[2] and his applications of this to wages, such as the following:

[1] Mr. Gary: "Senator, I believe there is only one who gets as high as $32.56."
[2] P. 178.

Mr. Gary: "I wish to state that there is no basic industry in this country, nor in the world, in my opinion, which has paid larger wages to its employees than the United States Steel Corporation, and perhaps not as large. . . .

"For the year 1914 in manufacturing the wages were $2.93; July, 1919, $6.27, an increase of 114 per cent. . . . all companies, 1914, $2.88; July, 1919, $5.99, an increase of 108 per cent.; unskilled labor, 10 hours, 1914, $2 per day; July, 1919, $4.62, an increase of 131 per cent. Twelve hours, in 1914, $2.40; in July, 1919, $5.88, an increase of 145 per cent. (p. 158).

"We have stood for the highest wages, invariably. We have been the first to increase wages and the last to decrease them." (Senate Testimony, Vol. I, p. 175.)

Altogether, Mr. Gary's figure of $6.27 per day as the average for the whole industry, his figures on wage increases in hundred percentages and exhibits of photographs of beautiful homes owned by steel workers, combined to leave with the public the impression that "steel may be mighty hard labor but its wages are mighty big," and that "whatever else the steel trust may be, it pays well." It might not be unfair to say that the impression is general that the Steel Corporation's reason for hiring 24 different races of foreigners was that they could stand the hours, not that the kind of wages these foreigners would take had anything to do with it.

Another means of misleading public opinion undoubtedly was the appearance in the press and in magazines during the strike of many articles such as the one entitled "Think of the 'Poor Steel Workers' Who Get From Four Dollars to Seventy Dollars a Day" in the *Current Opinion* of January, 1920. The article is taken from the *N. Y. Sun* and goes on to say:

"According to a writer who has been investigating conditions in the Pittsburgh steel mill district for the *New York*

*Sun,* the worker on an ice wagon or on a moving van in any large city does more real hard work in a day than the average mill laborer does in two or three days. . . . Wages of from $8.26 to $9 a day have been made right along by semi-skilled workers, a large number of whom are foreign born.   For what are known as skilled workers in the steel mills, to which positions all workers may aspire and many of which are held by aliens, the average daily wages are, at this writing:

| | |
|---|---:|
| Steel rollers | $28.16 |
| Sheet heaters | 21.12 |
| Roughers | 11.92 |
| Steel pourers | 12.84 |
| Vessel men | 14.65 |
| Engineers, manipulators, etc. | 12.63 |
| Blooming mill heaters | 17.92 |
| Skelp mill heaters | 18.18 |
| Skelp mill rollers | 21.73 |
| Lap welders | 16.08 |
| Blowers | 13.76 |
| Bottom makers | 12.91 |
| Regulators | 13.52 |

"It is stated authoritatively that employees of the United States Steel Corporation now are the highest paid body of men in the steel industry in the world."

The list of employees given above, " rollers," etc., constitutes a fraction of 1 per cent. of all employees.   Of these in turn, the " aliens," or immigrants who " may aspire " to such jobs, constitute a fraction of 1 per cent.   It was " stated authoritatively "—on behalf of steel companies,—many times during the strike that steel workers were highly paid, on the basis of such citations as the above.

The result was that most persons had the impression that " wages were not an issue in the strike."   Even public spirited citizens who conferred with Mr. Gary on the strike remained under this misapprehension. Persons who took the trouble to mingle with strikers, however, found every other man complaining of wages. Half the strikers interviewed by the Senate investigating committee talked of "low wages."

It is entirely possible that the Steel Corporation heads sincerely believe their workers are well off, financially. No such analyses as the following were obtainable from the Corporation's statisticians.

Analysis shows that the misconception of steel as a high wage industry arises from:

(a) The existence of a very small highly skilled and highly paid body of American workers prominently visible at the top of the industry.

(b) Failure to realize that the amounts earned by the low-skilled, (the bulk of the labor) are determined chiefly by the extraordinary long hours rather than by a high rate per hour.

That is: steel rates are the same or lower than in similar industries if earnings are compared on a basis of equal hours. As regards common labor steel is a low wage industry. Comparison of common labor earnings in steel with common labor earnings in five other major industries in the Pittsburgh district for the latter part of 1919 on the basis of a common standard week shows *steel labor the lowest paid of the six.*

" This class (common labor) is of the greatest importance in the industry, not only because of the very large proportion employed, but even more because their wage forms the base rate of the entire industry, above which the wages of the other employees are graded." (Senate Document, 110, Vol. I p. xxxix.) This finding of the Labor Department's famous study of the steel industry in 1910 is admittedly true today. The steel wage, as well as the organization of the steel business, (see next section of this report) is pyramided on a broad and tremendous base of common labor, restlessly drifting and with a high turnover while the industry is held together by the tight and almost unbreakable skilled organization at the apex. Yet the high pay rates at the top depend largely on the rates which the mass at the bottom are willing to take.

True understanding of the wage complaints of thousands of steel workers depends on analyzing the huge wages budget of the Corporation to show how the earnings are divided. It is no comfort to the underpaid worker to learn that the Corporation paid in wages and salaries for 1918, $452,663,-524.; and for the first eight months of 1919, to manufacturing employees, $255,861,264. The following figures make the matter plainer than gigantic totals, though *the figures are based on the totals,* which include many salaries in the administrative force, admittedly larger than the run of producing employees' wages. (Reference is made to tables in sub-reports.) These figures are maxima, too high to be representative. The figures cover approximately the union organizing period of a year before the beginning of the strike, September 22, 1919.

In 1918 the the Corporation's wage and salary budget " for the manufacturing properties," $344,907,626 went to the 198,968 employees as follows:

60,486 skilled (30.4 per cent. of all) got 41.6 per
    cent., or .................................... $143,581,571
62,675 semi-skilled (31.5 per cent. of all) got 30.6
    per cent., or .................................... 105,531,733
75,807 unskilled (38.1 per cent. of all) got 27.8
    per cent., or .................................... 95,884,320

In 1919 the Corporation's wage and salary budget ($255,-861,264 for eight months) went to 191,000 employees as follows: (eight months budget multiplied by 50 per cent. for an annual basis):

58,064 skilled (30.4 per cent. of all) got 41.6
   per cent., or ............................ $159,657,328
60,165 semi-skilled (31.5 per cent. of all) got 30.6
   per cent., or ............................ 117,440,320
72,771 unskilled (38.1 per cent. of all) got 27.8
   per cent., or ............................ 106,694,145

That is, individual average earnings were not higher than as follows, since the above totals contain administrative salaries:

*In 1918:*
Skilled annual earnings averaged under...... $2,373
Semi-skilled annual earnings averaged under.. 1,683
Unskilled annual earnings averaged under..... 1,265
*In 1919:*
Skilled annual earnings averaged under..... $2,749
Semi-skilled annual earnings averaged under.. 1,952
Unskilled annual earnings averaged under.... 1,466

With this must be compared what the workingman is always comparing with his wage—his cost of living. Before taking up detailed discussion of standards of living, it will be convenient to set down here brief definitions of two standards, (disregarding a third commonly called the pauper line, because the latter has not been defined with scientific exactitude comparable to)—(1) the *minimum subsistence level,* and (2) the *minimum comfort level*) both for families of five.

These standards, derived from the most exhaustive extant analysis of cost of living statistics, incorporated in government reports and used in government wage awards, are defined as follows:

1. The minimum of subsistence level.  This is based essentially on *animal well-being,* with little or no attention to the comforts or social demands of human beings.

2. The minimum comfort level.  This is somewhat above that of mere animal subsistence, providing in some measure for comfortable clothing, insurance, a modest amount of recreation, etc.  This level provides for health and decency, but very few comforts, and is *probably much below* the idea had in mind in the frequent but indefinite expression, " *the American standard of living.*"

In other words, these standards applied to families, mean first, the level at which a wage-earner can keep himself and his dependents healthfully alive; second, the lowest level at which scientists would be willing to put "the American standard of living."  (The detailed calculations of these standards, chiefly on the basis of the work done for the government by Prof. W. F. Ogburn, the best known American authority on costs of living statistics, will be set forth later in an appendix.)

It must be noted that as standards for wages, these levels are bitterly protested by organized labor.  The whole principle of limiting wage rates to their relation to bare standards of *subsistence* or of *minimum* comfort has been denounced again and again by Mr. Gompers.  The following figures therefore may be considered simply at the rock bottom of calculation for those who wish to grasp the meaning of existing wage rates, not as representing rates which organized labor considers just.

*For 1918,* Family of Five (June)
Minimum of subsistence level...................... $1,386
Minimum of comfort level...................... 1,760
*For 1919,* Family of Five (August)
Minimum of subsistence level...................... $1,575
Minimum of comfort level...................... 2,024

These figures,—which are hammered down to the most conservative possible levels—may be compared with the (highest possible) individual averages based on the Corporation's payrolls above, as follows:—

|                                      | 1918    | 1919    |
|--------------------------------------|---------|---------|
| Minimum of comfort level             | $1,760  | $2,024  |
| Minimum of subsistence level         | 1,386   | 1,575   |
| Unskilled labor's annual average     | 1,265   | 1,466   |

That is, in 1918, the unskilled worker's annual earnings were more than $121 *below* the minimum of subsistence level and more than $495 below the "American standard of living" for families.

In 1919 the unskilled worker's annual earnings were more than $109 below the minimum of subsistence level and more than $558 below the "American standard of living."

Comparing the semi-skilled earnings and the minimum of comfort level:

|                                      | 1918    | 1919    |
|--------------------------------------|---------|---------|
| Minimum of comfort level             | $1,760  | $2,024  |
| Semi-skilled labor's annual average  | 1,683   | 1,952   |

That is, in both years the semi-skilled's annual earnings were below the lowest "American standard of living" for families.

*These two groups,* unskilled and semi-skilled, *comprise 72 per cent. of all* manufacturing iron and steel workers.

If, leaving *average* annual earnings for a moment, comparison is made between (a) the two standards of living cited and (b) the wages of those groups of workers whose highest earnings just fail to reach these standards, the following curious and significant revelation results. That is, the labor force of 191,000 men for 1919 can be classified by gradations upward, beginning with the group earning $3.36 a day or approximately $1,000 a year, then the group earning

$1,200, then $1,300, etc.   The level at which $1,575 (the minimum of subsistence standard) appears in this classification leaves just 38 per cent. of the workers below it.   If the classification is continued on upward, through $1,600 annually, $1,700, $1,800, etc., the level at which $2,024 (the minimum of comfort standard) appears leaves just 72 per cent. of the workers below it.   But 38 per cent. marks the limit of unskilled labor and 72 per cent. the limit of semi-skilled.

That is, as if by the workings of a law, all in the unskilled class fall just short of the level of living to which common labor ordinarily feels it is entitled and should attain,—the level of a healthful animal existence.   And all in the semi-skilled class (workers in steel jobs usually from 1 year to 5 years or more) fall just short of the level of living to which more steady workers feel they ought to attain—the level of decency and at least a few comforts.

Such a " law " might be put thus: that the " labor market," if left only to " supply and demand," uninfluenced by trade union or other forces, tends to leave the top level of possible earnings for each class of worker just out of reach.   Each class of worker must always be striving for the level of livelihood which seems " due " him and always be just short of it.   He must, therefore, always be working his hardest.

The worker is, therefore, by the workings of such unrestricted industrialism, " speeded " to the limit by the hope of attaining the standard which *seems* surely attainable. Employers capitalize the situation, partly consciously,—" if you pay 'em too much, they won't work "—and partly unconsciously, by making each wage raise just enough to meet " increased costs of living."   Consciously, employers have utilized this " law " to speed workmen by skilfully adjusting reductions in piece-rates of payment to increases in output.   This is the practice of " increasing output by ' shaving ' rates, a method raised to perfection by the steel trust," [1] as observed by Prof. Carleton Parker in 1914.

The wage averages given above, it should be noted again, were based on the *money actually paid out*. The true averages for each class of work, therefore, could not be *over* the figures given. How much lower than the given averages the true averages should be is hard to determine. It depends mainly on the extent to which the Steel Corporation has lumped into its totals for wages for the labor force, the sums spent for salaries for the great office and administrative organizations. That these have been lumped in is obvious; [2] but to what extent can only be estimated. Besides the administrative salaries which must be paid out of the industry's productiveness, there are such items as the thousands of " plant police " and other adjuncts of anti-union policies, whose pay must also be earned by the productive steel workers. This percentage of deduction for administrative overhead, etc., should be, judging by the only statistics available, about 9 per cent. In 1910 the indicated average for all Steel Corporation employees, obtained by dividing the given total payroll of $174,995,130 by the 218,435 employees, was $801 per man annually. But the actual average annual earnings, as determined by the government's exhaustive survey of that year, were about $726 per man, or 9 per cent. below the Steel Corporation's indicated average. In 1919 the Corporation's indicated average, obtained by dividing the given manufacturing plant payroll by the number of manufacturing employees, was $2,009 per man. If this " manufacturing

[1] " The Technique of American Industry," *Atlantic Monthly*, Jan., 1920.
[2] The fact is plainly indicated by analysis of the figures cited by Mr. Gary to the Commission in the letter of Jan. 30. This gives $344,907,-626, as the " total payroll " for " the employees of the manufacturing plants." If this excluded administrative salaries, etc., these salaries should raise unduly the average annual wage for the rest of the Corporation's 70,000 employees. Instead the average for the remaining 70,000 is $200 lower than the average given as for " the employees of the manufacturing plants " alone.

payroll " contains the same proportion of overhead as the Corporation's customary " total payroll," as seems to be true, this average of $2,009 should be 9 per cent. too high as a true average. But the $726 true average of 1910, increased by 150 per cent., (the actual increase in iron and steel wages according to government reports [1]) would be $1,815 and this is also just 9 per cent. below the Corporation's indicated average. This would mean that the true average annual earnings of iron and steel workers for 1918 and 1919 would be as follows:

|  | 1918 | 1919 |
|---|---|---|
| Unskilled ............................ | $1,152 | $1,335 |
| Semi-skilled ......................... | 1,534 | 1,777 |
| Skilled ............................. | 2,178 | 2,502 |

That is, if a survey were made of company payrolls, it would probably indicate the above as the actual average earnings of steel workers.[2]

These facts, then, should be borne in mind in considering the following recapitulating table. The above averages are probably much truer estimates of actual annual earnings than the averages given below which, on the companies' own statistics, are maxima. The true averages for semi-skilled and unskilled are farther below the standards of living than this table indicates:

|  | 1918 | 1919 |
|---|---|---|
| Skilled ............................ | $2,373 | $2,749 |
| Minimum of comfort ................. | 1,760 | 2,024 |
| Semi-skilled ........................ | 1,683 | 1,952 |
| Minimum of subsistence ............. | 1,386 | 1,575 |
| Unskilled .......................... | 1,265 | 1,466 |

[1] Increase in average hourly earnings 1910 to 1919 is 150 per cent. Bulletins U. S. Bureau of Labor Statistics No. 218 and *Monthly Labor Review*, November, 1919, p. 192.

[2] An increase of 10 per cent. for common labor with proportionate adjustments for skilled was granted by the U. S. Steel Corporation at the close of the strike. This was immediately met by increases from the independent companies.

In each of two classes, in each year, the average earnings were below the standard of living which each class normally feels to be the least " due " him.  How far one class, common labor, was below the minimum comfort or lowest " American standard of living " was striking.

For many years this was so in the industry; decency, or comfort, just out of reach, for two-thirds of the workers. Therefore many strikers, who looked blank at mention of " Bolshevism " and who knew little even of the A. F. of L., insisted on talking a great deal about wages to this Commission's investigators and to the Senate Committee.

Such were the hard facts of which all but skilled steel workers were more or less conscious year in, year out.  They realized that by the long day, and its overtime they could earn considerable sums, but, what with exhaustion due to overwork and what with lay-offs due to shut-downs, the annual income was disappointing.  Though they were laid off, they must eat and their families be kept alive.  Iron men, with plants running full time, could earn much more than the $24.32 (1918) or the $28.19 (1919) maximum weekly averages actually paid to common labor in those years.  For example, the following is an Open Hearth gang actual schedule for a Pittsburgh District plant, July, 1919:

Hours: ten-hour day, fourteen-hour night
(Alternate 6-day and 7-day week)

|  |  | Weekly |  | Rate |
|---|---|---|---|---|
| Common labor | ...unskilled | .....$35.28 | ................ | $  .42 |
| Pit | ..............unskilled | ..... 36.12 | ................ | .43 |
| Third-Helper | ....semi-skilled | ... 45.00 | (6 wks. to learn) | .45 |
| Second-Helper | ...skilled | ....... 45.00 | (8 mo.-2½ yrs.). | 7.00 a day |
| First-Helper | .....skilled | ....... 69.00 | ................ | 10.07 plus |
|  |  |  |  | tonnage |
|  |  |  |  | ($1 or $2) |

17 (hours) ✕ 45 (cents) ✕ 6 (days) = night week
11   "     ✕ 45   "    ✕ 6   "    + (32 ✕ 45) = day week

The mathematics of overtime for the semi-skilled man at the end illustrates the story.  This Third-Helper makes his total on his "night week," 14 hours for 6 nights, by multiplying his hourly 45 cents by 17 hours by 6.  He makes his "day week" total by multiplying 45 cents by 11 hours by 6 plus one 24 hour turn, or (overtime pay, 32 hours in all), $14.40.

If this semi-skilled man kept this up for 52 weeks he would, being allowed only 26 days rest in all that year of 12-hour dáys, earn $2,340 or $216 over the minimum of comfort level for 1919. And if the common laborers *who make up* 49 *per cent.* of Open Hearth employees, worked this 12-hour schedule for all but 26 of the 365 days in the year, they would still be *nearly* $200 *below the lowest "American standard."* But few men can stand it and few plants run without a lay-off,—many are "down" from 8 to 20 weeks a year, and the years' earnings are never "full time." Thus common labor's income is annually below healthful existence for families.

It is these possibilities of overtime on 12 to 24-hour shifts which give to steel jobs the reputation of "high pay" which they actually enjoy among a considerable class of husky unmarried immigrant workers. This touches one of the real reasons why the 12-hour day has persisted in the steel industry: 30 per cent. of steel workers are unmarried, with no responsibilities and with the strength and desire to pile up as much as they can for a few weeks or months, then "lay off" to enjoy life or take an "easy job" until "broke." From this 30 per cent. the steel companies recruit their 12-hour gang in considerable part, irrespective of whether the development of such intermittent working is good for the industry or the community. The long overtime constitutes the bait to this class and to many a simple foreign laborer who sees what one day *can* bring in but not what the years *do* bring in, to him and his class. Moreover 68 per cent. of the "foreigners" are married, *with an average of* 6.63 *members to each household,* and 81 per cent. of the "foreigners" in the industry are paid the unskilled or semi-skilled wage rates. These married and familied "foreigners" are the ones who desire to keep their money and themselves here, to be "Americans;" and these are the immigrants most worth while and yet most penalized by steel's long hours and un-American wage rates.

It must be noted too that 15 per cent. of immigrant steel workers have families of ten members or over; of the Croatians 37 per cent. have families of 10 or over; of the Magyars, 21 per cent. With large families, with the unskilled jobs where the " lay offs " strike first in slack times, with the communities such that none other than steel jobs are near, with the work such that " old age at forty " is its watchword, the average immigrant steel worker, after a dozen years at it, often finds himself contemplating not the " long overtime " which first tempted him but actual conditions nearer the following:

This is the official family budget and verbal report made by the Home Service Division of the Pittsburgh Red Cross for the only case of relief growing out of the strike that had come to it by November 26, 1919. (The question of helping a *striker* was the subject of very serious debate by the Pittsburgh Red Cross.)

Polish worker living in Braddock, employed by American Steel and Wire Company. Father, mother, and nine children. Oldest boy, 21, was making about $60 a month, went into army service.

Father, 42, common laborer, was making $80 to $90 a month on the average. His employment was irregular, although his foreman reported that he was a good, steady workman and worked every day there was a job. Last summer his monthly earnings went up, being $129 in July, and $118 in August. There is no record of the family ever having been a charity case.

Another boy makes about $15 per month, and some of the girls occasionally pick up some money.

The father went on strike; since the strike he has applied

for other jobs and *was refused them because he belongs to the union.* At length he got a job on a government dam.

*Minimum Budget* for the above family of father, mother and eight children, worked out specially with reference to the special needs of the family for milk, medicine, etc.:

| | |
|---|---:|
| Rent ......................... | $ 20.00 |
| Food ......................... | 101.65 |
| Clothing ...................... | 42.00 |
| Fuel ......................... | 3.00 |
| Spending money ................ | 5.00 |
| Medicine ...................... | 4.00 |
| Education ..................... | .60 |
| Polish tuition ................. | 1.50 |
| Insurance ..................... | 2.00 |
| Recreation .................... | 1.00 |
| | $180.75 |
| Family income in normal times.... | 143.00 |
| Actual relief needed before the strike ..................... | $ 37.75 |

Comment: Almost any ordinary workman's family has a hard time to get along at present prices. The worst problem is housing. Not only are rents high, but there is an absolute shortage of fit housing.

In this case the " decency budget " *set by local authorities* was $2,168 a year, *or over* $700 *more than the average actual earnings of common labor* for that period; and over $1,000 more than the average earnings of the father himself.

Before making detailed comparisons with costs of living, reference should be made to the other of the two comparisons which the steel worker is always making in regard to his wages—the comparison with the wages of his neighbor miner, builder, railroader, etc. Detailed comparisons of hours and wages in nine industries are given in Appendix B, based on the " earnings per full week," not on the actual annual earnings.  With this is a comparison of weekly earnings in six principal industries, besides steel, in the Pittsburgh District, on the basis of a common standard-length week.  The earnings of (1) steel workers, (2) bituminous coal miners, (3) metal trades, (4) railroad employees, (5) building trades, (6) street railwaymen, (7) printers, are compared on the basis of the same week for all, in this case a 44-hour week.[1]  In the comparison steel earnings due to overtime for the customary excessive hours *are averaged in,* but even so the following facts are brought out:

*Comparative earnings for 44-hour week at prevailing hourly rates* (Pittsburgh District, 1919) :
> *Common labor—*
>> Iron and steel ..................... $21.12
>> Bituminous coal .................... 25.30
> *Building trades*
>> Building laborers ................ $22.00
>> Hod carriers ...................... 30.80
>> Plasterers' laborers ................ 30.80
>> Average for laborers .............. 27.85

The comparison makes it plain that *steel common labor has the lowest rate of pay of the trades* for which there are separate statistics for laborers.  The two principal factors to be considered in the comparison are, of course, (a) seasonal influences; (b) unionism.

Excluding laborers the main comparisons run as follows: (still on 44-hour week basis) :

Iron and steel—
> Skilled and semi-skilled................... $38.32

[1] It could be any week for the purposes of comparison, 44-hour week, 90-hour week, 120-hour week; the comparison would result the same.

Bituminous coal miners—
    Hand miners .............................. 34.50
    Machine miners ........................... 41.67
Metal trades—
    Blacksmiths .............................. 30.80
    Iron molders ............................. 33.00
Railroad employees—
    Machinists ............................... 31.68
    Boilermakers ............................. 31.68
Building trades—
    Bricklayers .............................. 49.50
    Carpenters ............................... 39.60
    Painters ................................. 38.50
    Structural iron workers................... 44.00
Street railwaymen ............................ 23.76
Printers—
    Newspaper linotypers ..................... 38.50
    Newspaper compositors .................... 33.88
    Book and job.............................. 26.58

With this should be noted the average for all steel workers
—$32.02; the whole comparison makes plain why steel work-
ers found that steel rates of pay were not " high " when compared with similar industries; that " high " earnings in
steel plants were due principally to long hours. Steel workers often carried the comparisons on to the causes of differences: e.g. to comparisons of the amounts of time lost by unemployment in steel, building, mining, etc.; and to the fact
that the building trades, street railways, railroads and mines
were more or less completely unionized and steel not at all.

A first and foremost item in living costs, conditioned by
wages, is *housing*. This Inquiry for adequate reasons did
not go extensively into two phases of housing: (a) the Steel
Corporation's housing provisions; (b) comparison of present
conditions with findings of investigations of a dozen years
ago.

(a) The Steel Corporation testimony on the houses, including whole towns, built for workmen and leased at low rentals, takes up over ten pages in the Senate Investigating Committee's record. It includes the millions expended for this purpose and this item as a total (Vol. I, p. 192):

Dwellings and boarding houses constructed and leased
    to employees at low rental rates.................... 25,965

But most of these houses, it was well known, were for the Corporation's miners, erected in hitherto uninhabited regions where towns had to be built before mining could go on. Inquiry of the Corporation determined the fact that less than 10,000 of these houses were available for steel workers. The facts were simple:

Total employees at manufacturing plants............ 191,000
Total Corporation houses near plants............... 10,000
                                            ————
    Employees not company-housed................. 181,000

That is, 181,000 steel workers had just as much chance to get a Corporation-built, low-rental house as they had to get Mr. Gary's New York mansion. Moreover most of the 10,000 houses were occupied by "American" workers.

(b) A dozen years ago the Pittsburgh *Survey* revealed conditions of housing of steel workers which shocked public opinion and which, Pittsburgh authorities state, have been improved practically not at all since then. It was impossible to conduct another such exhaustive housing survey in this investigation but sufficient observation was made to bear out the local statement, that housing was as bad as ever. The U. S. census, taken in January, 1920, should reveal complete statistics of conditions. The census takers found in Braddock, for example, that in this steel suburb of Pittsburgh 200 families were living in 61 houses; 35 boarders were in one house where three different persons occupied each bed in the 24 hours of each day, sleeping in eight-hour shifts.

It was of Braddock that Senator Kenyon, chairman of the Senate Investigating Committee, was quoted as saying: "This is the worst place I have ever seen and I have watched the living conditions of many immigrants."

A sub-report [1] contains the detailed findings of an investigator for this Inquiry who spent three weeks in November, 1919, in the Pittsburgh District collecting data on the actual living conditions of steel workers' families. The investigator obtained, as far as the workers could supply them, data on the family budgets of expenditures for rent, food, clothes, children's education, benefit societies, etc. and observed the housing conditions. Questions were also asked, principally of the wives, dealing with the strike, what were their ideas of its causes, whether they approved the strike. Strikers and non-strikers, "foreigners" and "Americans," were interviewed. The visits were haphazard, including neighborhoods in Pittsburgh, Braddock, Homestead and Monessen, sometimes with an interpreter, sometimes with a member of the strike relief committee or with a settlement worker, frequently alone. The neighborhoods were principally those of the immigrant semi-skilled and unskilled workers who constitute the bulk of steel communities. At the end of the investigation, tabulation of the results proved that this haphazard inquiry had achieved a representative survey inasmuch as the average of income for the families visited approximated the average income for the semi-skilled and unskilled workers for the whole industry. The semi-skilled and unskilled actual average for the eight months of 1919 before the strike was not over $128 monthly. The average income of the forty-one immigrant strikers' families visited was $132 a month. The excerpts from the investigators' family reports, given herewith, are representative of the forty-one immigrant households.

[1] Family Budgets and Living Conditions," by Marian D. Savage.

These families ran from four to eight members. The tabulation of the forty-one immigrant families brought out the first characteristic of steel communities,—overcrowding:

Living in 1 room ............... 2 families
Living in 2 rooms............... 22 families
Living in 3 rooms............... 14 families
Living in 4 rooms............... 2 families
Living in 5 rooms............... 1 family (with two boarders)

Over half of these four to eight-member families lived in "apartments" of two rooms; over one-third in three rooms. The resultant physical and moral conditions are not sufficiently portrayed by the bare figures. An excerpt from the report reads:

The first thing which strikes the attention of one who visits the homes of the strikers is the shocking overcrowding. The majority of families which I have seen live in only two rooms, and only four of them have more than three rooms. As the families are composed of from four to eight people, this means that the air space necessary for hygienic living is wholly lacking, and the right kind of home life is made impossible. It means that frequently a bed must stand in the kitchen all the time, taking up space greatly needed for other things. In a few cases the crowding is due to the presence of lodgers, but usually it is not. In one case I was told that the family had tried to find an apartment with three rooms instead of two, but had been unable to, as many landlords objected to having such a large family of children in their houses. Such a policy, of course, means that the largest families may be forced into the smallest accommodations. In general, however, the burden of paying rent for an additional room seemed too great for the family to undertake. In many cases the apartments have no water in them and several families are forced to use a single pump in the court yard. In still a larger number of cases there are no toilet arrangements except dilapidated water closet sheds in the yard.

In a few places there are open unsanitary drains in the court yard, around which the wooden houses are built. Many of the strikers live in alleys which are very dirty and cluttered with rubbish collected by the authorities at infrequent intervals. In one place in Homestead I found what appeared to be drainage water flowing down the middle of the alley. In a good many cases families live in rear houses which can only be reached by narrow dark passageways or ramshackle wooden staircases leading in from the street.

Although the wages in many departments of the industry have more than doubled in the last five or six years, the women are quite convinced that the cost of living has risen very much higher in proportion, so that they are worse off than they used to be. According to the Associated Charities of Pittsburgh, a food order which in 1914 cost $5.88 in New York City (where prices are not very different from those here), in 1919 cost $11.10 in Pittsburgh. This food order, though intended as a minimum standard for a family of five for one week, is not considered adequate by the Pittsburgh A. C., which substitutes a food budget of $17.04 that makes it possible to have meat twice a week instead of once. Compared with this minimum standard, the amount spent for food by the women visited seems to be enough to sustain life, but in most cases, especially in the larger families, to do little more than that. Considering how hard and long-continued the work of a man in the steel industry is, a food budget which does not allow him meat more than twice a week is hardly sufficient, so even in the cases where somewhat more than $17.04 is spent for food for a family of five every week the amount seems far from exorbitant.

Out of forty-eight families from which data could be obtained for estimating each family's budget of expenditures, twenty-eight of the budgets fell below the minimum of subsistence level for 1919 and ten below the minimum of comfort level.

Following are the tables of hours, wages and budgets for the immigrant strikers and for native-born strikers:

## HOURS, WAGES AND BUDGETS OF FOREIGNERS ON STRIKE

| Occupation | Hours per day and turns per week | Wages per month | No. in family | No. of rooms | Rent per month | Food per month | Balance for other necessities | Insurance or lodge per mo. | Miscellaneous items per mo. |
|---|---|---|---|---|---|---|---|---|---|
| Laborer | 11 and 13 | $136. | 8 | 2 | $10. | $100-$120 | $ 6-$26 | | |
|  | .... | 120. | 5 | 2 | 10. (½ paid by mother-in-law) | 76- 88 | 27- 39 | | |
| Laborer | .... | 136. | 6 | 2 | 10. | 100- 115 | 11- 26 | | |
| Wireman | 12 (5 turns) | 114. | 7 | 2 | 10. | 80. | 24. | $6. | |
| Worker in foundry | 10 and 12 | 150. | 5 | 2 | 10. | 90. | 50. | 5. | $10, shoes |
| Laborer | 12 (6 or 7 turns) | 142.+ | 6 | 2 | 10. | 80. | 52. | 8. | |
| Laborer | 12 | 160.+ | 4 | 3 | 15. | 80. | 70. | 5. | 9, coal |
| Worker in rolling mill | 12 (6-7 turns) | 127.50 | 5 | 3 | 15. | 120. | 32.50 | | |
| Laborer | 11 and 13 (6-7 turns) | 130. | | | | | —5. | | |
| Laborer | 8 (6 turns) | 78. | 6 | 2 | 8. | 42. | 28. | 28. | |
| Laborer | 12 (7 turns) | 145. | 4 | 3 | 11. | 80. | 54. | | |
| Pipe worker | 10 (5-6 turns) | 100. | 5 | 2 | 10. | 85. | 5. | .60 | |
| Laborer | 12 (5-6 turns) | 111. | 6 | 2 | 11. | 90. | 10. | | |
| Laborer | 12 (5 turns) | 100. | 4 and 2 boarders | 5 | 15. (—$10.) | 70. | 25. | .50+ | |
| Roll hand | 12 (6 turns) | 120. | 8 | 3 | 10. | 100. | 10. | | |
| Laborer | 10 and 11 | 95. | 5 | 2 | 11. | 60. | 24. | 2. | |
| Laborer | 10 (4-6 turns) | 89.- | 4 | 3 | 8. | 60. | 21.- | .50+ | 1, school |
| Worker in spike mill | 10 (6-7 turns) | 130. | 7 | 3 | 14. | 80. | 36.50 | 7.35 | |
| Laborer | 8 | 90. | 5 | 2 | 7.50 | 50. | 32.50 | 2.25 | |
| Mechanics' helper | 10 | 90. | 4 | 3 | 8. | 40. | 42. | .90 | 5, gas |
| Laborer | 12 (7 turns) | 120. | 5 | 3 | 9.50 | 70. | 40.50 | 2-3 | 1.50-2, gas and elec. |
| Hooker of steel | 10-11 (6 and 7 turns) | 145. | 8 | 4 | 21. | 110. | 14. | 1.50-2 | 0.70-2.10, gas |
| Craneman | 12 (7 turns) | 140. | 5 | 2 | 10. | 105. | 25.50 | | |
| Laborer | 11 and 13 (6 and 7 turns) | 120. | 6 | 1 | 4.50 | 60. | 55.50 | | |
| Laborer | 12 (6 turns) | 135. | 5 | 3 | 14. | 80. | 41. | 1.90 | |
| Wire-drawer | 8 (6 turns) | 90. | 5 | 2 | 11.50 | 100. | —21.50 | | |
| Millwright helper | 12 and 13 (7 turns) | 175. | 5 | 4 | 15. | 115. | 45. | 2.25-4 | 1.80, oil |

## HOURS, WAGES AND BUDGETS OF FOREIGNERS ON STRIKE

| Occupation | Hours per day and turns per week | Wages per month | No. in family | No. of rooms | Rent per month | Food per month | Balance for other necessities | Insurance or lodge per mo. | Miscellaneous items per mo. |
|---|---|---|---|---|---|---|---|---|---|
| Pipe fitter | 10½ (7 turns) | $200. | 4 | 3 | $18. | $100. | $82. | $5. | $1.75+, coal |
| Millwright | 12 (6-7 turns) | 205. | 9 | 2 | 10. | 94-95 | 100. | 6.20 | 2, gas |
| Repair worker | 12 and 13 (6-7 turns) | 157.50 | 5 | 2 | 16. | 70-75 | 66.50— 71.50 | 14.60 15.60 | |
| Machinist helper | 7 turns | 270. | 4 | 3 | 9. | 75. | 186. | | |
| Furnace keeper | 11½ and 14 | 180. | 3 | 2 | 10. | 75.+ | 95. | | |
| Worker in engine house | 10 (7 turns) | 154. | 3 | 1 | 6. | 60-65 | 83-88 | 1.85 | |
| Millwright helper | 11 and 13 (7 turns) | 200. | 6 | 3 | 15. | | | 5. | 5, shoes |
| Laborer | 10 and 12 (6 turns) | 111. | 4 | 3 | 15. | | | 3.25-4 | |
| Laborer | 12 (4 turns) | 100. | 7 | 3 | Owns house | | | 1. | |
| Packer of bolts | 11½ (6-7 turns) | 98-114. | 3 and 4 boarders | 2 | 14. | | | | 0.50, school (Boy earns $40 per mo.) |
| Laborer | 10½ (5½ turns) | 69. | 5 | 2 | 8.50 | | | 1.06 | 0.85, school (Girl earned $20 a mo.) |
| Laborer | 12 (7 turns) | 162. | 8 | 3 | 9. | | | .50+ | |
| Boiler worker | 10 (6 turns) | 100. | 8 | 2 | 8. | 110. | Deficit | 10. | |
| Roller in hoop mill | 12 (3-5 turns) | 80. | 5 | | | | | | |
| Piece worker in mill | 8 | 175. | 7 | 3 | 18. | | | 20. | |
| Engineer | 10 and 14 (7 turns) | 208. | 4 | 5 | | 60. | 130.+60 from sons | | 1, school |
| Pipe worker | 10 and 13 (7 turns) | 149. | 4 | 4 | 15. | 67.50+ | 66.50— | | 2+, coal or 7, gas in winter Meat not included in food |
| Craneman | 12 or 8; 7 or 5 | 114-150. | 4 | 4 | 20. | 125. | —31 to +5 | | 2, coal 4+, doctor 1.45-4.75, gas |

Following are typical excerpts from the investigator's note-books, giving a little better idea, than do the tables, as to what such budgets means to strikers:

Place—Braddock
Nationality—Slavish

G—— is a laborer in a blast furnace. Earned $34.00 a week. Worked 11 hours on day shift, 13 hours on night shift. Has 6 children. Before prices were so high he could save, but cannot now. Groceries cost from $48.00 to $60.00 a month, and meat just about as much. The rent for the two rooms in which the family lives is $10.00 a month, and the landlord is soon to raise it to $11.00. A "tax" of $5.09 also has to be paid. The wife, when asked in the presence of her husband if she wanted him out till the strike was won, replied that she did.

Place—Braddock
Nationality—Slavish

L—— earned $4.62 a day and worked 13 days in two weeks. Has two children. The mother-in-law lives with them and pays half the rent, which is $10.00 a month for the two rooms. Food costs from $76.00 to $88.00 a month. They were unable to save anything. The man, who seemed more intelligent than most, declared vehemently that the union was the principal thing he cared about—more even than wages and hours. His wife said little, but agreed that she wanted him to stay out on strike.

Place—Braddock
Nationality—Slavish

E. is a laborer in rail mill. Earned 42 cents an hour ($80 in two weeks when working 14 turns). Worked 12 hours, sometimes on day shift, sometimes on night. Worked 7 days a week about twice in two months. Has four children. Rent for their two rooms costs $10 a month. Food costs about $80 a month; $5 a month was paid to the lodge to insure man and his wife. He had bought a $100 Liberty Bond, but has only paid $50 on it; $10 a month was deducted from his pay for it. He cared more for shorter hours than anything else, though he needed higher wages, too.

Place—Braddock
Nationality—Slavish

S. worked in engine house of Carnegie Steel Co.  Earned 48 cents an hour; $77 for 15 turns was the most he ever earned. Worked 10 hours a day, 7 days a week.  Has one child.  Rent for one room in which family lives is $6 a month.  Food costs from $60 to $65 a month; $1.85 a month is paid to the lodge. Shoes cost on an average $5 a month.  The wife wants the man to stay out on strike till it is won.  She cares most about reduction of hours, provided the weekly pay is not reduced.

Place—Homestead, Pa.
Nationality—Russian

K. worked as an open hearth laborer in one of the Carnegie Steel Mills, 11 hours during the day, 13 hours at night.  Every second Sunday he worked also.  His wife said that when he came home at night he was so tired that he just lay down and slept.  As one of the neighbors explained, when a man works as long as that "he can't see his babies, he can't see the daylight—all he can do is just to come home and lie and sleep." Shorter hours seemed more important to him than anything else, provided the weekly wages were not reduced.  He could get along after a fashion with his present wages, but could not stand the long day.  His wage was 45 cents an hour, and $60 or $70 in two weeks, according to whether there were 12 or 14 turns.  This amount did not permit any permanent saving, however.  He had one Victory Bond of $100 which he was forced to sell after the strike began in order to live.  A Liberty Bond which he had bought last year he had been obliged to sell again last fall in order to live.  He had nothing in the bank and he had not been able to afford membership in any lodge.  Rent for the three rooms in which he and his wife and three children lived was $15 a month.  The rooms were well lighted and the kitchen had running water.  He was obliged to pay for papering and painting them, however.

Place—Homestead, Pa.
Nationality—Austrian

C. worked as a laborer in one of the Carnegie Mills, 10 hours on the day shift, 12 hours at night, 6 turns a week, and earned from $53 to $58 in two weeks. He has two children. The family lives in three rooms, which are light, pleasant and well cared for. Rent is $15 a month. The wife said she wanted to move somewhere where rent was cheaper, but could find no other rooms. I was unable to discover how much food and clothes cost, as she kept no record of them. From $3.25 to $4 a month was paid to the lodge, according to the number of members who were ill. If a member is obliged to omit three monthly payments he is dropped from the lodge. The man was ill with influenza for 12 weeks last year and was obliged to sell the $200 Liberty Bond which he had in order to pay expenses. The bond was sold to the storekeeper, who only gave $180 for it, much to the indignation of Mrs. C. Since the strike began C. has had to sell the only other bond which he had—a $50 one, on which he had only paid $30. The family have no other savings, and the money from the bond is almost gone.

Last spring the family bought a load of coal for $13, but that is all gone and they have nothing but wood to burn. They cannot afford any more coal.

I asked Mrs. C. if she wanted her husband to go on strike, and if she now wanted him to stay out. She said she did not know anything about the strike before the men went out and knows little about it now. She does not want her husband to return to work while the strike is going on for fear he might be hurt. She does want better conditions, however. Shorter hours seem to her more important than anything else, provided there is no reduction in pay, as her husband is very tired when he comes home—too tired to do anything but eat and sleep. She also feels that more money is needed.

I asked if she liked living in Homestead. She replied that she had lived there ever since she came to America thirteen years ago and could not compare it with other places. She was too young when she left Austria to know much about conditions there.

### Place—Pittsburgh
### Nationality—Polish

S. is 45 years old. Six children in the family, the oldest 15 years old. The father was the only supporter. He was a laborer in the J. & L. mill, but did not have steady work. Worked 12 hours a day about four days a week frequently. Earned on the average about $25 a week. Was able to save nothing. Paid $1 a month to the lodge. He owns the house—a ramshackle wooden building—lives in three rooms. According to the wife, all that is earned goes into food. Though wages were quite inadequate, the long hours seemed most serious to the woman. When asked if she wanted him to stay out till the strike is won replied, " Yes—what a question ! "

### Place—Pittsburgh
### Nationality—Polish

P. is 56 years old. Has three children, one of them is a boy who is now earning $10 a week. Has worked as a laborer, putting screws on bolts at the Oliver Iron & Steel Co. for 10½ hours a day, 5½ days a week. He earned 30 cents an hour. Before the strike, he was sick for ten weeks and hence had no savings. He paid $1.05 a month to the lodge, however. Rent for the two rooms in which the family lives is $8.50 a month. The man wants a permanent union most of all, but better wages and hours are both very important.

### Place—Pittsburgh
### Nationality—Lithuanian

J. has six children, one of whom, a girl, is earning $7.50 a week. The man worked as a laborer at the J. & L. mill, 12 hours a day, 7 days a week. (Since the strike was declared the week has been shortened to 6 days for that job.) He earned $5.80 a day. Rent for three rooms in rear building costs $9 a month; 85 cents a month is spent for schooling. He pays 50 cents a month to the lodge, and $1 more when a member dies. He was unable to save anything else, because he was forced to buy at the company store, where prices were higher than elsewhere. Sometimes nothing remained of his wages when things purchased there—clothes, groceries, etc.—were deducted. Those who refused to trade with the company had things made unpleasant for them.

Place—Homestead, Pa.<br/>Nationality—Irish

S. has two children. He was a pipe worker in the Carnegie Steel Mill, with 10 hours on the day shift, 13 hours on the night shift, 7 days a week. Every second week he was obliged to work from 7 A. M. on Saturday to 7 A. M. on Sunday, with only one hour off for rest and food. Then he had to begin work again at 3 P. M., and continue until 7 the next morning—thus working 39 hours out of 48. (Both he and Mr. C., another striker, complained that no time was given for eating meals when a man was on a 12-hour shift. He was expected to snatch a bite of food as he worked. Mr. C. said he was obliged to work 15 hours every Sunday, and often did not get time to eat a mouthful during that period. This, he considered, one of the most serious grievances.) There is no chance for advancement in the plant. The boss brings in his friends, relatives, or people who have pull with him, and gives them the better positions instead of advancing others.

Mr. S. earned 47 cents an hour, and from $74 to $75 in two weeks. He was discharged from the Canadian Army about a year before the strike, and during that period he had been able to save nothing. He bought one $150 Liberty Bond, but had only paid $100 on it, and was obliged to dispose of it for $90 when the strike began. The company had forced him to buy it and deducted $15 a month from his pay for it. During the strike he had a few odd jobs, but for the most part they had been living on credit.

They pay $15 rent for 4 rooms. This rent is lower because of the fact that the house is close beside the railroad and is noisy

and dirty. The landlord threatened to raise it soon. Groceries
for the family cost from $25 to $30 in two weeks. This pur-
chases a very small and inadequate supply. They do not know
how much meat costs. Horlich's milk for the small baby costs
about 25 cents a day. The mother thinks it necessary to pay
this, as she lost another baby because of improper feeding. She
says that she can spend very little on clothes. She has had only
one suit in six years. Friends have given her clothes for the
children to help out. She says she wishes the strike had never
happened, and is rather discouraged about it. Nevertheless, she
thinks the men ought to have better conditions and wants the
men to win out. She is indignant that so many of the higher
paid men are still at work, and thinks they ought to come out
to help the others.

Place—Homestead, Pa.<br>
Nationality—Slav from Austria-Hungary

D. did repair work on machines and furnaces, working 12
and 13 hours a day, and sometimes 36 hours at a stretch. Once
he objected to doing overtime work when he was very tired and
was laid off for a week as a penalty. His work was dangerous,
yet he earned only 45 cents an hour. He has three children.

Rent for three rooms, a parlor, kitchen and bedroom, is $16.
There is water in the kitchen, but the room is so dark that the
gas must be kept burning all the time. The woman cooks with
it, and also heats other rooms with it in winter. Groceries cost
$40 a month, meat from $25 to $30, milk $4.50. Shoes for the
children last only one or two months and cost from $5 to $6 a
pair. The man and his wife both belong to two lodges, and
pay from $14 to $15 a month to them. The children are also
insured, and 20 cents a month is paid for them. The lodge pays
$5 a week in case of sickness, $1,000 in case of death of the
man, $250 in case of death of a child.

They had bought bonds worth $450, $350 of this they had
spent before the strike for necessary food and the expenses of
the baby's christening. The remaining $100 they had spent dur-
ing the strike. They have no savings.

I asked the woman if she thought she was better off in Amer-

ica than if she had stayed in Austria-Hungary and she said she
didn't know.  She had lived in Homestead for fifteen years and
could not afford to move anywhere else in order to get better
conditions.  She knew nothing about other parts of America.
Her husband said he has his first citizenship papers, but had
not yet gotten his second.  He told me indignantly that some
strikers had applied for their second papers in Pittsburgh, but
had been refused because they were on strike.

The wife told me she wanted her husband to stay on strike
till he got shorter hours and better conditions.  She did not
"want a bad name on her children."

Place—Homestead, Pa.

Nationality—Slavish

V. was a millwright in the open hearth department, working
12 hours a day, and sometimes 7 days a week.  He earned 45
cents an hour, or from $100 to $105 in two weeks.  There are
seven children in the family.

They pay $10 a month rent for two rooms in a rear house.
There is running water in the kitchen, but the only toilet is
in the yard, which also has open drains.  They have tried to get
a better apartment with three rooms, but cannot find one, for
landlords object to such a large family of children and will not
rent to them.  Groceries cost them about $60 a month, meat
about $29 or $30, milk $5.  One of the daughters works in the
grocery store, earning $10 a week, and the family are obliged
to trade there, so she will not lose her position.  Coal costs
them $20 a year—perhaps more.  Monthly dues to the "so-
ciety" which pays sick benefits and death benefits are $5 for
the man and his wife, $1.20 for the children.  The children
go to Slavish school, and something must be paid for their
tuition also.

They have been unable to save anything with the exception of
$800 in Liberty Bonds, which they had at the beginning of
the strike.  These have all been sold since then, with a loss of
$4 or $5 on each one.  The company deducted $50 a month
from the man's pay while he was buying his bonds.  The wife

has been sick a good deal for the last ten years and her illness has cost money.

She says she wants her husband to stay out on strike. Shorter hours seem to be most important, but better general conditions are also necessary.

Place—Homestead, Pa.<br>Nationality—Slavish

E. was a laborer, working 12 hours a day with a 24-hour shift every other Sunday (one hour being allowed off for breakfast). He earned 42 cents an hour, or $60 in two weeks. He has four children.

Rent for the one room in which they live is $4.50 a month. Food cost $60 a month even when they had little but bread and potatoes. They sometimes had meat, but never any cakes or pies. Three years ago, when wages were only $1.60 a day, they could buy more than they can now because of the high prices. The shopkeepers find out beforehand when a rise in wages is to come and put up the prices at once, the man says. They cannot buy any clothes without going hungry, and cannot afford insurance or lodge membership. He says he has never been able to save anything. He was forced to buy a $50 or $100 bond of each loan, but had to sell them again at once. He told of one case where a man who said he could only afford a $50 bond instead of the $100 one, which the boss ordered him to take, was tarred and feathered by men whom he was sure the company had stirred up to do it. This story was also told me by two American strikers—Mr. S. and Mr. C.

The family had been living on his last pay ever since the strike began. Higher wages seem as important to them as shorter hours. The wife said she wanted him to stay out on strike.

One great grievance was that there was no chance to get ahead or change to better work. He had tried hard to get a chance to do more skilled work, which he was sure he could do just as well as anyone, but though he had worked there for thirteen years, he was never given a chance. The foreman kept people back because they were hunkies and brought in his relatives and those who treated him to booze to take the better positions. If anyone complained he was fired.

The man lost his thumb at the mill and was out for three months a while ago. The company paid him $75.

He has his first citizenship papers and sends his children to the public school.

Place—Monessen, Pa.
Nationality—Russian

T. worked as a pipe fitter in the machine shop of the Pittsburgh Steel Co., 10½ hours a day, 7 days a week. Sometimes as often as twice a week he was obliged to work 29½ hours at a stretch. For this period he was given overtime pay for only 5½ hours. He earned 46c. an hour or about $100 in two weeks. He has two children.

Rent for three good rooms is $18. Food, which is quite ample, costs $100 a month. Insurance costs $62 a year. He had saved about $100 before the strike. He evidently considered himself much more prosperous than many of the strikers. His principal objection was too long hours.

During the organizing campaign a company official had asked him to go around and find out what "Bolsheviks" there were among the men, and what men had joined the union, so they could be discharged. He refused but someone he knew undertook the job.

## V

## GRIEVANCES AND CONTROL IN A NO-CON-
## FERENCE INDUSTRY

ANALYSIS of the data gathered in this Inquiry on the grievances of workers and the companies' methods of control of employees in the iron and steel industry warrants the following conclusions:

The Steel Corporation's "arbitrary" control of hours and
   wages extends to everything in individual steel jobs, resulting in daily grievances.
The Corporation, committed to a non-union policy, is as
   helpless as the workers to prevent these grievances.
The grievances, since there exists no working machinery of
   redress, weigh heavily in the industry because they incessantly remind the worker that he has no " say " whatever in steel.
The strike was the workers' revolt against the entire system
   of arbitrary control and for trade unionism.

The Steel Corporation, here as in hours and wages, is the determining factor for the whole industry. "Independent" companies, however, have shown far more tendency to break away from the Corporation's methods in the case of control than in the case of wages and hours.

This section deals with the *industrial* effects of a policy of "no conference," and arbitrary control; its effects on the worker in relation to his job, especially inside the mill; its inevitable consequences of rebellion and the means taken to soften rebellion.

Section VII will deal with the *social results* of such a labor

119

policy; the means taken to combat rebellion when softening fails; the effects on the worker in relation to the community; the effects on the community and state; and will try to determine to what extent social institutions in towns, counties or states, i.e. the executive government, the judiciary, the church, the press, etc., were bent to the business of maintaining one corporation's policy of " not dealing with labor unions."

The evidence for both sections is drawn principally from public records, private labor files of companies, interviews with Corporation officials, also with officers of " labor detective " concerns and from affidavits or statements from over five hundred strikers and non-strikers.

This section deals mainly with conditions before the strike, with the normal conduct of the industry, with the problem raised by a friendly critic of Mr. Gary who said:

" The trouble is that the Corporation's labor policy is still in the stage of detectives and toilets."

That is: a stage of arbitrary control naturally causing unrest which is met with espionage on the one hand and sanitation and welfare on the other.

It is important to grasp clearly the distinction between the two aspects of control in this or any other industry. The distinction is that between " personnel management " and " industrial relations "; the one confined within the plant, conditioned primarily by each job's requirements; the other, labor policy or the system of relations between the labor force and the owners. The first aspect concerns the job,—who gets it, how he shall do it, how it shall be safeguarded if hazardous, who shall meet the emergency requirements always fringing the job, the running of the job for production. The second aspect concerns the relations of the workers as a whole to the sum of jobs: it concerns the profits of work (wages), the length of work (hours) and the *vesting* of authority over the separate jobs (control proper,—whether autocratic control, trade union control, shop committee control, etc.). The first aspect is the primary concern of employment managers, or scientific managers or production engineers; the second aspect is concerned primarily with who shall control the employment manager or production engineer and for what purposes. Each function tends to encroach on the other and is generally nullified when it does. In the steel industry the typical employment manager is helpless when he tries to deal with industrial relations; he can get the workers a day off or a change of job, but he cannot influence hours, wages or the foreman's authority. Likewise the Finance Committee of the Steel Corporation can decree hours and wages but is helpless to direct workers on the jobs. But always *the second aspect stretches back with decisive effect over the first.* In the steel industry this is peculiarly so.

Section VII therefore deals with the more important phase: with the non-union policy of the Corporation, the resultant attitude of the workers, the means,—such as espionage, discharge for unionism, blacklists, police, " labor detectives" etc.—used to combat the workers, the use made of civil authorities, courts, press and pulpit, particularly during the strike. It analyzes *the actually existing alternative to " the kind of conference the labor unions wanted."* But before the present section's analysis,—which must begin at the opposite pole, the organization of the jobs for production,—can be grasped, some of the facts concerning the other greater aspect of control must be set down.

The character of the control in the Steel Corporation is plain: it is arbitrary control. The workers called it " autocratic." Mr. Gary's word,[1] spoken to the Senate investigating Committee, was " arbitrarily," used by him in reference

---

[1] Senate Testimony, Vol. I, p. 226.

to fixing wages, but applying equally to the whole system. With this Mr. Gary coupled his recognition that there was possible at least one other system of control—by conference —in the statements that " his workmen knew that they were always free to come to him or any plant officer or to send committees." Coupled with this, investigation proved, were the facts that no workers, individuals or committees, do confer with Mr. Gary, and that actual conferences with plant officers, higher than foremen, fell into either of two categories: (a) individual or committee conferences which did not deal with hours or wages or authority of control, but with comparatively minor matters; or (b) conferences by temporary committees concerning hours or wages, of such a rare character as to prove themselves the exception, the exhibition of temerity, almost like strikes. The few instances of such, discovered in this Inquiry, are detailed in a sub-report.

The practice of Corporation plants was by no means uniform, but all practice conformed to the Corporation's policy, as perfectly understood and as set forth by Mr. Gary, for example, publicly to his own officials as follows:[1]

"  .  .  .  treating the whole thing as a business proposition, drawing the line so that you are just and generous and yet at the same time keeping your position and permitting others to keep theirs, retaining the control and management of your affairs, *keeping the whole thing in your own hands,* but nevertheless with due consideration to the rights and interests of all others who may be affected by your management."

In practice, it was found, Corporation steel workers wherever questioned, recognized that the control of " the whole thing" was absolutely in the Corporation's " own hands." Surprise, that the inquirer should be so naïve, or contemptu-

[1] Proceedings of meeting of presidents of subsidiary companies of Steel Corporation. Empire Building, New York, Jan. 21, 1919. (Senate Testimony, Vol. I, p. 242.)

ous jeers greeted any serious question concerning the "right to see Mr. Gary or the Superintendent."

A number of "independents" have parted company, to slight or great degree, with the Corporation in the matter of installing some conferring. This is considered later, but there is no question that the iron and steel industry, as a whole, will change its manner of control only as the Corporation does.

The Corporation, of course, has been assailed for many years for its "autocratic methods of handling workmen," and in one instance, after due self-investigation, has gone on record approving the policy; Mr. Gary put this record into the Senate investigation.[1] This was the "Report of Committee of Stockholders," dated April 15, 1912, which under the heading, "Repression of the Men," said that if the term "repression of workmen" involved "the question as to what measures the Corporation should adopt for the *suppression* of organizations that in the past have, at times, proved irresponsible and incapable of self-control," then, the Committee finds that "while we do not believe the final solution . . . has been reached," still, "we do believe . . . that the Steel Corporation, in view of the practices often pursued by labor organizations in steel mills in past years, *is justified in the position it has taken.*"

Repression justified and the whole control in their own hands is a policy so long practised by Corporation officers that they rarely really question it except when disrupting strike times compel them to discuss it. So customary is it that Mr. Gary cited with satisfaction one example of its workings, quoted elsewhere from the Senate testimony, and reset down here in part:[2]

For instance, to mention a somewhat trivial circumstance, some three or four years ago—not to be exactly specific as to date—

[1] Senate Testimony, Vol. I, p. 232-233.
[2] Senate Testimony, Vol. I, pp. 161-2.

one of our presidents telephoned to the president of our Corporation, who is in general charge of operations, that a certain
number of men—it may have been a thousand or it may have
been two thousand men—in a certain mill had all gone out, and
his report was that there was no reason for their going out . . .
And he said, " It is very easy for me to fill this mill, and I
will proceed to do it." The president of the corporation came
to me immediately and reported this. I said, " Tell him to wait
and to come to New York." He came the next morning and he
made substantially that same statement to me. I said, " Have
you taken pains to find out; has anybody spoken to you? " " No,"
he said, " I have not received any complaint whatever." I said,
" Are you sure no complaint has been made to anyone? " He
said, " I will find out." I said, " You had better do so before
you decide what you are going to do or what you propose to do."
He went back; got hold of the foreman. A committee of men
had come to the foreman and said that they thought three
things, if I remember, were wrong—not very important, but they
claimed they were wrong. And the president came back the
second time and reported that; and I said, " Well, now, if they
state the facts there, isn't the company wrong? " " Well,"
he said, " I don't consider it very important." I said, " That is
not the question. Are you wrong in any respect? It seems to
me you are wrong with respect to two of those things, and the
other, not. Now, you go right back to your factory and just
put up a sign that with reference to those two particular things,
the practice will be changed."

The incident represents completely the Corporation's
working system of control;—the un-asked-for grievances of
thousands, the perilous strike, the arbitrary intervention, and
the episode ended with " just put up a sign." This section's
analysis centers on the post where signs are put up and the
foreman who had ignored a committee. But the causes for
such a system of industrial control must be sought behind
the post and the foreman.

Those reasons involve a phase of which Mr. Gary seemed unconscious and which indicates that personal will or personal powers of arbitrary intervention may after all be less controlling than other forces. These forces molded modern industrial development and in two senses they left the Corporation comparatively helpless. In the first place the trend of development forced, or at least made easier, the Corporation's first choice of fundamental non-union policy. The mere concentration of private financial power tended to oust collective bargaining. Professor Carleton Parker put the matter as follows: [1]

In the words of Mr. A. D. Noyes . . . "We are in the presence of a novel and striking condition of things in American finance, whereby active or potential control of a very great part both of our financial institutions and our industrial institutions is concentrated in the hands of a comparatively small group of financiers."

How does this affect the labor problem in America?

First, it brings the most complete temperamental and geographical divorce of management and worker in industrial history.

Second, it leaves the final control of industrial enterprises in non-industrial, and in the end, abstract financial, hands.

Third, it means that the only information from the industrial plants which these boards of directors care for or understand is that of statistics of output and costs.

Fourth, it turns over the formation of wage—and labor—policies to men supersensitive to the stock market, a market notoriously panicky over labor disturbances.

In a word, it turns industrial affairs, one of whose major characteristics is the human quality brought by the worker, over to a group of financial minds whose education, environment, and ambitions make it impossible for them to obtain an accurate perspective of the human side of industrial production. The condition is potential for danger.

[1] "The Technique of American Industry." *Atlantic Monthly*, Jan. 1920. (Written in 1914.)

In a second sense the helplessness of the steel masters is daily emphasized by their inability to keep from creating grievances.  It was not an original object of the Corporation when organized in 1901 to go into either the detective business or the welfare business.  It was going to make money out of plants which were to make steel as much as possible and as cheap as possible and it deemed the best way of keeping down labor costs was to control arbitrarily hours and wages.  Since unions try to cut hours and increase wages the Corporation adopted the anti-union policy which was not so widespread in the steel industry in 1901 as the Corporation has made it now.  After twenty years of this kind of control the Corporation finds that in making steel, it must spend five to seven millions a year for sanitation, stock participation, pensions and welfare, and sums for watching its workers which are not revealed to investigators.

It is not merely that the Corporation Executive Committee on June 17, 1901, passed the resolution:[1]

" That we are unalterably opposed to any extension of union labor, and advise subsidiary companies to take a firm position when these questions come up and say they are not going to recognize it, that is any extension of unions in mills where they do not now exist that great care should be used to prevent trouble and that they promptly report and confer with this Corporation."

But on the basis of this fundamental labor policy, laid down at the start and pursued so that all unions were eliminated from the Corporation's mills, the Corporation developed its whole productive organization, trained its great staffs of executives, superintendents and foremen, organized the jobs and picked the labor force until now it makes steel through a machinery which makes trouble too.  A policy or system of industrial relations, on the employing side, becomes

[1] Minutes Executive Committee, see Senate Document 110, Vol. III, p. 118 and pp. 497-499.

visibly a body of executives and their methods of action. The Corporation's executives are trained anti-union men who convert the Corporation's labor policy into action by organizing labor forces which shall be primarily "tractable."[1] They translate the 1901 resolution into orders such as the following, for handling labor:[2] "Catch 'em young, treat 'em rough, tell 'em nothing." The Corporation's executives, in order to meet the Corporation policy, are *forced* to grind the faces of the "hunkies" and to trust to "welfare" to salve the exacerbations.

The system, of course, is not new. It was typically American in the heyday of the Captains of Industry; but no big corporation has developed it so drastically or clung to it to so late a date as has the Steel Corporation.

The system, in which both sides, employers and employees are enmeshed, is subject to two viewpoints appallingly different: and the viewpoint of the employees is what caused the strike. The viewpoint of the directors of the Steel Corporation is based on examining the reports of millions spent for "welfare," the picture books of company houses, clubs, hospitals and towns, photographs of groups of smiling old pensioners, and finally the Corporation's annual payroll, as big as a small nation's national debt: viewing the total the directors naturally feel, "the Corporation does a tremendous lot for its workmen." The viewpoint of the workman is based not on totals but first on the percentage of all these things touching him personally. The bulk of employees— the unskilled and semi-skilled—have had simply no experience of the company houses, "welfare" and pensions, and their percentage of stock profits do not impress them. But

---

[1] Letter of manager of Edgar Thomson works, quoted in "Inside History of Carnegie Steel Co.," by J. H. Bridge, p. 81. "My experience (in 1875) has been that Germans and Irish, Swedes and what I denominate 'buckwheats' (young American country boys), judiciously mixed, make the most effective and tractable force you can find."

[2] Quoted by R. S. Baker, N. Y. *Evening Post*, Dec. 31, 1910.

in the second place, they, as well as the skilled, experience the Corporation's hours and wages, about which they have as little "say" as about the weather, and were hitherto hopeless about getting a "say"; and they experience daily grievances about which they cannot help *trying* to "have a say." Now if the system is such that the grievances are excessive, and if the grievances seem to them to be met mostly by detectives and "welfare" in place of machinery for redress, and if the grievances *perpetually remind them of the great grievance of no control over hours and wages,* it is obvious that the workers may come to look blackly on what the directors regard blandly.

The data will be analyzed first as to the causal relation between the customary organization of the steel industry and grievances.

A Pittsburgh professor of economics, an admiring student of the steel industry, described its organization to the Commission as "highly militarized." Several steel masters agreed that his description was fitting.

"The general staff of the Carnegie Company," he said, "is one of the most efficient in the whole world of business. The superintendents, department managers and foremen are splendidly loyal efficient officers with high morale.

"Bound to them are the non-commissioned officers, such gang leaders as rollers, blowers, melters and the other top-skilled Americans, who are part bosses, part workmen. Altogether this administrative group, almost a third of the force, has a real military efficiency, bound to the company by stock participation, bonuses, loans, house-rentals and pensions."

The "army" under this group is, of course, almost altogether made up of low-skilled "foreigners." They are the smallest participants in the Corporation's stock offers, tonnage bonuses, company houses and pensions. Before considering how this system impinges on them, let us view it in relation to the skilled Americans.

The first characteristic of the militaristic system is promotion: promotion by seniority. From the upper half of the semi-skilled class on up every steel worker has his eye on the next higher job. He is in line for it, but he has no guarantee that he will get it. Seniority is a custom only. The man who incurs the displeasure of the Company is not promoted. Let him be suspected of " agitating in the mill " or of being a " trouble maker " and he has no way of enforcing his complaint when others are promoted over him. Merely making the complaint may be deemed proof of being " undesirable " and cause for demotion. In the absence of any enforceable rule favoritism results and where it may not exist, it is suspected by the workers. The following from the diary of a steel worker at Gary in the summer of 1919 is paralleled by many other statements to the Commission's investigators:

" Old hand here tells me: ' Superintendent of this department? He's the cousin of the general superintendent. His assistant? Married to his sister. Boss's assistant on this floor is his son-in-law.' And so on down a long list of the better jobs. It is the universal impression of the lower ranks that favoritism rules."

There is then an inherent grievance touching the skilled worker's most precious possession under this system—his *right* to promotion.

The second characteristic is " speeding up." An object of this militarized organization is the attainment of the highest production. Tonnage bonuses are the commonest method of accomplishing it. Supplementary is the incited rivalry between teams or crews, between furnaces, between departments, between plants. The " record " made by a rival outfit is the unceasingly applied spur. Against " speeding up " the skilled worker feels he has no defense. All the while he feels that his success in attaining unexampled tonnage—and unexampled bonus—may be the excuse for a cut in bonus rates. He feels that rates are "shaved," as it is called, just to "speed" him harder by egging him on to the attempt to regain his former earnings' total. "Speeding" is most marked as a grievance in the Pittsburgh District.

Third, because of their obvious relation to control, the Corporation's stock sales, loans, bonuses and pensions are viewed as a grievance by many highly skilled. They gradually see what these mean. If they complain on any score whatever they may be told directly: "You own stock in the Corporation? Well, then you don't want to damage that stock's price by making trouble for the Company. This complaint of yours makes trouble." Many workers, taking Company jobs, living in Company houses, buying at Company stores, obtaining Company loans, holding Company stock, working toward a Company pension, feel "all sewed up." Every "lay-off" they ask, to recuperate from speeding or long hours, depends on the favor of a Company boss and reminds them of all their company entanglements.

Freedom from arbitrary control, then, which was generally given by the skilled Americans who did strike as their object in going out, seems by the organization of the steel job to be denied them. In Youngstown, Johnstown, Wheeling, Cleveland, as well as in many Calumet District mills where great numbers of Americans struck, the basis of their peculiar grievance, aside from long hours, was the system of absolute control. These men earned from $8 to $30 a day. Their willingness to imperil this and all their prospects indicated how strongly some of them rebelled against having no "say."

Add to this the eternal and increasing grievance of excessive hours and the state of mind of even the skilled American tended to become more violent than clear. Here is a

page from the diary of the Gary worker, made in August,
1919, recording the talk of a group of skilled workers:

" A heater who works eleven hours by day and thirteen by
night, making $400 a month, says, ' Why shouldn't we get the
eight-hour day without striking for it? I'd be glad to give
up three or four dollars a day to get eight hours.'

" An engineer many years on the job says, ' Count me in
for a six-day week too, like a civilized man. This fourteen hours
a night, seven days a week, is hell.'

" The gang boss says, ' Who the devil is this man Gary to tell
our representatives to go to hell. Somebody's going to get him
for that.'

" Another says, ' Gary thinks we've worked his old twelve and
fourteen hours so long we'll stand for anything.' "

This was before the strike. The following, one of many
statements made by skilled men during the strike, was obtained in Youngstown, October 25, from a gray-haired
stationary engineer:

" The other day the boss called on me and told me I was
too valuable a man not to be working for the company, that all
the places were filled except mine, and that he wanted me to
come back. I told him I would think it over. The next day
he came back again and asked me how much was owing on my
house. I told him it was none of his God damn business. I told
him there was not a cent owing on my house, but if there was
my wife and family would follow me into the street before I
would touch any of his dirty money. There *is* money owing on
my house, but I would not give him the satisfaction of knowing
it. I would rather lose it than go back to work before this
strike is won. I had relatives in the Revolutionary War, I fought
for freedom in the Philippines myself, and I had three boys in
the army fighting for democracy in France. One of them is lying
in the Argonne Forest now. If my boy could give his life
fighting for free democracy in Europe, I guess I can stand it to

fight this battle through to the end. I am going to help my
fellow workmen show Judge Gary that he can't act as if he was
a king or kaiser and tell them how long they have got to
work!"

All the foregoing analysis, finally, applies to only about
one-third of the employees, and that third the better paid,
shorter-houred, better treated, the skilled, the "Americans."
If the Corporation's "welfare," which applies principally to
this third, leaves so many with such a viewpoint, it becomes
practically negligible, as an emollient in consideration of the
two-thirds, the "hunkies," particularly *if the Corporation's
system of production and control creates even more grievances
among the immigrants* than among the Americans.

How does the basic organization of the steel industry affect
the "hunky job"? Below the skilled, who form the apex of
the pyramid, comes the indefinable mass of the semi-skilled;
beneath these, the mass of the unskilled, mainly classed as
common labor. The loyalizing forces of the militarized
organization are loose among the semi-skilled and scarcely
exist at all among the unskilled. The bulk of both sections,
of course, is recruited from the fifty nationalities, more or
less, making up the foreigners, mostly Slavs.[1] At the top
of the semi-skilled there is no sharp dividing line from the
skilled. Heaters' helpers, melters' helpers, the helpers closest
to rollers, blowers, etc., hold jobs requiring a training which
takes years; in these jobs the influence of possible promotion,
the pull of seniority, is almost as strong as among the highly
skilled jobs. In the jobs below these, where pay and skill
are less, the influence of possible promotion is also less, and
so on, down through the whole range of jobs beneath the

[1] Some idea of the number of races in the steel industry is given by
the following table, submitted to the Senate investigating committee
by the superintendent of the Homestead plant. It is not typical of the
industry in two respects: (a) the small proportion of Slavs, Greeks
and Italians; (b) the large proportion of Americans, due to the un-

hierarchy of the skilled and the upper half of the semi-skilled, the prospect of promotion becomes more and more remote, the militarizing influence rapidly lessens, until at the bottom the whole mass of common labor, the broad base of the pyramid of steel, is fluid. The jobs are not clearly defined, the capabilities for the jobs are largely brawn, and the holders of the jobs can be and are switched about. Not but that even the heavy common labor jobs in steel require a certain degree of training, rather knack, but the "know-how" can be learned in a few days or weeks at most, and if not learned the job can still somehow be done, though badly and with

usual number of negroes. Fifty-four races are given, or 52 non-American. (Senate testimony, Vol. II, p. 480.)

*Nationality report, Homestead Steel Works, Howard Axle Works, Carrie Furnaces, Oct. 8, 1919.*

| Nationality | Number | Per cent. | Nationality | Number | Per cent. |
|---|---|---|---|---|---|
| American | 5,799 | 39.45 | Kreiner (Slovanian) | 6 | 0.04 |
| Armenian | 15 | .10 | Lithuanian | 238 | 1.62 |
| Austrian | 42 | .29 | Macedonian | 4 | .03 |
| Arabian | 5 | .30 | Mexican | 130 | .89 |
| Albanian | 25 | .17 | Negro: | | |
| Austro-Servian | 1 | .01 | American | 1,734 | 11.80 |
| Belgian | 3 | .02 | British | 1 | .01 |
| Bohemian | 2 | .01 | East India | 1 | .01 |
| Brazilian | 1 | .01 | West India | 1 | .01 |
| Bulgarian | 67 | .46 | Norwegian | 4 | .03 |
| Canadian | 20 | .14 | Polish | 432 | 2.94 |
| Croatian (Horvat) | 299 | 2.04 | Portuguese | 1 | .01 |
| Cuban | 2 | .01 | Porto Rican | 18 | .12 |
| Dalmatian | 9 | .06 | Roumanian | 49 | .33 |
| Danish | 6 | .04 | Russian | 628 | 4.28 |
| English | 424 | 2.89 | Ruthenian | 1 | .01 |
| Filipino | 1 | .01 | Saxon | 4 | .03 |
| Finnish | 7 | .05 | Scotch | 226 | 1.54 |
| French | 7 | .05 | Slovak | 2,373 | 16.15 |
| German | 219 | 1.49 | Servian | 26 | .18 |
| Greek | 267 | 1.82 | Spanish | 48 | .33 |
| Hebrew | 11 | .07 | Swede | 74 | .50 |
| Hindu | 1 | .01 | Swiss | 11 | .07 |
| Hollander | 6 | .04 | Syrian | 9 | .06 |
| Hungarian (Magyar) | 574 | 3.91 | Turk | 53 | .36 |
| Indian | 3 | .02 | Welsh | 91 | .62 |
| Irish | 443 | 3.02 | | | |
| Italian | 264 | 1.80 | Total | 14,687 | 100.6 |
| Japanese | 1 | .01 | | | |

bad effects on the clumsy worker. Every sort of long, hard, hot, heavy work, from shoveling weighty substances into the maws of white-hot furnaces or sledging to pieces still-hot masses of metal or slag, to picking up or putting down or heaving or carrying pipes, hot bricks, planks, great iron hooks, sheets of metal, largely with an accompaniment of grease, noise, sweat or danger—these make up the steel jobs and the dirt, grease, heat and long hours generally increase the lower the job is in the pyramid. Finally, the pay-rate of the common labor at the bottom, the lowest of all, of course, is the base from which all other wage rates are ranked.

The semi-skilled is the growing group in the whole industry. The mechanizing of processes in the past two decades has revolutionized the industry, each new machine displacing skilled men at the top and unskilled at the bottom. More and more the steel job tends to become the job of a machine, each new machine tending to abolish either the occupations of a dozen common laborers in favor of one semi-skilled man or of a few skilled men in favor of one not so skilled. More and more the making of steel requires a type different from either the brawny Fafnir who used to wield the " peel " or the versatile brainy man who could do many things with many complicated machines. The new type is the slighter, weaker man with intelligence a little above the common laborer, who can handle with accuracy a few levers on some crane, charging machine, or " skip." He must not have too much brain or he will revolt at the deadly monotony of moving his few levers on his one machine ten to fourteen hours a day and from three hundred to three hundred and forty days in the year.

In these jobs, of the lower half of the semi-skilled and all of the unskilled, two things are all-important: the disagreeableness of the job and the length of time the worker is kept at it. The lure of immediate promotion is small, one or two cents more an hour, no change in the length of the day and mainly the added satisfaction of slightly greater security, inasmuch as it is always forty-two-cent common labor that gets laid off or fired first when work is slack. Hours and wages, then, are the great grievance of common labor, with denial of promotion entering in according to the job's height in the scale of the semi-skilled. In the upper half of the semi-skilled the lure of promotion takes hold of the worker out of all proportion almost even in comparison with the skilled American worker higher up; for it is this almost-skilled worker, of five to fifteen years' experience in the business, who remembers most keenly the dirt, heat and drudgery from which he ascended and who feels most poignantly the failure to win promotion still higher if the discrimination against him is based solely on the one thing he cannot get away from,—his race.

For common labor, then, grievances primarily concern too low wages, too long hours and the arbitrariness of the foreman; he feels little their connection with the company's labor policy; for the semi-skilled, grievances are less concerned with wages, more with hours and most sharply with discrimination based on race and preventing promotion, and through this, a great deal with the company's labor policy.

Here is the sum of grievances and the life and progress of the immigrant steel worker as determined from hundreds of interviews: The Slav, Pole, Serb, Croat, Russian, Greek, Magyar, Jew, Roumanian or Turk is nine times out of ten, a peasant, taking an industrial job for the first time. At the start, only as the wages fail to keep him and his family as he wants them to be kept, or the hours break down his health, does he care much about " controlling " either wages or hours. What matters most to him is that if the mill is shut down he is the first to be laid off; if the job is unusually hot, greasy or heavy, he is the first to be set to

it.  He is the most arbitrarily, often brutally, shifted and
ordered about; if he takes a lay-off, he is the most likely to
pay for it with his job; if he is late a few minutes he is
the most likely to be heavily docked and he is the most likely
to be kept beyond his hour with no additional pay.  If there
is sickness in his home or he is otherwise kept away, his
excuses get the shortest shrift.  If he is the butt of unusual
prejudice in either his foreman or some fellow-worker,
evinced in profanity or the penalties of always the nastier
task, he knows least where to go for redress or how to speak it.

As the years go on and he works on up, the right to his
job, the fear of losing it or of being shifted become more important and he is the one to value most his security in promotion.  He finds he is the one whose personal preference
counts least and the bar that stands out strongest in his mind
is not being an " American."  " That job is not a hunky's
job; you can't have it," is the answer that destroys his confidence in himself.  He can't change his race; he can't change
his foreman and he cannot get above the foreman.  By this
stage in the progress he has become sufficiently Americanized
to want higher wages and shorter hours, he wants better
living and more recognition as a human being and less as a
hunky, but he finds himself in the grip of a system which
regulates his hours by whistle, his wages by bulletin-board,
his grievances by rebuff.  In this stage the union organizer
found tens of thousands in the steel industry to whom the
strike was very considerably a revolt against arbitrary control, as it was principally for the Americans and hardly at all
for the common laborer.  Of the " foreigners," this class is the
one left by the strike in the most rebellious frame of mind
and most likely to answer another strike call.

It is entirely possible that this state of things is almost
unknown to the corporation officials who assured the public
and the Senate investigating committee that the steel workers

were " satisfied " and " contented," and that " there was no
cause for the strike." It has been pointed out elsewhere that
Mr. Gary has admittedly no functioning open and above-
board system of learning what his workmen think. If the
Corporation even had an efficient system of redressing daily
grievances, leaving totally out of consideration hours and
wages, Mr. Gary would inevitably learn these things. Most
of the companies now have employment systems which are
efficient in turning out statistics concerning the labor force
gleaned from two points of contact; hiring and firing. In
between, the most important time of all, these systems admittedly have no contact. The employment managers rely
on the foremen, " cooperate " with the welfare workers and
fundamentally are powerless to do anything. Consideration
of wages and hours is clean out of their province, and as more
than half the remaining grievances deal with the foreman,
who is their co-worker, they are a futility as far as any
redress is concerned and not only do they know it, but the
mass of steel workers know it too. The general test of an
employment manager's success, in the estimation of his superintendent, is whether or not he is successful in keeping complaints from bothering the superintendent. What with his
powerlessness and with the prevalence of the system, the employment manager, whatever his human desires, quickly falls
into the way of steel—to refuse, rebuff, browbeat, or, finally,
to " get-to-hell-out," that is, fire.

Here are typical statements of grievances of the lesser
skilled taken from Inquiry investigators' notebooks or from
Senate Committee testimony, just as the workers disjointedly
spill them out. They could be duplicated to the point of
boredom.

J—— W——, a Czech, (Homestead) was a miner during
his first two years in this country. Learned to speak
English in the mines. Is married, with two children, owns his

own home and has his first citizenship papers. In the steel mills he is a pipe fitter, $8.50 a day, of 10½ hours day shift and 14 hours night shift. Thinks the hours are altogether too long but the pay is fair. During the war the workers were paid, he said, for every hour they put in; now they are paid for 10 hours during the day but must work 10½ hours. At night they are paid for 12 hours but work 14. Those who complained were told to get-to-hell-out if they did not like it.

W—— declares that the workers have *never been able to learn the rate of pay* which they get. The foreman does not tell the worker, who must wait until pay day to see how much he will receive. Once W—— found out from the timekeeper what his hourly rate was but soon after it was announced that the rate of pay was increased although no definite rates were posted. When he applied again to the timekeeper for information he was refused.

He had never heard about the I.W.W., until the present strike when the newspapers told about it in their attack on the union. He believed in the A. F. of L., as he thinks they have shown results at the mines.

M—— U——, a Czech, (Homestead), in this country eight years and is married but he " never could find time to take out citizenship papers since he would have to go on a week day to Pittsburgh, which would mean that he would have to pay the wages of his two witnesses and lose his own." While he was out on strike he would have taken out papers but he understood from the newspapers that the strikers were not granted citizenship. He owns his own home and a little Company stock. He can read, write and speak English fluently. Chief grievance the unbearably long hours. He wants an 8-hour day with present pay, $8.50 a day.

This man feels that he is discriminated against because he is a hunky. Several times when he has asked for promotion he has been *told that the good jobs are not for hunkies.* He feels that the clean, decent jobs are for Americans only.

A—— T——, a Czech, millwright's helper, 47 cents an hour. During the war he worked as a millwright but *has been demoted since* and feels that he is discriminated against *because he is a hunky*.

Would be willing to forego a raise in wages if the hours were shorter. He thinks the long hours the worst part of the steel work.

M—— (of Donora) feels that he is being cheated by the Company officials in regard to the pay for tonnage. He says he has *never been able to find out how much tonnage he is entitled to* and that the rest of the workers feel that the count is not accurate but they have no means of checking it.

M—— is a Lithunian who speaks English fluently and reads and writes it; electrical craneman, 12 hours a day, 13 hours at night, at 50 cents an hour and tonnage. "The hours are altogether too long; eight hours a day is long enough for any man to work."

That the long hours are unendurable and destroy family life is the grievance of J—— McG——, born in Scotland, (now of Natrona). He works 10½ hours a day and 14 hours night, alternating each week, at $5.50 a day, which he says is inadequate to support his family.

P—— Y——, a Lithuanian (Vandergrift), 6 years a citizen, family, rougher at $6 a day of 8 hours, declares that while the wages are insufficient his chief grievance is discrimination and contempt. The foreigners are given the dirtiest and hardest jobs and are lorded over by the skilled American workers. He is always *told to wait by the foreman* when he asks for a better job, although his hands are maimed because of the hard work which he must do. In the meantime young Americans who have worked in the mills only a short time are promoted over him to the better jobs.

W—— S——, Russian-Pole (Natrona), in America six years, first papers and served in the A. E. F. Works as a laborer, $5.50

for a day of 10 hours and 14 hours at night, alternating each week.

Although he was in the Army he feels that he is now being discriminated against and is very bitter about it. He says that the Americans call him a "foreigner." He was unable to get his old work back when he came out of the Army but finally after getting to the superintendent with his complaint he did receive back his old place.

S—— G——, a Neapolitan, water-tender at $7.50 for a 12-hour day (New Kensington), joined the union because the foremen are arbitrary and *won't listen to anyone's grievances* and because the hours are altogether too long for any man to work. He has never heard about the I. W. W., or Socialism, cannot tell what they mean and knows almost nothing about the A. F. of L. Never heard the term "closed shop" and does not know what it means. Never has read any literature on trade unionism either in Italian or English.

K——, a Pole, works in galvanizing shop, 12-hour day for $5.00 (East Vandergrift), says that the foreigners get the hardest and most unpleasant jobs and are always discriminated against. Says it makes no difference about the foreigner's ability or whether he speaks English, he is looked down upon and considered fit only for jobs Americans won't take.

Says he has a younger brother, born in this country, who had a knack for learning and was sent to the high school up on the hill in the American section. But the other children would not play with him because he was a hunky. Now he is at work in the mills.

K—— complained that the shop is very unhealthy, full of acid fumes and the vapor was so thick a person could not be seen a few feet away. Everybody in it has complained again and again to the *foreman who promises relief* but nothing ever happens. *Nobody dares go to the superintendent* for fear of angering the foreman.

L——, a Russian, (Natrona) naturalized, laborer, $5.50 a day, 10 hours days and 14 hours nights, declared he cannot support himself and family on $5.50 a day. Complained at great length about the hours being much too long. Finds it does not help to complain to foremen or superintendent because *" all the higher-ups have offices somewhere else."* Unions seemed to him the only way of getting anything done.

Two Poles, (Vandergrift) both roughers, 8 hours at $5.50 a day, complained bitterly that the foreigner has no chance at the better jobs, that they are looked upon with contempt and considered fit only for the dirty and heavy work that Americans would not do. They feel they are exploited by the heater and roller who can rest at intervals while the remainder of the gang, the foreigners, must work steadily and even snatch bites of their lunch while working. *" Always when they ask for better jobs they are told to wait."*

Again and again investigators found this attitude of the immigrant worker repeated with an added intensity of bitterness by the son of the immigrant, the native born " foreigner," speaking English, dressing and largely living like an " American." In the steel mills he is a " hunky." One of these, a striker, released a few months before from the army, summed up the attitude of many when, asked what his job was in the mills, he answered, " Oh, the same as the *other* hunkies."

It is the same story on examining the volumes containing the testimony offered by the Senate Committee's investigation:

*George Mikulvich,* a Dalmatian, in the coke works at Clairton, complained to the Senate Committee which interviewed a group of strikers on a street corner that the " reason why these people went out on strike and he went with them was because they want to work shorter hours and get more money and better conditions; better treatment from the bosses and the foremen."

He worked on shifts of 12 hours and 14 hours for 42 cents an hour straight, no time and a half for overtime, and none in his gang got overtime pay.

(Senate Testimony, Vol. II, p. 524.)

George Miller, a Serb, thirteen years in the mill at Clairton, a naturalized citizen, was interviewed by the Senators as follows:

*Mr. Miller:* If my family gets sick and I ask my foreman that I want off that day, because my woman is sick at home, he say " All right," and he will go around and get another man if he can, and if he cannot he will let me off.  The next day I will come back and there will be a man in my place and I say to him " My woman is better."  He will say " You can go home and stay home . . ."

There is not enough money for the workmen.  We work 13 hours at night and 11 hours at day, and we get 42 cents an hour.

*Senator McKellar:*  And how much is that a day?

*Mr. Miller:*  For a 12-hour day it makes $4.20 and for the longer day it makes $5.04  . . .

Why did we strike?  We did not have enough money so that we could have a standard American living  . . .

I have a wife and two children  . . .

And take all I make and I can not put one penny aside, and if my family gets sick and I call a doctor, he won't come down for nothing, and I do not make enough money to pay a doctor and he won't come for nothing  . . .

There is another thing.  If I get in the mill but three-quarters of a minute late in the morning, they take off an hour, off of me.  Then if I stay five minutes over the hour I should quit in the mill, they won't give me an hour for the five minutes at all.

(Senate Testimony, Vol. II, pp. 524, 525.)

Frank Smith, a Hungarian, testified as follows (Clairton):

*The Chairman:* How long have you been in this country?

*Mr. Smith:* Thirteen years. The reason that I am not naturalized is that I have never stayed long enough in one place; stayed long enough to get my papers.

*Senator McKellar:* Do you expect to be naturalized?

*Mr. Smith:* Yes; I expect to be naturalized, of course, because I have got my family here, my woman, and I have five children; and I have that family, and I would like to know how a man is going to make a living for himself and his wife and five children on $4.75 a day.

*The Chairman:* How many hours do you work?

*Mr. Smith:* I work 10 hours a day and I get paid for straight 10 hours time.

*The Chairman:* And how many days in the week do you work?

*Mr. Smith:* Seven days—sometimes six days and sometimes seven days.

He was asked about treatment by the corporation on joining a union.

*Mr. Smith:* Oh, they won't allow us in there if they know that we are union men.

*The Chairman:* And you want the right to belong to the union, too?

*Mr. Smith:* Yes, sir; we do. This is the United States and we ought to have the right to belong to the union . . . We were all for the United States. We worked day and night for that.

*The Chairman:* And how many of you contributed to the Red Cross and the Y.M.C.A.?

*Mr. Smith:* Every one of us contributed $3 to them.

(Senate Testimony, Vol. II, pp. 526, 527.)

# VI

## ORGANIZING FOR CONFERENCE

In this section are analyzed the Commission's data on how steel workers were organized as trade unionists, the plan, methods, aims and personnel of the organizing campaign, the object and conduct of the strike, its successes, if any, and the causes of failure inherent in the organization, if any. The evidence was drawn from union records, interviews with labor leaders and talks with the rank and file and with company officials and government agents. Findings may be summarized thus:

The organizing campaign and the strike were for the purpose of forcing a conference in an industry where no means of conference existed; this specific conference to set up trade union collective bargaining, particularly to abolish the 12-hour day and arbitrary methods of handling employees.

No interpretation of the movement as a plot or conspiracy fits the facts; that is, it was a mass movement, in which leadership became of secondary importance.

The strike failed in its object; part of the failure was due to defects in the labor movement.

In analyzing the organization resulting in the strike it is necessary to draw a distinction which however cannot be clearly kept throughout the discussion; that is, the distinction between the leadership and the body of strikers. The leadership came from the organized labor movement, the American Federation of Labor, having comparatively few footholds in the steel industry. The labor movement initiated the organizing campaign, invited by the steel workers, according to the

144

labor leaders, invading where it was not wanted, according to the employers. Both statements are correct and neither lays emphasis on the principal fact—the isolation of the mass of immigrant steel workers, unable to unite their thirty nationalities, ignorant of, or fearful of, the ways by which workmen act to change their conditions of labor. These steel workers are more important than their leaders, in analyzing causes of the strike, and in this section of the report the emphasis laid on the leadership must be clearly grasped as over-emphasis, due to the fact that it is *organization* which is being analyzed. Such analysis must begin with the list of the twenty-four [1] participating A. F. of L. unions, whose officers composed the National Committee for Organizing Iron and Steel Workers, of which John Fitzpatrick, President of the Chicago Federation of Labor, became chairman, with William Z. Foster as Secretary-Treasurer. The list whose relative unimportance compared with the hundreds of thousands of nameless steel workers must not be forgotten is as follows:

Blacksmiths, International Brotherhood of; J. L. Kline, president, Chicago, Ill.

Boiler Makers and Iron Ship Builders of America, Brotherhood of; L. Weyand, acting president, Kansas City, Kans.

Brick and Clay Workers of America, The United; Frank Kasten, president, Chicago, Ill.

Bricklayers, Masons and Plasterers International Union of America; William Bowan, president, Indianapolis, Ind.

Bridge and Structural Iron Workers, International Association; P. J. Morrin, president, Indianapolis, Ind.

Coopers International Union of North America; A. C. Hughes, president, Newton Highlands, Mass.

Electrical Workers of America, International Brotherhood of; J. P. Noonan, acting president, Springfield, Ill.

[1] The list, as officially furnished to the Senate Committee, includes a 25th union, added in the latter months of the organizing campaign.

Foundry Employees, International Brotherhood of; A. R. Linn, president, St. Louis, Mo.

Hod Carriers, Building and Common Laborers' Union of North America, International; D. D'Allessandro, president, Quincy, Mass.

Iron, Steel and Tin Workers Amalgamated Association of; M. F. Tighe, president, Pittsburgh, Pa.

Machinists, International Association of; L. H. Johnston, president, Washington, D. C.

Metal Polishers International Union; W. W. Britton, president, Cincinnati, Ohio.

Mine, Mill, and Smelter Workers, International Union of; C. H. Moyer, president, Denver, Colo.

Mine Workers of America, United; Frank J. Hayes, president, Indianapolis, Ind.

Moulders' Union of North America, International; J. F. Valentine, president, Cincinnati, Ohio.

Pattern Makers' League of North America; James Wilson, president, Cincinnati, Ohio.

Plumbers and Steam Fitters of the United States and Canada, United Association of; John R. Alpine, president, Chicago, Ill.

Quarryworkers, International Union of North America; Fred W. Suitor, Barre, Vt.

Carmen of America, Brotherhood Railway; M. F. Ryan, president, Kansas City, Mo.

Seamen's Union of America, International; Andrew Fureseth, president, San Francisco, Calif.

Metal Workers' International Alliance, Amalgamated Sheet; J. J. Hynes, president, Chicago, Ill.

Firemen, International Brotherhood of Stationary; Timothy Healy, president, New York, N. Y.

Engineers, International Union of Steam and Operating; Milton Snellings, president, Chicago, Ill.

Switchmen's Union of North America; S. E. Heberling, president, Buffalo, N. Y.

Steam Shovelmen and Dredgemen, International Brotherhood of; W. M. Welsh, president, New York City, N. Y.

One man, it was generally admitted inside and outside of this heterogeneous group, stood out among his fellows and was so far as personal characteristics went the central dominating influence. This was John Fitzpatrick, the chairman. His broad human qualities, it seemed to observers, justified his national reputation. An uncalculating idealism, quite simple, but quite determined, was in him.

It is much easier to give an accurate surface record of the strike than to detail the underlying essential facts which are largely facts of psychology. A list of all committees, a chronological history of all the organizing mass meetings, transcripts of executive meetings held, copies of correspondence between Mr. Gompers and Mr. Gary, might conceivably shed no light on the fundamental question:—

What made 300,000 steel workers leave the mills on September 22nd and stay away in greater or fewer numbers for a period up to three and a half months?

It cannot be too strongly emphasized that a strike does not consist of a plan and a call for a walkout. There has been many a call with no resultant walkout; there has been many a strike with no preceding plan or call at all. Strike conditions are conditions of mind.

The frame of mind of steel workers in late 1918 and early 1919, first and foremost, as detailed in other sections of this report, grew out of their conditions of labor, things with which Mr. Gompers, Mr. Fitzpatrick and the strike organizers had little to do. That three quarters of steel employees, who were forced to work from 10 to 14 hours a day, developed a frame of mind of more or less chronic rebellion, largely the physical reaction from exhaustion and deprivation. Rebellious reactions from having no " say " in the conduct of the job was also chronic, though less so. These were fundamental facts in steel workers' minds, of which they were constantly reminded by endless " grievances "; these facts Mr.

Foster was thinking of when he said that if the steel companies had shortened hours and granted some sort of representation, " this movement would never have had a show." In this respect the Finance Committee of the U. S. Steel Corporation was the principal organizer of the strike.

This rebellious state of mind had existed a long time without a mass strike. The high labor turnover in steel plants[1] means that thousands of steel workers have been going on " individual strikes " for several years. The " labor shortage " which steel companies experience is a persistent evidence of this " strike " frame of mind. The high rate of absenteeism is another evidence. Whetting this state of discontent were two other psychological factors, both growing out of the war and previously referred to in this report. Together they were far more important than Mr. Gompers or Mr. Foster or anybody possibly except Mr. Gary.

The first factor was the increased consideration accorded steel workers, by foremen daily and by high company officials frequently, in the course of the national war effort. The steel worker was made to feel that he was mightily helping to win the war, with his steel shells, steel guns, gun carriages, ship plates, etc., etc., etc., in short, with his maximum production. The " foreigner " found himself sworn at less by the foreman, actually conversed with, finally promoted to semi-skilled or even skilled jobs, periodically solicited by the plant superintendent himself to buy Liberty Bonds, subscribe to the Red Cross, the Y. M. C. A., etc. More especially the American worker read in his newspaper that he was an important person, that President Wilson, General Pershing and other great men were relying on him and were telling him so in " greetings," " appeals " and " proclamations " in which " labor " and especially " organized labor " was " recognized "

[1] Labor turnover in Homestead Steel Works for 1919 was 575 a month or 6,800 a year to maintain the force of 11,500. Testimony of Homestead Superintendent, Senate Testimony, Vol. II, p. 481.

in a fashion hardly recognizable to the old steel worker. Most important of all, the Government was putting its seal of recognition on Mr. Gompers personally, and the War Labor Board was making " collective bargaining " and the " right to organize in trade and labor unions " the text of business awards. The mistake was quite natural for the worker to suppose that this recognition was based on his worth as a steel maker, not on the coincidence of war time needs. Naturally, on November 11, 1918, he made a mistake about the armistice which seemed to him to have no connection with this recognition.

The data before the Commission show that at the beginning of the strike steel workers in great numbers had the liveliest expectation of governmental assistance in getting their organization " recognized " by the Steel Corporation. Particularly the " foreigners," with their tradition of awed respect for constituted authority, talked about the government coming to the rescue; some believed " Mr. Wilson will run the mills." Months before, others of the " foreigners " had been disillusioned; they lost the skilled jobs, the foremen resumed swearing and reminded them in so many words that they were " hunkies." The solicitous superintendent and the published proclamations vanished. Instead there was rumor of cuts in wages. Once again the vital link between the steel worker and the steel employer was the wooden board where notices were posted. During the strike instead of Mr. Wilson, Mr. Palmer came and the Senate Committee's report. Thus, in two aspects, the Federal Administration was an organizer of the strike.

The second psychological factor growing out of the war, with which American labor leaders had even less to do, sprang from events in Europe. The news of two years happenings there deeply influenced all labor, of course, but the evidence indicates peculiar influence on steel workers.

English speaking workers were impressed by what happened in England; the mass of Slavic workers, constituting from 30 per cent. to 70 per cent. in many mills, were stirred by Russia.

The evidence supports no sweeping conclusions about exact effects of British and Russian influence. Weeks of careful interviewing in the Pittsburgh and Chicago districts indicated that it was results rather than methods which " got over " to the American worker from London and Moscow. The inference is not warranted that all " American " steel workers become converts to political action by labor and all Slav workers to a dictatorship of the proletariat. " Americans " talked about British labor a great deal but they were vague on the details of organizing labor parties. The one big thing they grasped was the news of the probability or possibility of a labor government of the British Empire, how to be obtained they did not exactly understand.

Slav workers were even more vague about Russia. A sub-report [1] demonstrates that the immigrant leadership in Russian, Slovak, Serb, Hungarian, Polish and Roumanian communities in steel areas has been largely conservative, middle-class, " characteristically bourgeois." It is the leadership of priests, editors, small business men, and officers of benefit societies; only lately has there been much labor leadership, and the little radical labor leadership has not been widely effective.

One or two nationalities, Magyars and Finns, for example, are politically Socialist by tradition and the Finns are economically of radical trend. The mass are principally concerned with " bettering themselves " in the fashion usual to pioneers,—better houses, better food, better hours and wages, better social recognition, especially from " Americans." But

---

[1] "Intellectual Environment of the Immigrant Steel Worker," by David J. Saposs.

they came from Eastern Europe and now Eastern Europe
means to them mainly the overthrow of autocracy. They
have a vague idea that big rich people who run things
" arbitrarily," even in mills, are coming down in the world.
Russia, moreover, means to them the rise of workingmen to
power. They have a vague idea that poor people who have
been run for a long time, on farms and in mills, are coming
up in the world and are beginning to run themselves.

Communists, looking for evidence of Lenin as an organizer
of the steel strike, found little to please them. Two students
of Lenin's method, one a Communist enthusiast, returned
from rather hasty investigations of the Pittsburgh strikers in
a state of dejection. They reported that the Slavic workers
" were mad enough but didn't know anything." They laid
the blame to the strike leadership and to the lack of propaganda. They recommended breaking down the influence of
A. F. of L. organizers, Foster especially, and " a campaign
of education by leaflets." They said the steel workers were
not ripe for " action " (Communist) but would be particularly ripe for " education " after the strike was lost. One of
these investigators termed Fitzpatrick " a menace because he
wanted to lead the workers away from economic direct action
and into a labor party, to follow the losing by-path of
bourgeois political action ; " he considered Foster " worse than
useless because his reputation as an old radical spoiled the
true picture of the strike—the worst kind of an A. F. of L.
strike."

The Commission's own investigators noted the following
fact which relates to the above gentlemen's discouragement
about " spreading knowledge of proletarian tactics:"

Slavs in this country have a high percentage of illiteracy;
and most of the papers of large circulation which they can
read don't even print " labor news," let alone revolutionary
methods. Radical foreign language papers to " counter-act "

these newspapers, seem to be few in number and without established means of circulation. There is plenty of evidence of a militant minority, informed on Russia, among the immigrant races, just as there is in any "American" community. But these militant immigrants, it is undisputed, had no connection and no power with the national leaders of the strike. The "Russian idea" imbedded in the minds of the great majority of immigrant workers, as revealed in many interviews, was this: That Russia now is a worker's republic. This, of course, is pretty much the "American" worker's conception, according to observers who have talked much with the rank and file of American workers:—that the Russian revolution was likely a bloody business and Bolsheviks are doubtless dangerous and wild but the Russian Government is a laboring man's government and it has not fallen down yet. Two years of newspaper reports that the Russian republic was about to fall seem to have given workingmen, even here, a sort of class pride that it hasn't fallen.

The above represents about the best that can be made in the direction of analyzing out the ingredients comprising "foreign influence" on immigrant workers. What is a common sense way of regarding it all? When Gen. Smuts said that now "humanity is on the march" and that men everywhere, workingmen too, feel that sweeping social readjustments are necessary, he spoke the every-day belief of sensible men in America. Steel workers felt that in this period workers everywhere were moving to get rid of things which chained them,—czaristic dynasties in some lands, in others slavish hours of labor and subjection to industrial machines. This is a rather more sensible view than to suppose that several hundred thousand immigrants, many of them illiterate, struck in 1919 because they had carefully read and mastered rules for forming soviets. Their intention, analysis seems to indicate, was to reach an agreement with the

Steel Corporation about hours, wages and bosses, rather than to send armed workers to seize the Allegheny County court house or the Pennsylvania railroad station.   What immigrant and native-born learned from Europe in 1919 was that it seemed a good time to end the autocracy which they knew— the Corporation's way of running its workers.

Therefore, from all these causes, the length of hours and arbitrary control inside the mills and the deep influences growing out of war events, steel workers were *individually* in a strike frame of mind; it was the job of the National Committee for Organizing Iron and Steel Workers to make a machine for moving these individual frames of mind into mass action.   Mr. Foster, its Secretary-Treasurer, could never have supplied the first part of the necessary conditions but he did furnish the second.

The overshadowing importance of basic states of mind is only emphasized by seeing how a strike machine works.   The vital thing about the Fitzpatrick-Foster campaign organization was that it dealt in psychological factors.   It wasn't so much the system of organization as the handling of states of mass-mind that counted.   To the very end the Foster machine was a poor thing as a system of control; the strike moved on its own legs, it was a " walkout " of rank and file.

Inspection of the records makes this plain; that while Mr. Foster's disposition of organizers and his series of mass meetings brought members into the unions, the thing that fetched steel workers to sign up in big numbers was the influence of an idea which Mr. Foster's men skilfully wielded. The idea was not culled from the " Red Book " nor from Mr. Gompers' speeches; it was the same idea which is the backbone of most American political campaigns, the idea that " this thing is going to succeed—this movement is getting somewhere—we're winning."   The fact is proved in such detail that it makes impossible the explanations of steel company officials that " the men joined because milk drivers and barkeepers tricked their wives into signing " or " the men were intimidated into joining." Steel officials who said " the organizers promised them everything " came a little nearer the explanation.

The union tabulations show how this psychology of success worked, how " red " ideas had as much to do with it as blue or green. The two great jumps in tabulated memberships came first when the strike ballot was ordered among those already signed up and word went round among the others, " they *are* doing something—they're off." During the strike-balloting the enrollment jumped 50 per cent. Setting a strike date brought in the next large increment. Likewise the two great drops in active membership had occurred, first, after the " flu ban " in the Chicago district had caused the National Organizers to be withdrawn, giving the rank and file the idea that " there was nothing doing after all; " and second, after the congress of 500 rank and file workers in Pittsburgh on May 25. The inexperienced delegates, eager for a strike, found that they were not empowered to call one, and immediately the whole movement sagged, again in the belief that the leadership was getting nowhere.

Herd psychology was far more powerful than any set of trade union doctrines preached in meeting. It proves, too, how essential to such a movement were the states of mind induced by long hours, arbitrary control and aspirations derived from the war. This business—of gauging the feelings of the masses in the mills—was the all-engrossing duty of Mr. Fitzpatrick and Mr. Foster, a task of which the public knew nothing and which Mr. Fitzpatrick did not promulgate.

Conversely, the leaders' greatest difficulty, beginning in the spring and almost unmanageable by August, was in withstanding the mass-feeling they had fostered. The " situation nearly got away " from them several times in Johnstown, and in places in Ohio and Indiana; that is, the men in these districts nearly went on strike before other districts were organized. As it was, "the dam broke before this district was more than half worked," according to one organizer in Pittsburgh. The movement, before getting to the 100,000 mark, reached a point where, by the working of the very idea that built it, it threatened to break out in sporadic strike-lets or break down altogther. That point was when Mr. Gary refused to confer: right then the "this-thing-is-succeeding" idea began to change to "this-thing-is-not-succeeding" along the negotiating line, and the leaders had to let it go on to a strike as the next means of success or let it go all to pieces.

The inside story of the strike puts out of consideration descriptions of it as a "plot" or "dark Bolshevik conspiracy." A strike movment of 300,000 men in a dozen states is about as secret as a presidential campaign.

Conversely again, the great blow to the strike in October and November was the growth of the feeling that "this thing is not succeeding." The steel companies' most powerful single weapon was creating and fostering the feeling that "it's a fizzle, we're making steel, strike's all over." That feeling, more than arrests or suppression of meetings or "Cossacks," wore down the strike. Mr. Foster built up the movement from the idea that "the steel trust can be beaten." The companies won out by restoring the idea that the Steel Corporation can't be beaten. During the campaign the I. W. W. used the same argument as the companies, with this difference: "Don't join the A. F. of L.; the A. F. of L. loses its strikes."

To these psychological facts, which are the nub of the history of the strike movement, many details can be added from the Commission's evidence by examining the plan of the organization movement, the industrial situation of the period, the men who formed the National Committee and their ideas of what they were after. Such examination must begin with Mr. Foster and his resolution to organize the workers in the steel industry passed by the A. F. of L. convention at St. Paul, June 17, 1918. This raises at once the matter of "radicals boring from within," over which public opinion was greatly exercised as the strike began. Organized labor, however, seemed to regard "boring" as an old story. Its explanation may shed light on why the trade unions have not "ditched Foster," as many "friends of labor" expected them to do and why the trade unions have no intention of ditching him.

Mr. Foster's business might be described as making the labor movement move. His main personal characteristic is intensity. When he followed the sea he is reported to have been intensely a sailor for he qualified an A. B. and learned all the knots on a 4-sticker. When he was a homesteader, in the Coast mountains, he was intense enough to stick at it alone for five years, prove his claim and clear twenty-two acres of land. When he took up making the labor movement move, he tried it first as a very intense syndicalist, an I. W. W. outside the trade unions. Little motion resulting, he "repudiated" syndicalist methods and joined the Railway Carmen's Union in order to "bore from within" the A. F. of L. In the steel campaign he was most intensely boring from within and the labor movement knew it and let him bore. It was considered that his boring might be *through* the unions but was certainly *against* the anti-union employers.

That is, he decided that the labor movement *was* the A. F. of L. and not the I. W. W. and that his job was making the A. F. of L. move. The A. F. of L.'s first job, he conceived, was organizing men. He saw that even the strongest A. F. of L. unions, the United Mine Workers, had only about half the coal miners organized; perhaps he noticed that Mr. Gompers' own union, the Cigar Makers, had

its industry only 25 per cent. organized. He saw the stockyards unorganized, the steel industry unorganized. Instead
of merely trying to sting the A. F. of L. into moving on
the stockyards, he thought out a plan of action which was
to get all the unions having " claims " on stockyard trades to
unite in one onslaught instead of attempting separate attacks
and being beaten separately. He took the plan to Mr. Fitzpatrick, who saw its possibilities, the A. F. of L. endorsed it
and they led the united unions triumphantly through the
stockyards. Then they turned to steel.

In each case besides offering the plan, Mr. Foster offered
himself, a liability from one viewpoint, an asset according to
the trade unionists backing the plan. For this reason: a new
kind of man was necessary: a large-scale promoter instead
of small salesmen. Mr. Foster's advent in the steel industry
was like Mr. Gary's. Mr. Gary came in from outside to help
consolidate the efforts of separate concerns. Twenty years
later Mr. Foster was the newcomer, to help consolidate the
efforts of a score of unions, not in the industry but trying to
get in; his, too, was a large scale business proposition. The
officers of A. F. of L. trade unions, it is alleged, tend to be
job holders rather than apostles; they are more expert, it is
asserted, in figuring out the scale of dues for their own
organizations than in figuring out what is due to laborers
outside their locals. Some of the unions in the steel drive
were stumped to the end by the following problem: how to
admit recruits at the $3 initiation fee, set for the drive,
when their union constitutions set initiation fees at from 5
to 3000 per cent. higher. Mr. Foster flattered himself on being a broad gauge executive, able to look past such details and
to offer a prospectus of " trust " magnitude. The officials
of the unions flattered him by regularly nominating and
electing him Secretary-Treasurer of the National Committee,
under two bonds, inspected by three auditors, responsible

for the minutes and more noting than noted during committee meetings.

Thus the supposition that "boring" is a Machiavellian
business does not seem to fit the facts. It does not mean joining the Republican party and boring from within throughout
a campaign in the confident expectation of having all the
Republicans on election day vote the Democratic ticket. It
did not mean a campaign among the steel workers at the end
of which they voted the I. W. W. ticket, or Mr. Gary's
ticket, or for anything but "strike" for their unions. It
does mean putting inside the trade unions radically minded
men who will make more trade unionists. It does involve the possibility that after all the unorganized are
gathered into the old-line trade unions, these radically minded
organizers may convert the trade unions, *if they can;* that
is the trade unions' lookout. Inside the unions the critics of
the "borer" are old officials who feel he is a reflection on
them; which he is. To Mr. Foster personally the steel
organization campaign was largely a matter of conciliating
old unionists who were not used to having the movement
move. Beyond that, his task was persuading the twenty-four
rival unions involved to obey Marshal Foch, *alias* Fitzpatrick.

Let this analysis of Mr. Foster and of "boring" be distinctly understood in its relation to the labor movement as a
whole; it is much the smaller side of the real problem which
confronts A. F. of L. trade unions. That problem is industrial unionism and the larger side of it is not "borers"
but economic conditions. Ten years ago "boring" was a
fairly live topic in the conventions of both camps—craft
union and industrial union—and both camps are now little
interested in it. The I.W.W. official decision was against it
on the ground that it would depopulate the I.W.W. and that
industrial unionists inside the craft union would become
denaturized. I.W.W.'s in 1919 pointed scornfully to Foster

as a " horrible example " of the emasculation of an industrial unionist. The A. F. of L. decision was to welcome the " borer " as a " convert from heresy," welcome to enter and act like other craft unionists. And there the American controversy has rested, revived occasionally, as during the steel strike or when some British exponent of " boring," like Tom Mann, is elected head of an old craft union, or when William D. Haywood proclaims that any real " borer " must ultimately bore to the outside, that is, must get out of the A. F. of L.

The far more important side of the labor movement's industrial union problem lies in those economic conditions which latterly have exposed weaknesses in craft unions and have driven them to essay " amalgamations " and other approximations of industrial organization. When a craft union on strike sees brother unions in the same industry sticking to work or even filling the strikers' jobs, that craft union begins to do a lot more thinking about industrial unionism than a hundred " borers " could inspire. When craft unions promulgate ambitions, as did the A. F. of L. in 1919, about " sharing control and democracy in industry," they are forced automatically to considering industrial union problems.

Neither in plan nor practice was the work of the National Committee for Organizing Iron and Steel Workers industrial unionism.

During a year of Committee meetings on the campaign there was never discussion of " general policy as regards ideas to be used " by the speakers, except once. There was no discussion because the international craft unions and the experienced organizers they supplied all knew what the ideas would be: the orthodox pure and simple trade union text of " organize." Heresies such as industrial control or industrial unionism or political organization or, least of all, " soviets," never were an issue in the Committee; the undisputed gospel was "organize and all these things shall be added unto you," with no speculation as to what "all these things" might turn out to be in actual terms of hours, wages and conditions for steel workers. The one exception was a reference at the start in 1918 when President Gompers warned "lest the movement be turned to other than trade union ends." Scenting the bare possibility of industrial organization, he wanted early to make it plain to the Committee, meeting for the first time, that his endorsement in no way meant any personal leaning toward One Big Unionism. But the twenty-four unions had no doubt about what they wanted,—more numbers for each of their separate craft organizations; and that is what they got. Mr. Foster, as the string around the package, might have been a very red string, and still he couldn't have incarnadined the multitudinous locals from Maine to Mississippi which put up the money to pay the organizers to get new craft unionists in steel towns.

Data were gathered by the investigators on whether the viewpoint expressed by Mr. Gompers and carried out by Mr. Foster resulted in the same harmony among the newly organized rank and file as among the National Committeemen. The evidence is clear that it did not. In many plants the instinct of the immigrant recruit was to associate with his shopmates of different "crafts" rather than with his "craft" mates from other shops. He fell more easily into a shop or plant union, which, however, would have been an industrial union. Some local leaders so organized him. Thus an internal conflict arose which had serious consequences (set forth elsewhere) for the strike. In local unions, the artificial harmony of the twenty-four International Unions conflicted with the "inexperienced" immigrant drift toward real industrial unionism. The twenty-four crafts smothered this drift. The end of the strike saw different unions pulling out of the National Committee, each with its separate booty of recruits and even the specious "industrial" effort represented by the Committee openly disrupted. If Mr. Foster, as a former industrial unionist, had still in the back of his head a hope of an industrial union in steel, the outcome was a joke on him as it was on those of the rank and file who moved with the drift.

Ideas of industrial control and the ideal of One Big Union were urged at different times *from the outside* by I.W.W.'s, by Socialists, by "friends of labor" in publications and personally. One of the Committeemen was told: "Don't answer the Bolshevik stuff by making yourself out so conservative. It's just a ruse of the Steel Corporation to make you admit you're conservative, so that those foreigner steel workers will distrust you. Those Slavic steel workers are radical and won't respond to conservative pleas."

The Commission's investigation of Slavic communities, as referred to before, indicates that the ideas influencing immigrant steel workers hitherto have not been radical. When the above theory was repeated to a national strike leader he displayed no interest beyond saying, "I don't think Mr. Gary is that smart." Mr. Foster's comment was: "That advice sounds like one of those intellectuals who are always telling Sam Gompers how to run trade unions. The trouble with all radicals is that they don't know the labor movement or the laboring man or what we're up against."

At the Commission's Pittsburgh hearings in November, Mr. Foster was asked directly whether he did not think the Slavic worker brought to this country radical leanings in industrial ideas. He replied that so far as knowledge of trade unions or any industrial organization was concerned, "they brought a blank in their skulls." The record of his conception reads as follows:

"They are really a new factor in American trade unionism. They are just learning unionism since the war started. They are just breaking into it. So far as I can see the foreigner wants more money. He is confronted with the immediate problem of life. His idealism stretches about as far as his shortest working day. The percentage of them that have any vision for future conditions is very small. It is not a determining factor at all. It is more wages, shorter hours—the regular trade union demands are the things that count.

" Take an organization like the brotherhoods—they have a vision among them far in excess of anything among these people. The American makes the best type of union man. He is hard to organize, and he hasn't got that collective sense so highly developed as the foreigner has. He is individualistic and critical, and he has some ten or twelve excuses why he shouldn't belong to an organization; but once you can win them, once you can get them on your side, you have a splendid type.

" The foreigner is a different type. He has that group idea very strongly developed. In his own country individualism plays a small part. He is labeled and tagged and oppressed, and he is classed, and his psychology is pretty simple over there. He knows what he is, and if there is any possible chance for him to do anything he feels that it is as a group, not as an individual.

" He comes over here and he seems to respond to an appeal better than Americans do. But he is very materialistic in his demands. You know you can convince the Americans and you can hold an organization for years in a plant without getting a cent benefit out of it directly. But the foreigner you can't hold that way. He comes in for increase of wages and shortening of hours. He comes in quite readily, but if you don't get him the results he drops away quite readily also.

" Then, a peculiar thing happens. When the fight occurs, he is a splendid fighter. He has the American beaten when it comes to a fight. I don't say that in criticism of the American, but I think it is due to the position he occupies in industry. The American usually holds the good job, and he has a home half paid for, and he is full of responsibility; whereas the foreigner is more foot-loose; has a poor job anyway, and he doesn't feel that so much is at stake.

"He will stick, while the American will go back to work. That is what happened in the mills just now. When the fight occurs the foreigner displays a wonderful amount of idealism, a wonderful amount of stick-to-it-iveness, that is altogether dissimilar to the intensely materialistic spirit he shows in his union transactions."

Question: "There has been a difference in response to your appeals in the district here between the unskilled foreign workers and the skilled American workers. Could you give any further explanation,—other than what you have given,—of why the skilled American in this district was slow to join the organization?"

Mr. Foster: "The reason is simply this: The most irresponsible elements rally first. Mr. Gary rules by fear—pure unadulterated fear; fear of losing their job; the fear of having their life's occupation taken away from them. That is what keeps them from joining the unions.

"If Mr. Gary would post a notice in his mills tomorrow that every man could join a union if he saw fit, they'd break down the doors all over the country trying to join. A first-class proof of this was shown by what occurred to the railroads. Our unions fought along for years and years and years in the face of no response at all from the workers. There was violent opposition on the part of the company to trying to organize the men, but as soon as the railroad administration took the position that the men could join the union, a million and a half joined in practically two or three months. The great Pennsylvania Railroad was organized in about two or three months, which for forty years they had worked on before and couldn't touch. As soon as the fear was removed they flocked in.

"When we came into the Pittsburgh district we were confronted with the proposition of breaking down this fear. Those men who had less to fear were first to respond. They are the unskilled, and naturally, the foreigner. They don't care whether they are discharged or not.

"Here is what usually happens to a plant. At first the American doesn't like to say he is afraid. No, he won't admit that, but he says the union can't do anything; it is no good. Naturally, every man likes to develop some philosophy to protect his own particular brand of weakness.

"But we go ahead and organize those who will come in, and we get more and more into the union, and the first thing you know the American begins to prick up his ears a little bit, and begins to be not quite so sure about the union being a failure. And so, as we go into the mill we get into the better class of men, and eventually get them all. We get the very best of them. But it is a question of time.

"The reason we didn't get them here was because our organization was immature. In this Pittsburgh district it was due to the fact that we couldn't hold meetings and couldn't reach the men. In Johnstown, where we had a free hand, we organized them right off the bat, and right up to the office. We had the office help in our organization up there.

"The creation of an organization among or in a group of workingmen is wonderful. After the bonds of organization are created it is just as hard to break them as to create."

Mr. Foster's testimony is cited because it typifies the statements of the National strike leaders investigated by the Commission. It is borne out by all the National Committee records accumulated by investigators. Whether its reasoning is based on fact or not, it seems to be a fair statement of the ideas actually carried out in the campaign, and so far as the strike's failure rested with ideas, these were the ideas responsible.

What ideas were responsible for the actions of the leaders in the next phase of such a movement—the attempt to accomplish something for the men when organized, by forcing a conference with the employers? This phase, from midsummer, 1919, on, is the story of continued attempts to arrange a conference or to mediate, attempts made by the Amalgamated Association of Iron, Steel & Tin Workers, then by the National Committee, then by Mr. Gompers, then by

President Wilson, then during the President's National Industrial Conference and last by the Commission of Inquiry of the Interchurch World Movement. All these attempts were successfully defeated. It seemed as if the public approved the denial of anything which might eventuate in "the kind of conference the labor unions wanted." What kind of conference was this? What exactly was in Mr. Fitzpatrick's mind in writing to Mr. Gary?

Mr. Fitzpatrick himself gave the Commission the clearest possible picture. The personal element was the first element in it. Mr. Fitzpatrick showed the most downright, unqualified, belief in the idea that "if only both sides could get together around a table, it could all be straightened out." Personalities as a stumbling-block did exist strongly in the minds of both sides. Mr. Gary objected to conference partly because of "the character of the leadership." He reminded the Commission that "Mr. Foster is a slick one." Mr. Buffington told the Commission that "Mr. Fitzpatrick is a bad lot." Mr. Fitzpatrick, in a discussion of general conditions, said, "When I think of those trust magnates and the conditions their workers live in and work in and die in—why their hearts must be as black as the ace of spades." But he seemed to think more deeply that "it could all be straightened out" if he could convince the other side that labor leaders were not bad men and that their plans were not bad.

What Mr. Fitzpatrick wanted was what he got at the end of the 1918 campaign to organize the stockyards of Chicago. Then he began attempting to arrange a conference with Mr. Armour, the leader of the packers. Mr. Armour's offices were on the seventh floor of a Chicago building, Mr. Fitzpatrick's on the sixth. The efforts reached the point where Mr. Armour's secretary acted as messenger, reporting to Mr. Fitzpatrick, "John, he won't meet you": and on being persuaded to go back again, reporting as a finality, "John, he says you're a very fine man and he has nothing against you, but he won't deal with union labor and he's very busy."

Just as happened later in the Steel Industry, Mr. Fitzpatrick set a stockyard strike date and President Wilson intervened to effect a conference. The President promised to do everything in his power to obtain that conference, just as he tried later to approach Mr. Gary. Meanwhile Mr. Fitzpatrick gave the President "two hours, two weeks, or two months" to get the conference, extending the strike limit indefinitely. The President ordered the five big packers and the union leaders to meet in the office of Secretary of Labor Wilson.

"There," Mr. Fitzpatrick said, "we all sat in a circle, about twenty of us, Armour and the packers on one side and our fellows on the other side, and the Secretary in the middle on a kind of pedestal. It was war-time and the Secretary made a most eloquent, patriotic speech. At the end, Armour's lawyer got up and began to argue against conferring with union men. I saw he was simply cutting the ground out from under the speech and out from under everything, so I just stood up and said, 'Gentlemen, it all seems to turn on whether or not Mr. Armour is going to meet anybody, and I want to say right here that I am now going to shake hands with Mr. Armour.' So I just walked across that circle, had to walk about twenty feet, over to where Armour was sitting, and I stuck out my hand. He got red and looked up at me very funny and then he stood up very courteously and shook hands and said, 'Of course I'll shake hands with Mr. Fitzpatrick.' And then I went right on down that line of packers and shook hands with every one of them, and the lawyer's argument and the whole conference went bust for twenty minutes.

"If the argument had gone on, we would have just got

nowhere.  But, after that twenty minutes of mix-up, we sat down and quickly arranged a conference between the packers and union labor."

There was the picture in the mind of the leader of the steel strikers.  His ideal was to overcome the personal refusal of Mr. Gary to deal with labor leaders personally and to bring about a peace meeting which should be first a simple meeting of men; and then what?  Mr. Fitzpatrick explained to the Commission his next idea.

"Suppose Mr. Gary had met us and had said, 'Let us negotiate.'  I wouldn't have been able to do it, I don't know steel.  Then we should have said, 'All we want to do, Mr. Gary, is to tell you with whom to confer to carry out the details.'  And these men would have been Mr. Gary's own employees, with the union leaders somewhere nearby to advise."

There, frankly set forth, is the union leaders' position, under Mr. Gompers' tenets.  To Mr. Fitzpatrick it was a very simple proposition.  He was undeniably surprised that the Government did not support it and that public opinion did not enforce it.

He might be surprised if reminded that in this frankness he had put his finger on two points which often, rightly or wrongly, leave pure and simple trade unionism, with so little support in "public opinion" and with such opposition from the employer.  "To tell him with whom to confer" typifies in many minds all that goes with the phrase "labor autocracy."  The second point, "I don't know steel," typifies all the repugnance in the mind of the employer conveyed by the phrase, "dealing with outsiders."  So far, A. F. of L. unions have answered the two objections in but one way, by saying that if you won't confer, we'll make you confer, we'll strike. That is, union labor's tactic simply accepts the gauge of "autocracy of labor" and sets to to fight it out against an

" autocracy of capital." Certain unions outside the A. F. of L., and abroad, have begun to formulate another,—not a substitute but an additional,—answer:—the acceptance of responsibility for production, the learning of the problem of production for public service and the clarified demand for a decisive share in control and in earnings.

What part had this limited " force against force " doctrine of the A. F. of L. in the responsibility for the failure of the strike? What were the causes of failure? It would be a serious mistake to consider causes within the labor organization without reference to other causes which were more important, for example, the active opposition waged by the U. S. Steel Corporation. 'And before analysis of either set of causes can be made, the character of the new steel workers' organizations and of the twenty-four-headed leadership must be clearly grasped.

The respective positions of the organized steel workers, the National Committee and the twenty-four International Unions, may be summarized as follows:

The raw recruits, particularly the immigrant workers, wanted to strike soon after they had joined up, since they could conceive of both protection and " results " only in a universal walkout.

The twenty-four old unions willingly put money into a campaign for new members but hesitated greatly over backing a strike in behalf of the new steel locals, which might possibly jeopardize their old membership outside the steel industry.

The National Committee tried to unify the twenty-four Internationals for (a) the organizing drive (in which it had difficulties); (b) the strike (in which it was partly successful); (c) the concerted conduct of business in the industry, through the establishment of a Steel De-

partment in the A. F. of L. (in which it was easily
beaten).

The facts are detailed with greater exactness than has
usually been attained in histories of strikes, in the sub-report
on "The National Committee," based on the Committee's
minutes.  It is the story of a conciliating body, made up
principally of representatives of the Internationals rather
than of the International presidents themselves, which persuaded and cajoled the twenty-four unions, all rivals for the
booty of new recruits, into subordinating their differences and
contributing a modicum of cooperative effort.  The Committee struggled with ancient jurisdictional disputes between
the Steam Shovelmen and the Stationary Engineers over
the disposition of cranemen; between the Amalgamated Association of Iron, Steel and Tin Workers and the Hod Carriers'
Union over the disposition of common laborers; it argued
unceasingly with constituent unions whose constitutions and
by-laws threatened to bar out steel recruits.  It tried to impress the wishes of the newly organized rank and file, clamor-
ing for action, upon the absentee officialdom of the International Unions and the conservative A. F. of L. overlords.
As an administrative machine the Committee never attained
a remarkable degree of perfection.  "This organization," one
of the strike officers said, "has as much cohesiveness as a
load of furniture."

The first meetings of the embryo National Committee were
held June 17-20, in St. Paul, Minn., coincident with the
1918 convention of the A. F. of L.  Organization meetings
were convened in Chicago August 1 and August 16, at which
W. Z. Foster was elected temporary, then permanent Secretary-Treasurer, in active charge of the organizing drive, and
John Fitzpatrick succeeded Mr. Gompers as Chairman.  It
was decided to make the campaign simultaneously nation-

wide; to use a uniform application blank and a universal low initiation fee of $3, of which $1 should go to the National Committee's fund, the other $2 to the International Unions; to obtain from each union a $100 initial contribution as an organizing fund ($2,400 to organize an entire industry!) and as many experienced organizers as could be donated. Organization was to be through mass meetings, at which applicants would be signed up, the applications then " segregated " according to crafts, and the segregated applicants then organized into separate locals or inducted into locals already existent in separate localities, thenceforward to be dues-paying members subject to the laws of the International to which they were assigned. The industry was divided into the following " Districts ": Chicago, Bethlehem, Johnstown, Pittsburgh, Youngstown, Cleveland, Wheeling, Steubenville, Buffalo, Pueblo (Colo.) and Birmingham (Ala.); in each was formed a " Steel Workers' Council," a Foster idea, resulting in the most effective organizing means outside the National Committee.

Inspection of the records demonstrates how the three main parties to the movement reached their differing positions.

(a) *Rank and file of new recruits.*

With the first mass meetings in September, 1918, the rank and file began to indicate their general attitude and their need,—protection. At the National Committee meeting of September 28, delegates reported " splendid mass meetings at South Chicago, Gary, Hammond, Joliet and Bethlehem." A delegate reported 1,500 signed up at one Chicago meeting. A delegate from Gary reported " fifteen boilermakers discharged for union affiliation."

From September, 1918, to September, 1919, the new unionists with increasing power urged action,—and the only action they understood was serving " demands " and striking. At the January 4 meeting reports were heard on "good movements on foot at the steel plants at Bethlehem, Coatesville, Sparrows Point, Steelton, Johnstown, Butler, Monessen, Wheeling, Youngstown, Buffalo, Cleveland, Lorain, Milwaukee, Gary, Indiana Harbor, Joliet, South Chicago, Minnesota, Pullman, Pueblo." The Secretary "announced that beyond all question the steel industry is being organized." The South Chicago workers asked " whether or not it was advisable for them to begin wearing the union button." Apparently even that much show of " action " was urged by the rank and file but the Committee advised holding buttons " in abeyance for the time being." Discharges of workmen for union activity began to be reported from the Pennsylvania districts.

At the March 8 meeting "hundreds" of Johnstown workers were reported as " discharged point blank "; affidavits were read of union men discharged "after ten to thirty-five years service." Similar " obstructionist " tactics had been reported from Youngstown. On May 25 a congress of 583 rank and file delegates from eighty steel centers, untrained in trade union practice, clamored their abuses and urged a strike which they thought themselves empowered to call. The Internationals' representatives counselled moderation. At the July 11 meeting the reports read that " in Johnstown, Youngstown, Chicago, Vandergrift, Wheeling and elsewhere great strikes are threatening. The men are letting it be known that if we do not do something for them they will take the matter into their own hands. Where they are not threatening to strike they are taking the position that they will pay no more dues until they can see some results from their efforts." From then on until September the records show a long tussle between the erupting rank and file and the International officers—with the National Committee as buffer—while demands were served, a strike ballot taken and a strike date set. In the last tense debates over postponing the date it was the impact of many telegrams like the following which forced the issue (meeting of September 17):

W. Z. Foster, 303 Magee Bldg., Pittsburgh, Pa.
We cannot be expected to meet the enraged workers, who will consider us traitors if strike is postponed.

Organizers Youngstown District.

The rank and file through the local leaders thus over-rode the Internationals, the A. F. of L. and President Wilson's request to wait for the October Industrial Conference.

(b) *The Internationals.*

The position of the twenty-four International Unions is indicated with similar clearness from the earliest Committee meetings. Few of the International Presidents, nominally members of the Committee, ever attended the meetings personally and at one meeting there were demands that the unions' representatives be at least a vice-president, rather than a powerless organizer. They agreed to the financing plan—pro-rata distribution of expenses in ratios of each union's total votes in A. F. of L. conventions—but, from September, 1918, on, many of the Internationals had to be "jacked up" persistently for moneys pledged. In organizers they contributed in all about 100; at the May 25 congress of rank and file, resolutions were passed that "there is sadly lacking a sufficient number of labor representatives" for the campaign and, "Whereas, without straining their resources all the various cooperating unions could easily increase" their organizers and "financial assistance," the Internationals were urged to "double the number of organizers now in the field in this work." Other resolutions called on Mr. Gompers and the A. F. of L. "to lend their assistance."

Particularly this conference, and the local leaders persistently, called on the Internationals to back up the National Committee's "free speech fight" in western Pennsylvania. Committee meetings from November, 1918, on, were much concerned with Pennsylvania's "time honored tactics of suppressing the right of assembly." In Pittsburgh, McKeesport, Braddock and Homestead, the Secretary reported, mass meetings were forbidden flatly or the money for rented halls was returned "under pressure of the steel interest" and the meetings "cancelled." The minutes of November 25 wax indignant:

In Rankin, the hall-owner having more than the usual share of independence, the city officials were unable to make him abandon the meeting. A lick-spittle Board of Health was called into service and gotten to arbitrarily close the hall.

The November 25 meeting of the Committee adjourned to go before the City Council of McKeesport to demand "the right of organized labor to have a hearing in McKeesport." They were rebuffed: the minutes add that "after this disgusting evidence of subserviency to the Steel Corporation" the Committee called on the A. F. of L. and all the Internationals to hold "a meeting as soon as possible in Pittsburgh" to test the right of assembly and settle the "free speech fight."

No such meeting resulted: the A. F. of L. took verbal action at its June convention and some International presidents promised to "fight it out in McKeesport" personally. The records, however, indicate no change in western Pennsylvania's administration of its laws of assembly, etc., as a result of "concerted action" by the Internationals and the A. F. of L.

The last and by far the most important positions taken by the Internationals, at variance with the new steel rank and file, concerned the strike—both as to calling the strike and as to supporting it.  It was natural that Internationals, such as the Machinists, with old established locals in a dozen other industries, should hesitate to burden these with a strike in behalf of their new machinist locals in steel.  They were divided between the desire to keep the steel locals, with their revenues, and the fear of possible consequences in carrying through to the limit what they had inaugurated.  At the May 25 congress it was the Internationals' representatives who quickly asserted their authority over the impatient rank and file.  At the critical July 20 meeting where the advisability of a strike ballot was debated, some of the Internationals, especially the Amalgamated Association of Iron, Steel and Tin Workers and the United Mine Workers, opposed the ballot and all impressed on the Committee that only the Internationals were authorized to take strike votes. After the locals' balloting,—resulting in a 98 per cent. vote for a strike—tense meeting followed meeting of the National Committee.  On September 4 President Gompers warned the Committee " of the great power of the steel trust, its ruthlessness and the glee with which it would deal Labor a heavy blow."  He advised " caution " and called a meeting of the twenty-four presidents.  Another message was sent to President Wilson, in the west, who telegraphed back his failure to influence Mr. Gary.  At the September 9 meeting for the twenty-four presidents, those present were divided, some urging " caution," some seeing " no way out," and all worried about financing so huge a strike.  By a vote of 14 to 4 it was decided to send a last telegram to President Wilson. The President's answer " contained no assurance of a conference " and the Committee set the strike date.  But when the President appealed to Mr. Gompers for a postponement, Mr. Gompers (minutes of September 17) wrote to " the International presidents requesting them to postpone action until after the Industrial Conference of October 6, if possible to safeguard the unions' interests while doing so." Mr. Gompers did not notify Mr. Fitzpatrick and Mr. Foster of his action in writing to the presidents on the Committee. " In consequence (of Mr. Gompers's letter) a number of delegates came to the conference (of September 17) with definite instructions as to how to vote on the postponement." Eight Internationals, it was revealed, either had instructed to vote for postponement or had telegraphed against the strike.

In opposition came a flood of telegrams and protests from local leaders urging that " it would be absolutely dangerous for our organizers to meet the men if the strike is called off." The Committee sent telegrams to the absent International presidents " requesting them either to come to Pittsburgh or to give their delegates the powers to act as the needs of the situation would seem to indicate." The debate lasted over a day and the consensus of those present was that if postponed the steel workers would " make short work of the organizations " and strike sporadically. Some of the International representatives wavered; the vote was for the strike, 12 to 3.

The record concerning the actual support of the strike by the Internationals is not clear. The Stationary Engineers and the Switchmen, two of the twenty-four Internationals, did not call their members out of the steel plants and yards, but a number of Switchmen's locals did. The Amalgamated Association of Iron, Steel and Tin Workers, after a month, began ordering its men back into " independent " plants, and, after the strike, withdrew from the Committee, taking away 70,000 to 90,000 members, all of whom were recruits from the drive. The United Mine Workers had their own strike of November on hand. Locals of the Internationals all over the country contributed to the strike relief fund but the bulk of this fund came from the Jewish clothing unions, one of which, the Amalgamated Clothing Workers, an industrial union fought by the A. F. of L., sent a check for $100,000 to the A. F. of L. for the steel strikers.

Thus the brunt of the strike lay on the steel workers who had forced it, not on "the organized labor movement of America" which had initiated the drive.

(c) *The National Committee.*

The position of the National Committee, in relation to the rank and file, has been indicated except in one matter. The Committee attempted to carry the temporary and artificial unity of the twenty-four Internationals into permanent organization in two directions. One was in setting up District Steel Councils, designed to maintain united, or quasi-industrial, action in dealing with separate plants. In most districts the weight of organizing and striking was carried chiefly by these councils; some of them survived the strike. The other Committee effort, specifically authorized by the May 25 congress, was toward setting up a national council, or Iron and Steel Department within the A. F. of L., like other trades departments in the A. F. of L. The A. F. of L. convention, on the recommendation of an administration committee, gave short shrift to this project.

With the foregoing analysis in mind, it is possible to summarize the principal causes of the failure of the strike, listing all but laying chief emphasis (in this section) on the apparent defects in the labor organization. To clarify the issue it is necessary to view the strike in two aspects: first, as the struggle of 300,000 newly organized workers against the Steel Corporation,—a limited aspect; second, the larger warfare of which the strike was a part,—the after-war battle for power between organized employers of the nation and organized labor, or as it has been termed, "between the money trust and the labor trust."

In the narrower aspect, the first cause of failure was the size of the Steel Corporation. The United States Steel Corparation was too big to be beaten by 300,000 workingmen. It had too large a cash surplus, too many allies among other businesses, too much support from government officers, local and national, too strong influence with social institutions such as the press and the pulpit, it spread out over too much of the earth—still retaining absolutely centralized control—to be defeated by widely scattered workers of many minds, many fears, varying states of pocketbook and under a comparatively improvised leadership. The " independent " steel companies gave the Corporation solid speechless support; not a spokesman was heard but Mr. Gary. In the crucial western Pennsylvania districts two decisive factors were the Governor of Pennsylvania, who sent in the State Constabulary, and the Sheriff of Allegheny County, who controlled an army of deputies. In a dozen towns the burgesses and police chiefs are salaried employees of the steel companies. It is impossible to pass over such facts as illustrating the *size* of the steel interests.

The second cause was the successful use of strike breakers, principally negroes, by the steel companies, in conjunction with the abrogation of civil liberties. As a fighting proposition the strike was broken by the successful establishment of, first, the theory of " resuming production " and, second, the fact of it. Production was maintained without any interruption in some plants. On this basis the companies created a *belief* that it was being resumed everywhere. Then by the use of strike breakers they spread the actual resumptions and reinforced the theory. Negro workers were imported and were shifted from plant to plant: in Gary the negroes were marched ostentatiously through the streets; in Youngstown and near Pittsburgh they were smuggled in at night. " Niggers did it," was a not uncommon remark among company officers.   Besides the comparatively small bands of avowed strike breakers, shifted from plant to plant, it is evident that the great numbers of negroes who flowed into the Chicago and Pittsburgh plants were conscious of strike breaking.   For this attitude, the steel strikers rightly blamed American organized labor.   In the past the majority of A. F. of L. unions have been white unions only.   Their constitutions often so provide.   Through many an experience negroes came to believe that the only way they could break into a unionized industry was through strike breaking.   The recent change in A. F. of L. official attitude toward negroes has not had time to be effective.   At Youngstown, for example, one lone negro machinist striker, who stuck to the end, was never admitted to the striking machinists' local.

Through strike breakers the companies played on one of the two great fears which always contend in workers' minds in time of strike.   One fear is, " My job, somebody will get my job."   The other fear is, " What will my neighbors say if I go back ? "   " Resuming production " makes the first fear overbalance the second.   Fears of other communities were played on.   In Pittsburgh the strikers heard, " They are going back in Chicago."   In Chicago they feared, " They are going back in Pittsburgh."   Committees of strikers, sometimes sponsored by mill officials or by Chambers of Commerce, went from Milwaukee to visit Chicago, and from Chicago, from Cleveland and from Wheeling to inspect Pittsburgh.   The newspapers kept reporting resumptions everywhere; other businesses were getting steel and were declaring they were getting all they wanted.

In their efforts to counteract this, in the pivotal Pittsburgh district, the strikers were in the main denied the rights of picketing and of assemblage.   The local leader could not reach them; he feared to visit strikers' homes lest he be arrested for " intimidation."   To counteract the newspapers they had only their strike bulletin, no local labor press. Constabulary and sheriff's proclamations kept them scattered. Separated, the great fear undermined them. By mid-November over half had forgotten the pure and simple trade unionist doctrine,—" organize and all these things shall be added unto you,"—and had gone back convinced that " this thing is not succeeding." Mr. Foster's dictum that " no worker is worth his salt who isn't willing to eat his hide in a strike " turned out to be " a counsel of perfection."

The third cause was the disunity of labor, limiting this consideration to the twenty-four unions involved and to the steel workers themselves. The skilled workers feared the semi-skilled, the semi-skilled feared the common labor: in the vast hierarchy of steel jobs each feared being put in a lower rank even if the strike were won. The Americans feared that the " foreigners " were pushing into the skilled jobs; the foreigners feared that the Americans were going back in the mill to conspire " to keep the hunkies down." Americans in the Pittsburgh district, who stayed at work, justified themselves on the ground that " the organizers had not appealed to them, only to the ' foreigners.' " The foreigners felt the newspaper criticisms that the strike was one of " un-American aliens." The strike's end saw the racial split deepened, many immigrants feeling that they had been " let down " by the American labor movement. Many immigrants told their leaders, " When you ' Americanize ' the Americans and the negroes, we'll strike again."

Among the twenty-four unions, besides the fights over segregating recruits, there came up in devastating form the unsolved problem of the " sacredness of contracts." The Amalgamated Association of Iron, Steel and Tin Workers, which had had agreements with certain " independent " mills, finally " remembered " these contracts and began " living up to them." The Amalgamated was acrimoniously charged with choosing between its contracts with employers and its contracts with fellow unions; its choice was called "treason." Rather, the difficulty was the recrudescence of an old dilemma hitherto unsolved by A. F. of L. unions in mass action.

Moreover there was no unity, at all comparable to that among the steel companies, as between the steel unions and the A. F. of L. The A. F. of L. sent out the strike fund appeal and Mr. Gompers battled for the strike in the Industrial Conference in Washington, but from the start the knowledge was widespread that Mr. Gompers had tried to have the strike postponed.

Three attitudes were distinguishable, at the end of the strike, concerning labor unity. One was that of Mr. Fitzpatrick and Mr. Foster, that "the strike had wonderful support from unions all over the country; Mr. Gompers and the A. F. of L. did everything that could have been expected in view of all the other strikes and troubles at the same period; the steel workers appreciate how the unions stood by them."

A second view was that expressed by an International president not involved in the strike: "The A. F. of L. doesn't *control* strikes and the International Unions are primarily business organizations for carrying on constructive negotiations for workers. Why should they bankrupt themselves for immigrants who originally took the steel jobs away from Americans and who wouldn't go on strike for Americans in the next trouble?"

A third view was put by a local strike leader, an experienced American unionist, without bitterness, as follows: "The A. F. of L. was not 'massed behind this strike.' The A. F. of L. didn't even hold a mass-meeting that I know of. When the hunkies tell me they were let down, I know it. The unions say they're 'always on the firing line' for labor and one reason they're *always* there is because they've never learned to fire together. If the railwaymen in the steel plant

yards had struck, this strike would have been won.   In
October the railway men's locals near Pittsburgh voted to
strike but they got no assurance of support from their
Brotherhoods.   In the Calumet district the Switchmen refused to pull out their men because, the organizer said, ' trade
control was at stake.'   The Switchmen were rivals of the
Trainmen for the men in the plant yards and if they'd have
struck the Trainmen would have stuck, filled up the places,
broke the strike and the Switchmen could never have got
back.   The Amalgamated's stand made them strike breakers.
When Mike Tighe [President of the Amalgamated Association of Iron, Steel and Tin Workers] ordered back his men at
that mill near Cleveland, he started an avalanche.   One Amalgamated organizer got four hundred men into one big union
with an Amalgamated charter at a mill near Steubenville
and they all struck.   Mike ordered them all back and tore
up that organizer's card.

" At Wheeling, after the gun riot there, some hunkie
strikers went to their A. F. of L. organizer for a lawyer to
get their fellows out of jail.   He told them he wouldn't use
union funds for that; let them hire their own lawyer.
Foster, I believe, made him move.   At Gary, Central Union
officials, jealous of the Steel Council, made speeches advising
the men to go back.   At Sparrows Point a big Amalgamated
official did the same thing.   I've heard Electrical International officers say their people didn't want steel organized,
because electrical workers, during slack times in union shops,
like to be free to get steel jobs, which they couldn't if steel
was organized.

" All these old habits of our unions played hob with the
strike.   There's no use denying it—the Steel Corporation
knows these things and counts on them.   And all the remedies
for them, like having all contracts date from the same day,
get tied up with radical proposals, like May Day.   During

the strike, Cleveland foreigner locals tried to get together in one separate steel industrial union. They got jumped on by the Internationals there. After the strike half a dozen towns' Steel Councils met in Gary to start an independent Steel Industrial Union. They'll get nowhere. If they take I.W.W. leadership, or W.I.I.U., they'll be outlawed. If they go it alone, secessionist, they'll be fought tooth and nail by the A. F. of L., with more success than the A. F. of L. fought the Amalgamated Clothing Workers.

" And all the while the twenty-four Internationals won't install the universal transfer card or the low re-installment fee or remit dues or do any of the things they've got to do to keep these new steel locals alive. They'll let 'em slide because there'd be no money in it.

" These selfish narrow habits wreck the movement. But we've got to take things as they are. Still there's no use being just optimistic like Foster. We'd better admit it since the steel companies just bank on our making the same mistakes."

The above is cited as a temperate statement of what many strikers and strike leaders expressed savagely.

The fourth cause of defeat was labor's failure to state its war aims, meaning, in the narrower aspect, the steel workers' plight and the unions' intentions in regard to steel jobs. Those most involved were the steel workers; they did the fighting; they seemed sometimes totally forgotten as workmen. The facts about their lives, their earnings, their jobs, were not set forth. The press may or may not have been hostile to such facts, but the facts were not prepared by the leaders and were not offered to the press. The facts mostly were not known to the leaders. Particularly when it came to actual knowledge of steel jobs and what changes might be necessary to make steel under union conditions and how the country's steel consumers might fare, such research had not been made by the unions. It was consciously ignored, partly on the ground that "the press and public opinion never count in a strike," and partly on the ground that the whole problem was not their business, which was solely "to organize the workers as they found them and any business can stand having its workers organized." But even this position was never clearly published. The leaders' overwhelming concern was with their strikers as union men. But the strike was to force a conference: that "public opinion" which *might* have helped to force it, never had an oversupply of facts on which to proceed; not even "workmen's opinion," outside of steel areas, was furnished with the facts.

As to the effects of unions on the steel industry, and labor's "failure to state its war aims," it is necessary to turn to the wider aspects of the strike, to that greater war in which the steel strike became engulfed and, in the public mind, almost forgotten as a separate entity after October.

This greater war was the clash between employer and employed experienced by each belligerent nation in the "readjustments" after the war, marked in America by more unthinking simplicity than in most countries. In England, for example, this clash was pressed by the workers, organized both economically and politically; in this country the drive seems to have been made by big industrial interests, bent on halting the unions' development or "encroachments." Particularly, big business associations were determined to end what they termed the "unfair gifts to labor in war time." The result was that a pretty solid association of manufacturers caught the inchoate body of labor at a time of crisis, split everywhere by a gulf between leadership and rank and file, split between old ideas and new, without a unifying program in terms of public service such as it had during the war, or even a plan of fighting for things that had been "given" to it during the war. Despite organized labor's boasts of power it was rather handily beaten everywhere in the fall of 1919.

Why did "public opinion" apparently join with the nation's employers generally to support a corporation, which in time past it had often attacked as the "menacing steel trust"?

First, because of the size and ramifications of the Steel Corporation. By its root connection with other businesses and especially with the sources of money-control, the Corporation has been, and is, naturally fitted to head the country's private producing employers. Its business ramifications lead:

(1) into the "independent" steel companies. Corporation men frequently head the "independents."

(2) into railroads. The Corporation operates thousands of miles of railroads, primarily for the transportation of ore. Also its directors are heavily involved in the directorates of the large railroads.

(3) into mines. The Corporation owns vast coal fields and limitless metal mines.

(4) into shipbuilding and ships. The Corporation owns ship lines, docks, etc.; it owns great ship-building yards.

(5) into general industries. The Corporation owns cement works, many by-product plants, and its regular product goes into a dozen basic utilities from railroads and buildings to farm implements and household utensils.

(6) into banks. The Corporation, primarily a great finance concern, is most closely tied into the country's financial reservoirs and in a directing capacity.

The Corporation owns towns. In many localities institutions, such as churches, schools and newspapers, are dependent on it for existence. Through its very size its social in-

fluence is enormous.  Its power over national legislation in
the past has been the text of voluminous criticism.  During
the war it paid no more attention to the national labor policies
as enunciated by the War Labor Board than as if the government had never made awards based on the " right to organize in trade and labor unions " and the " right to collective
bargaining."

Apart from its size, what *ideas* obtained for the Corporation such support?  Analysis indicates why so many smaller
business men, employers who had " scorned to take their labor
policy from trusts," and representatives of public opinion
generally supported Mr. Gary in all sincerity.

In the first place, employers all over the country were
paying higher wages than they were used to before the war
and as consumers were paying prices which seemed to them
unreasonable, for all sorts of commodities from " labor " to
laundry.  Especially was this true of little employers and
what may be called middle business men.

These new wage scales, *insofar as they were set by the
action of labor,* resulted from the operation of Mr. Gompers'
theory of pure and simple trade unionism.  The theory considered nothing but wages, hours and conditions, and jacked
these up as high as the traffic would stand, having little
regard to comparisons with other industries, or to the inherent
value of the service rendered, or to any standard (with the
exception of roughly approximating rises in the cost of living).  Comparative standards were " not labor's business."

Moreover, organized labor was showing no disposition to
share responsibility for production, nor had it had opportunity to demonstrate marked ability to " share industrial
control," an ambition newly proclaimed by it.  Labor was
emphatically refusing the kind of " responsibility " advocated by employers, that is, incorporation of trade unions and
making them subject to the courts, whose tradition, rooted in

the old conspiracy laws, is far from friendly to labor unions. For all that, labor was showing no disposition to supply any other schemes for assuming responsibility for production or responsible share in control. As the steel strike broke, the American labor movement was definitely opposed to any harness of "responsibility." This was a big fact in the consciousness of the country's employers and of the public.

Then came (1) the threat of the steel strike, and the strike itself; (2) a month later the great coal strike; (3) all along the threat of great railroad strikes. The upshot was that the country's employers as a class took fright at what seemed to be the rolling up of uncontrolled power by trade unions. Because the government after the war, as before, had shown no ability to formulate any plan for having labor share responsibility and control, employers were afraid of the government. They saw no leadership there.

The only leadership they saw was Mr. Gary's. Employers who feared the sweeping character of his statements about labor, men who were getting along very well with trade unions in their own businesses, "supported Mr. Gary" because they could not see where it would all end if labor won the steel strike, the coal strike, the railroad strike and every other strike.

Moreover, all through the country, the middle classes, or great body of consumers outside of organized labor, were mainly conscious that prices of everything consumed were getting beyond reach. In considerable part they accepted the explanation that labor was partly to blame; "high wages, high prices." They too "supported Mr. Gary," though many expressed fear as to what the outcome would be if they supported Mr. Gary to the hilt. Against him they saw only Mr. Gompers; they never really saw the steel workers or learned anything about the hunkies and the twelve-hour day.

It is quite true that "public opinion," especially in these

days of organized propaganda, may be a singularly meaning-
less, vague and artificial thing.  It is notorious that public
opinion is ordinarily "roused" in behalf of strikes chiefly
by murder, preferably murder of women and children, by
flame and machine gun for choice, as at Ludlow, Colorado.
In this sense too few strikers were killed, or those killed
were not young enough or not the right sex to "rouse public
opinion" for the steel strikers.  So far labor leaders of the
old type merely retort, "When unions are strong enough we'll
take care of public opinion."

On the other hand it is possible that the unions' present
lack of strength is caused considerably by failing to take
thought for the public now.  When labor thinks out where it
purposes to go and publishes its fair intent and even its clear
ambition, it may demolish much adverse public opinion.
Otherwise another 300,000 strikers in another industry may
find their justified cause hopelessly entangled in another lost
battle over the "open shop" or some even more indefinite
shibboleth.

In England, in the same week in which the steel strike
started, the labor unions, far more powerfully organized than
the American unions, spent $100,000 in six days for pub-
licity to "care for public opinion" and by forcing that publication of their case they added a weight sufficient to save
their national railroad strike against the government itself.
The steel strike leaders in 108 days did not spend 100,000
cents to present the steel workers' case to "public opinion."
In taking care of public opinion, moreover, the British
leaders were automatically informing and fortifying their
own forces, the workingmen's public opinion, which nowadays is becoming decisive.  The American steel leaders tried
to maintain their strikers' morale with a lonely weekly bulletin, which however good, was not good enough to offset the
same strikers' reading of hostile newspapers.

Conclusions, which are not so remote as they seem from the hunky in the steel towns, may be summed up as follows:

Causes of defeat, which were second in importance only to the fight waged by the Steel Corporation, lay in the organization and leadership, not so much of the strike itself, as of the American labor movement.

The immigrant steel worker was led to expect more of the twenty-four Internationals than they, through indifference, selfishness or narrow habit, were ready to give.

" Public opinion " cannot reasonably demand consideration or generosity from trade unions as long as trade unions are kept fighting for existence or for ordinary human rights, denied them under the sanction of " public opinion."

## APPENDIX TO SECTION VI

### *Organized by the National Committee*

The following extracts from the duly audited and approved final report and accounting of the Secretary-Treasurer of the National Committee give illuminating statistics on the strike.

The first tabulates, by districts and by crafts, the recruits obtained by the National Committee directly, based on the financial accounting. That is, each direct recruit is represented in the Committee's finance accounts by $1, the Committee's share of the $3 initiation fee. The Committee claims that the number of workers " swept out " with the walkout of new union members was 100,000. It seems probable that half that number was nearer correct.

The first extract reads:

" 250,000 members enrolled by the National Committee for Organizing Iron and Steel Workers during the American Federation of Labor organizing campaign in the steel industry, from August 1, 1918, to January 21, 1920.'

| Location | Black-smiths | Boiler Makers | Brick and Clay Wkrs. | Brick Layers | Coopers |
|---|---|---|---|---|---|
| South Chicago ............ | 153 | 143 | 9 | 21 | ... |
| Chicago Heights .......... | 41 | ... | ... | 2 | ... |
| Misc. Chicago Dist. ....... | 128 | 23 | ... | 22 | 1 |
| Pittsburgh ............... | 571 | 99 | ... | 43 | ... |
| Johnstown ............... | 503 | 137 | 156 | 122 | ... |
| Butler ................... | 75 | 30 | ... | ... | ... |
| Monessen, Donora ......... | 145 | 25 | ... | ... | ... |
| New Castle .............. | 18 | 3 | ... | 1 | ... |
| Homestead ............... | 136 | 63 | ... | 2 | ... |
| Braddock, Rankin ......... | 91 | 110 | ... | 10 | ... |
| Clairton ................. | 39 | 48 | ... | 21 | ... |
| McKeesport .............. | 109 | 33 | ... | 4 | ... |
| Gary .................... | 129 | 285 | 1 | 95 | ... |
| Indiana Harbor .......... | 161 | 95 | 3 | 11 | 1 |
| Joliet ................... | 52 | 50 | 18 | 48 | 71 |
| Milwaukee ............... | 4 | 2 | ... | ... | ... |
| Waukegan ............... | 8 | ... | ... | 3 | ... |
| De Kalb ................. | 1 | ... | ... | ... | ... |
| Aurora .................. | 1 | 1 | ... | ... | ... |
| Pullman ................. | 157 | 3 | ... | 2 | ... |
| Kenosha ................. | 4 | ... | ... | ... | ... |
| Hammond ................ | 62 | 11 | ... | 4 | ... |
| Wheeling District ........ | 38 | 57 | ... | 2 | ... |
| Farrell, Sharon .......... | 106 | 231 | ... | 22 | ... |
| Cleveland ............... | 2,230 | 35 | ... | 1 | 65 |
| Sparrows' Point ......... | ... | ... | ... | ... | ... |
| Brackenridge, Natrona ..... | 23 | 5 | ... | ... | ... |
| East Pittsburgh .......... | ... | ... | ... | ... | ... |
| East Liverpool ........... | ... | ... | ... | ... | ... |
| Warren, Niles ........... | ... | 5 | ... | 40 | ... |
| Minnesota Dist. .......... | ... | ... | ... | ... | ... |
| Pueblo .................. | 37 | 17 | ... | 10 | ... |
| Coatesville .............. | 3 | 40 | ... | ... | ... |
| Steuben, Mingo, Wierton... | 41 | 35 | ... | 16 | ... |
| Birmingham ............. | 36 | 13 | ... | 67 | ... |
| Canton, Massillon ........ | 65 | 56 | ... | ... | ... |
| Vandergrift ............. | 37 | 2 | ... | 1 | ... |
| Buffalo, Lackawanna ...... | 91 | 101 | ... | ... | ... |
| Youngstown ............. | 389 | 336 | ... | 11 | ... |
| Peoria .................. | 3 | 3 | ... | ... | ... |
| Decatur ................. | 12 | ... | ... | ... | ... |
| Total by Trades ...... | 5,699 | 2,097 | 187 | 581 | 138 |

| Elect. Wkrs. | Foundry Employees | Hod Carriers | Iron, Steel and Tin Workers | Iron Workers | Machinists | Metal Polishers | Mine, Mill and Smelter Workers |
|---|---|---|---|---|---|---|---|
| 1,078 | 139 | ... | 2,112 | 326 | 676 | ... | 798 |
| 16 | 27 | ... | 145 | 2 | 148 | ... | 4 |
| 73 | 228 | ... | 212 | 1,673 | 657 | 5 | 3 |
| 402 | 444 | 787 | 4,089 | 280 | 965 | ... | 320 |
| 719 | 108 | ... | 4,452 | 731 | 1,131 | ... | 437 |
| 21 | 26 | ... | 290 | 15 | 126 | ... | 236 |
| 320 | 7 | ... | 5,543 | 103 | 451 | ... | 792 |
| 12 | ... | 60 | 1,116 | 6 | 317 | ... | 221 |
| 216 | 178 | 71 | 2,307 | 144 | 237 | ... | 8 |
| 148 | 184 | 102 | 1,265 | 276 | 353 | ... | 1,022 |
| 136 | 11 | 105 | 947 | 70 | 166 | ... | 1,158 |
| 91 | ... | 14 | 2,452 | 69 | 249 | ... | 500 |
| 761 | 121 | 83 | 2,855 | 353 | 929 | ... | 534 |
| 270 | 407 | 26 | 1,494 | 235 | 473 | ... | 212 |
| 152 | 66 | ... | 1,814 | 180 | 142 | ... | 444 |
| 21 | ... | ... | 547 | 16 | 19 | ... | ... |
| 11 | 139 | ... | 758 | 9 | 73 | 21 | 22 |
| 4 | 1 | 2 | 256 | ... | 24 | ... | ... |
| 3 | 13 | 31 | 3 | 15 | 119 | ... | ... |
| 193 | 12 | ... | 106 | 4 | 255 | 5 | ... |
| 42 | 17 | ... | 187 | 34 | 165 | 7 | ... |
| 207 | 6 | ... | ... | 2 | 34 | ... | ... |
| 127 | ... | ... | 3,109 | 28 | 226 | 226 | 535 |
| 150 | ... | 10 | 2,386 | 22 | 118 | ... | 403 |
| 434 | ... | 33 | 7,820 | 38 | 1,296 | 85 | 2,599 |
| ... | ... | ... | 93 | ... | ... | ... | ... |
| 154 | 22 | 492 | 1,007 | 18 | 108 | ... | 63 |
| ... | ... | ... | ... | ... | 146 | ... | ... |
| ... | ... | ... | 50 | ... | ... | ... | ... |
| 22 | ... | ... | 240 | 27 | 36 | ... | 24 |
| ... | ... | ... | ... | ... | ... | ... | 185 |
| 61 | ... | ... | 2,281 | 26 | 143 | ... | 279 |
| 48 | ... | ... | 632 | 21 | 32 | ... | ... |
| 238 | ... | ... | 2,499 | ... | 288 | ... | 319 |
| 26 | ... | ... | 115 | 174 | 195 | ... | 691 |
| 397 | ... | 63 | 1,929 | 208 | 335 | ... | 16 |
| 92 | 3 | 13 | 1,560 | 16 | 87 | ... | 60 |
| 539 | 191 | ... | 2,242 | 242 | 477 | ... | 1,033 |
| 1,273 | ... | 443 | 10,364 | 449 | 1,019 | ... | 2,305 |
| 23 | 11 | ... | 746 | 17 | 71 | ... | ... |
| 1 | 45 | ... | 3 | ... | 120 | ... | ... |
| 8,481 | 2,406 | 2,335 | 70,026 | 5,829 | 12,406 | 349 | 15,223 |

| Location | United Mine Wkrs. | Molders | Pattern Makers | Plumbers | Quarry Wkrs. | Railway Carmen |
|---|---|---|---|---|---|---|
| South Chicago | ... | 46 | ... | 195 | ... | 38 |
| Chicago Heights | ... | 13 | ... | 8 | ... | 17 |
| Misc. Chicago Dist. | ... | 94 | ... | 38 | ... | 267 |
| Pittsburgh | ... | 168 | ... | ... | ... | 22 |
| Johnstown | 1,427 | 71 | ... | ... | ... | 566 |
| Butler | ... | ... | ... | 24 | ... | 329 |
| Monessen, Donora | ... | 51 | ... | ... | ... | ... |
| New Castle | ... | 11 | ... | ... | 616 | ... |
| Homestead | ... | 3 | ... | ... | ... | 20 |
| Braddock, Rankin | ... | 56 | ... | ... | ... | ... |
| Clairton | ... | 2 | ... | ... | ... | 17 |
| McKeesport | ... | 31 | ... | ... | ... | ... |
| Gary | ... | 98 | ... | 210 | ... | 20 |
| Indiana Harbor | ... | 211 | ... | 78 | ... | 42 |
| Joliet | ... | 12 | ... | 39 | ... | 2 |
| Milwaukee | ... | ... | ... | ... | ... | ... |
| Waukegan | ... | 14 | ... | 2 | ... | ... |
| De Kalb | ... | 1 | ... | ... | ... | ... |
| Aurora | ... | 4 | ... | ... | ... | ... |
| Pullman | ... | 11 | ... | 103 | ... | 2,819 |
| Kenosha | ... | 1 | ... | 23 | ... | ... |
| Hammond | ... | 17 | ... | 2 | ... | 751 |
| Wheeling District | ... | 2 | ... | 6 | ... | ... |
| Farrell, Sharon | ... | 6 | ... | 21 | ... | 30 |
| Cleveland | ... | 319 | ... | 25 | ... | 50 |
| Sparrows' Point | ... | ... | ... | ... | ... | ... |
| Brackenridge, Natrona | ... | 14 | ... | ... | ... | ... |
| East Pittsburgh | ... | ... | ... | ... | ... | ... |
| East Liverpool | ... | ... | ... | ... | ... | ... |
| Warren, Niles | ... | ... | ... | 19 | ... | ... |
| Minnesota Dist. | ... | ... | ... | ... | ... | ... |
| Pueblo | ... | 1 | ... | 87 | ... | ... |
| Coatesville | ... | ... | ... | ... | ... | ... |
| Steuben, Mingo, Wierton | 111 | ... | ... | ... | ... | ... |
| Birmingham | ... | 1 | ... | 45 | ... | 17 |
| Canton, Massillon | ... | 41 | ... | ... | ... | ... |
| Vandergrift | ... | 14 | ... | ... | ... | ... |
| Buffalo, Lackawanna | ... | 38 | ... | 84 | ... | ... |
| Youngstown | ... | 31 | ... | 354 | 109 | 38 |
| Peoria | ... | ... | ... | 4 | ... | ... |
| Decatur | ... | ... | ... | 2 | ... | ... |
| Total by Trades | 1,538 | 1,382 | ... | 1,369 | 725 | 5,045 |

| Sea-men | Sheet Metal Wkrs. | Station-ary En-gineers | Station-ary Fire-men | Steam Shovel-men | Switch-men | Unclassi-fied | Totals by Localities |
|---|---|---|---|---|---|---|---|
| ... | 19 | 116 | 585 | ... | 68 | 94 | 6,616 |
| ... | 64 | 4 | 6 | ... | 1 | 71 | 569 |
| ... | 14 | 7 | 18 | ... | ... | 408 | 3,871 |
| ... | ... | 43 | 196 | ... | ... | 541 | 8,970 |
| ... | ... | 324 | 441 | ... | 207 | 314 | 11,846 |
| ... | ... | 1 | 9 | ... | ... | 1,337 | 2,519 |
| ... | ... | 32 | 52 | ... | ... | 1,144 | 8,665 |
| ... | ... | ... | 41 | ... | 1 | 287 | 2,710 |
| ... | ... | 47 | 118 | ... | 10 | 11 | 3,571 |
| ... | ... | 19 | 300 | ... | ... | 108 | 4,044 |
| ... | ... | 66 | 73 | ... | ... | 111 | 2,970 |
| ... | ... | 20 | 64 | ... | ... | 327 | 3,963 |
| ... | 23 | 99 | 250 | 2 | 34 | 210 | 7,092 |
| ... | 5 | 105 | 298 | ... | 40 | 487 | 4,654 |
| ... | 9 | 84 | 255 | ... | 14 | 45 | 3,497 |
| ... | 11 | 3 | 27 | ... | 2 | 29 | 681 |
| ... | ... | 2 | 50 | ... | 2 | 98 | 1,212 |
| ... | ... | 1 | 22 | ... | ... | 20 | 332 |
| ... | 16 | ... | 6 | ... | ... | 30 | 242 |
| ... | 38 | 48 | 48 | ... | ... | 269 | 4,073 |
| ... | 2 | 3 | 12 | ... | ... | 88 | 585 |
| ... | ... | 3 | ... | ... | ... | 3 | 1,102 |
| ... | ... | 287 | 233 | ... | ... | 152 | 5,028 |
| ... | ... | 156 | 10 | ... | ... | 123 | 3,794 |
| ... | ... | 28 | 509 | ... | 4 | 1,734 | 17,305 |
| ... | ... | ... | ... | ... | ... | ... | 93 |
| ... | ... | 16 | 78 | ... | 19 | 91 | 2,110 |
| ... | ... | ... | ... | ... | ... | ... | 146 |
| ... | ... | ... | ... | ... | ... | ... | 50 |
| ... | ... | ... | 5 | ... | ... | 56 | 474 |
| ... | ... | ... | ... | ... | ... | ... | 185 |
| ... | ... | 77 | 80 | ... | ... | 14 | 3,113 |
| ... | ... | 52 | ... | ... | ... | ... | 828 |
| ... | ... | 205 | 206 | ... | ... | 150 | 4,108 |
| ... | 19 | 64 | ... | ... | ... | 7 | 1,470 |
| ... | 17 | 32 | 15 | ... | 4 | 2,527 | 5,705 |
| ... | ... | 30 | 20 | ... | 8 | 43 | 1,986 |
| ... | ... | 148 | 366 | ... | ... | 627 | 6,179 |
| ... | 119 | 71 | 900 | ... | 25 | 804 | 19,040 |
| ... | 5 | 1 | 26 | ... | 1 | 73 | 984 |
| ... | 16 | ... | 2 | ... | ... | 119 | 320 |
| ... | 377 | 2,194 | 5,321 | 2 | 440 | 12,552 | 156,702 |

"This detailed report includes only those members signed up by the National Committee for Organizing Iron and Steel Workers and from whose initiation fees $1.00 each was deducted and forwarded to the general office of the National Committee. It represents approximately 50 per cent. to 60 per cent. of the total number of steel workers organized during the campaign and is a minimum report in every respect.

"The report does not include any of the many thousands of men signed up at Bethlehem, Steelton, Reading, Apollo, New Kensington, Leechburg and many minor points which felt the force of the drive but where the National Committee made no deductions upon initiation fees. In Gary, Joliet, Indiana Harbor, South Chicago and other Chicago District points, the National Committee ceased collecting on initiation fees early in 1919, hence this report makes no showing of the thousands of men signed up in that territory during the last few months of the campaign before the strike. Likewise, at Coatesville and Sparrows' Point, during only a short space of the campaign were deductions made for the National Committee. Many thousands more men were signed up directly by the multitude of local unions in the steel industry that were not reported to the National Committee. These do not show in this calculation. Nor do the great number of ex-soldiers who were taken into the unions free of initiation fees—in Johnstown alone 1,300 ex-soldier steel workers joined the unions under this arrangement. Of course no accounting is here included for the army of workers in outside industries who became organized as a result of the tremendous impulse given by the steel campaign.

"In view of these exceptions it may be conservatively estimated that well over 250,000 actual steel workers joined the unions during the campaign, notwithstanding the opposition of the Steel Trust, which discharged thousands of its workers, completely suppressed free speech and free assembly in Pennsylvania and used every known tactic to prevent the organization of its employees."

In publishing this report, Mr. Jay G. Brown, who succeeded Mr. Foster as Secretary-Treasurer, made the following claims (undiscouraged, to say the least):

"It represents an accomplishment without a parallel in the history of the labor movement. This report will forever silence if not shame the class of men who are fond of saying, 'The steel industry cannot be organized.' It was organized. It also furnished a crushing answer to Judge Gary who asserted that only about 10 per cent. of the steel workers were organized. This report represents an irreducible minimum. Local unions when organized did not as a rule make accounting to the National Committee for additional members enrolled."

"The National Committee began its work on the theory that any men in any industry could be organized if they could be reached with the message of unionism. This report proves the correctness of this theory. This report should convey a lesson and furnish an inspiration to the labor movement of this country. It means that with the application of those same principles any industry in America can be organized.

"The report of the Relief Fund is equally noteworthy. It must be remembered that at the beginning of the steel strike, there were, as nearly as could be calculated, 367,000 men involved. 100,000 of these men were still on strike when it was called off."

Another extract is from the twenty-four-page printed financial account dealing with strike relief. It includes the following summaries of the moneys contributed through the A. F. of L. officials to the steel strikes. Note the late date at which efforts to raise a fund were inaugurated; six weeks after the strike began (September 22).

### "REPORT ON RECEIPTS AND DISBURSEMENTS.

"All moneys contributed to the undersigned for the Steel Strike Relief Fund, except those from organizations regularly affiliated with the National Committee for Organizing Iron and Steel Workers, were forwarded to Mr. Frank Morrison, Secretary of the American Federation of Labor, and appear in his report. The moneys contributed by the affiliated organizations are duly accounted for in the regular monthly reports of the Secretary-Treasurer of the National Committee for Organizing Iron and Steel Workers.

1919                              RECEIPTS

| | | | | | | | |
|---|---|---|---|---|---|---|---|
| Nov. | 4 | From Frank Morrison per John Fitzpatrick | | | | ......$ | 2,400.00 |
| " | 15 | " | " | " | " | " " | 5,000.00 |
| " | 19 | " | " | " | " | " " ...... | 17,665.13 |
| " | 20 | " | " | " | " | " " ...... | 13,783.50 |
| " | 21 | " | " | " | " | " " ...... | 57,835.70 |
| " | 21 | " | " | " | " | " " ...... | 8,387.53 |
| " | 23 | " | " | " | " | " " ...... | 107,067.39 |
| " | 23 | " | " | " | " | " " ...... | 17,438.56 |
| " | 28 | " | " | " | " | " " ...... | 45,208.82 |
| Dec. | 1 | " | " | " | " | " " ...... | 9,658.47 |
| " | 6 | " | " | " | " | " " ...... | 10,807.28 |
| " | 9 | " | " | " | " | " " ...... | 8,522.03 |
| " | 9 | " | " | " | " | " " ...... | 12,845.73 |
| " | 11 | " | " | " | " | " " ...... | 19,918.10 |
| " | 15 | " | " | " | " | " " ...... | 9,519.12 |
| " | 26 | " | " | " | " | " " ...... | 24,147.04 |
| " | 27 | " | " | " | " | " " ...... | 9,738.92 |
| 1920 | | | | | | | |
| Jan. | 3 | " | " | " | " | " " ...... | 15,125.76 |
| " | 8 | " | " | " | " | " " ...... | 11,043.30 |
| " | 30 | " | " | " | " | " " ...... | 12,028.76 |

Total Receipts ...................................$418,141.14

### DISBURSEMENTS

| | |
|---|---|
| Meat and Groceries ......................................$178,695.64 | |
| Commissary Checks for points outside Pittsburgh District .. | 93,082.82 |
| Labor and Expenses .....................................: | 3,612.44 |
| Freight and Drayage .................................... | 3,757.24 |
| Bread .................................................. | 46,739.54 |
| Potatoes ............................................... | 22,622.04 |

Total .........................................$348,509.72

RECAPITULATION

Total Receipts from Nov. 4, 1919, to Jan. 31, 1920 (comprising total fund) ................................$418,141.14
Total Disbursements from Oct. 27, 1919, to Jan. 31, 1920 .... 348,509.72

Bal. Deposited in Gen'l Fund of Nat'l Com. for Organizing Iron and Steel Workers ...........................$ 69,631.42

In addition to the above extracts it may be noted that the bulk of the strike relief fund came from the Jewish clothing and furriers' unions, principally of New York, some of these unions being outside the A. F. of L and long opposed by it.

Approximately $100,000 additional to the above was contributed by the twenty-four unions affiliated with the Committee. The year's organizing campaign cost the Committee approximately $75,000. It was reported that the financial cost of the year's work to one or two of the twenty-four unions of the Committee, in maintaining organizers, contributions, meetings, etc., approximated $200,000 apiece.

# VII

## SOCIAL CONSEQUENCES OF ARBITRARY CONTROL

In this section are analyzed the data obtained by the Commission on the second or larger phase of control, i.e. industrial relations, outlined in Section V. Analysis warrants the following conclusions:

Inasmuch as the Steel Corporation never offered plans or developed a working substitute for arbitrary control, present conditions in the industry constitute the *actually existent alternative* to " the kind of conference the labor unions wanted."

Maintenance of this non-unionism alternative entailed serious social consequences for steel communities and for the nation. The consequences were normal in the industry; they became pronounced and grave during the strike.

Maintaining the non-unionism alternative entailed, for the employers, (1) discharging workmen for unionism, (2) blacklists, (3) espionage and the hiring of " labor detective agencies' " operatives, (4) strike breakers, principally negroes.

Maintaining the non-unionism alternative entailed, for communities, (1) the abrogation of the right of assembly, the suppression of free speech and the violation of personal rights (principally in Pennsylvania); (2) the use of state police, state troops and (in Indiana) of the U. S. Army; (3) such activities on the part of constituted authorities and of the press and the pulpit as to make the workers believe that these forces oppose labor.

In sum, the actually existent state of the steel industry is
a state of latent war over rights of organization conceded by public opinion in other civilized countries.

The analysis centers around the Steel Corporation because
" independents " such as the Midvale-Cambria, Youngstown
Sheet & Tube, Inland Steel, Harvester and Colorado Fuel
& Iron, have offered or developed other alternatives to arbitrary control in the shape of shop committees or company
unions; and smaller " independents " have signed trade
unionist agreements.

The analysis attempts to investigate to what extent the
Steel Corporation's policy of non-unionism modifies American
social institutions.   The following problem, at once larger
and more specific, is not dealt with: the relation between the
facts that (1) America's trade union movement is, relative to
industrial populations, the smallest, with the possible exception of that of France, among the Atlantic industrial nations;
(2) America's private industrial monopolies or trusts are the
largest among the western industrial nations.

The social consequences of arbitrary control by corporations are set forth in the present Main Summary Section,
which attempts to analyze the subject as a whole, and in the
following sub-reports:

1. *Civil Liberties,* in western Pennsylvania; including an
   analysis of some 300 affidavits or statements from
   strikers.
2. *Blacklists, Evictions and Discharges for Unionism;* including several hundred signed statements from strikers
   and letters and lists sent out by steel companies.
3. *" Under-cover " Men;* being a study of 600 reports in the
   " labor file " of a steel company, together with affidavits,
   interviews and revelations by " labor detectives."

4. *The Press and the Strike;* being an intensive analysis of the Pittsburgh newspapers.
5. *The Pulpit and the Strike;* an analysis of the Pittsburgh Protestant churches, including the answers to a questionnaire sent out during the strike.
6. *History of Steel Corporation's Labor Relations,* including developments during preceding strikes.

To be considered with these are many separate interviews or observations made by the Commission or its investigators and public records, etc.

Consideration of social consequences is consideration of that larger, decisive aspect of industrial relations outlined in Section V on "Grievances and Control." Two aspects of control were distinguished; one, the problem of personnel management, lying largely within the plant and centering in the separate jobs; the second, the problem of industrial relations, extending outside the plant, decisively influencing the first problem, and concerned with the relation of the mass of workers to the sum of jobs. Bringing this distinction to a statement of conclusions (a) hitherto discussed and (b) treated in the present section, the following is warranted by the analysis:

The system of arbitrary control—the actually existent alternative to trade union collective bargaining—resulted in—

(a) markedly *excessive hours* for half the workers, *underpayment* for three quarters of the workers and daily *grievances* due to arbitrary management of personnel; and—

(b) opposition and repression, exerted primarily by the companies and secondarily by governmental officers and social institutions, against workers' organization for change of their industrial relations.

Viewed chronologically, in normal times the Steel Corporation's system of industrial relations functioned under the dominating idea of opposition to workers' organization. In strike times the Corporation's opposition was more actively supplemented by similar repression by organized society. This section, then, concerns—

1. The causes and characteristics of the Steel Corporation's opposition to trade union collective bargaining;
2. The effects of such opposition on the worker as citizen and on executive and judiciary authorities and pulpit and press, particularly during the strike.

A record of the minutes of the Corporation's Executive Committee meetings preceding and during the strike would, of course, shed much light on the personal character of arbitrary control. Lacking such data it is necessary to use the Executive Committee minutes which the Government obtained and published ten years ago, giving the financial control's ideas and debates in adopting the Corporation's labor policy in 1901; comparison seems to indicate that the same ideas govern the present-day execution of that policy.

The minutes [1] record the Corporation's manner of adopting a labor policy (previously quoted) in the following resolution:

That we are unalterably opposed to any extension of union labor and advise subsidiary companies to take firm position when these questions come up and say that they are not going to recognize it; that is, any extension of unions in mills where they do not now exist; that great care should be used to prevent trouble and that they promptly report and confer with this corporation.

[1] Printed in Senate Document 110, Vol. III, pp. 497-506.

The following extracts from the minutes give the ideas adopted by the Committee. (The names, of course, are the names of the original financial control whose formulation of policies has since been followed by the Steel Corporation.)

April 20, 1901.

Mr. Edenborn thinks it expedient to inform the newspapers and the public generally that the United States Steel Corporation is not the one employer, but that the *individual companies are distinct and separate for themselves* [1]*;* that the labor troubles of any one company must be settled by that particular company as an individual company, and a strike in one must be settled independently of any other company.

Attention was called to the fact that certain newspapers seem to publish any and everything that will create sufficient sentiment to influence newspaper sales; that we ought to do all we reasonably can to keep public sentiment right and the facts before the public. It was the opinion of one member that he would like to have the workmen understand that *we do not purpose to allow them to run our mills,* but that we do purpose always to treat the men fairly as individuals and give them good, liberal wages.

At the close of this whole discussion it was decided that the sense of this Committee is that the general policy should be to *temporize* for the next six months or year until we get fully established, and that the prevalent conditions of labor and labor unions at the different plants should be undisturbed, and that *if any changes do occur later they can be handled individually.*

Three members of the Committee have very positive ideas on the expediency of permitting any change in the labor relations now prevailing at the different plants. They insist that they believe we must accept whatever conditions now exist at our plants; that *it is not wise at this time to institute any change ourselves;* that any attempt on the part of anyone else to bring about an alteration in a certain direction should be *promptly*

[1] Italics are the editor's.

*discouraged by the ordinary means;* that if it is found and desired that *changes be brought about later by our companies* they can be done when business reasons would permit. These gentlemen further maintain that long experience in these matters has taught them that if certain situations which naturally arise from time to time be not quickly disposed of on the spot with a firm hand, *you will then witness the beginning of the end.*

They favored the *prompt reporting here of any trouble* and stated that matters that were serious or are likely to cause trouble should be handled upon the advice of this Committee. They do not approve of the local manager attempting to decide any and all questions of this kind that may arise at the plant, but these small affairs that require nipping in the bud should be disposed of by him and then reported here.

One gentleman thinks this whole question is so big and grave in its possible effect to the United States Steel Corporation that we ought to proceed with great caution and if necessary *consult with some of our associates* on the subject.

He believes that *it would be a great mistake if it were understood we had adopted a policy of antagonism:* that the effect might be disastrous; that we must not lose sight of the financial interests of the corporation and must endeavor to keep clear of anything that might be prejudicial to these interests.

June 17, 1901.

The next question is, Should we establish a r le and announce that rule to presidents, viz., that they are authorized to take up the question and dispose of it promptly on the basis that *under no circumstances will any union be recognized where there are no unions?* . . . It has been suggested in this Committee that when that question comes up the president of the subsidiary company should reply that he wished to consider and would make answer the next day, and in the meantime could take it up with the president of this company, and then finally report to the representative that the matter had been carefully considered and the decision reached is so and so.

To this last proposition the president commented that it would then be perfectly clear that such president had taken it up with this corporation.

Mr. Converse feels . . . that *public opinion would be with us inasmuch as we had not attempted to crush unions,* but had simply accepted the various situations as they were; that we had left the management at the individual plants just as heretofore and advised the local officers to use their judgment. He pointed out that we are assured by certain presidents that they *can run everything in their non-union plants.*

(The following lines in the minutes occur immediately after an expression by the one member of the Finance Committee expressing any toleration for unions.)

The president informs the Committee that there is in the air a well defined feeling that the corporation is indifferent as to fighting the extension of the labor unions.

(The situation before the Board on June 17, 1901, was the threat of a strike by the Amalgamated Association of Iron, Steel and Tin Workers. In this the labor union for the first time grappled with the new conditions of consolidation brought about by the formation of the Steel Corporation. This Association had agreements in about one-third of the Corporation's mills.)

Mr. Converse put this proposition that as a matter of fact it is not a question of finessing the situation except up to a certain point; that the very worst the Association can do is with about 33 1-3 per cent., and he believes it will not do it with that low percentage; that if our president says to the presidents that they will please understand that the United States Steel Corporation is a large financial institution and it expects you to go ahead now and handle this situation just exactly as if the United States Steel Corporation did not exist, *they will be very careful not to get into trouble.*

This met the unqualified approval of the president, Mr. Steele, and Mr. Reid.

(The following from the minutes of July 2 refer to the growing threat of a strike by the Amalgamated Association and the specific statement of the understood remedy hinted at throughout the minutes.)

The chairman stated that he would be willing to concede two mills as union mills, *to sign the scale for the McKeesport mill and to keep it shut down.*

July 2, 1901.

The chairman stated that probably the men would be satisfied if they gained a point; that while it is very humiliating, nevertheless it is a critical period and we had better temporize if it can be done.

(After a decision to send representatives to confer with the Amalgamated Association.)

The chairman stated that it should be clearly understood that the United States Steel Corporation has nothing whatever to do with it; that the representatives of the three subsidiary companies are *not to state that they are acting in concert, or even by consultation, with any of the officials of the United States Steel Corporation.*

The chairman explained his opinion that the men who go should be pretty big men and able men, who if necessary might be competent to decide pretty promptly what to do; they should be men with sense enough *not to be antagonistic to the views here* without full consultation with New York.

In response to an inquiry from the chairman, the president stated that he had been *assured by the head* of the financial house that he will stand by whatever action the president thinks best. The president has also stated that the junior partners expressed themselves as very anxious to have this matter settled, but did not at any time state that it should be settled.

The chairman called attention to the fact that it seems from the statements made to be clearly understood what policy ought to be pursued.

(The tense situation between the Amalgamated Association and the Corporation over signing the new scale was greatly increased by the episode recorded in the minutes of July 8, 1901.)

The president reported that the superintendent of the Wells-ville sheet mill down on the Ohio River had *discharged twelve men who were endeavoring to institute a lodge.* Later in the meeting the chairman read an Associated Press dispatch referring to this and stating that the men were discharged on Saturday last and that Shaffer [1] had announced that the men would have to be reinstated before any conference could be had.

Mr. Edenborn believes that we have the matter well in hand and that even if we have to face a tin-plate strike we *should not give in to labor.*

The mill is not a union mill because it has *not been recognized by the owners* as a union mill.

The president would now approve of meeting the people and making the best arrangement possible *and learn what they wanted.*

The chairman stated that we all labored under the impression based on the statement of the president that we could keep so close track that we would know pretty well what the men were doing; but that if this union at McKeesport mill had been formed between last April and the time the presidents were here we did not have the information.

July 12, 1901.

Mr. Steele reported to this meeting that an informal talk over the labor situation had taken place this morning between such of the directors as could be reached at that time, and there were present Messrs. J. P. Morgan, H. H. Rogers, Robert Bacon, Abram Hewitt, Charles Steele, and the president of this company; that during this talk the whole labor situation was again gone over; . . . that it was the unanimous opinion of those present that we should say we were willing to sign the scales in all of our union mills as we had last year as submitted, but that we *refuse to negotiate with the association in any particular for the mills known as non-union mills.*

Analyzed, these minutes indicate that—

[1] President of the Amalgamated Association.

1. The Executive Committee (financiers) control absolutely the Steel Corporation's labor policy.
   Mr. Gary told the Senate Investigating Committee that this was true today.
2. The nature and extent of the Executive Committee's control was to be kept secret from the public and the announcement made that each subsidiary company controlled its own labor policy.
3. Opposition to labor unions by the financial control was instinctive and complete. The bases of opposition were pride and fear; e.g. " we do not purpose to allow the workmen to run our mills." " If certain situations which naturally arise be not disposed of with a firm hand, you will then witness the beginning of the end." Fear of colleagues' opinion existed, e.g. the president's reference to the feeling in the air that " the Corporation is indifferent as to fighting the extension of labor unions."
4. Opposition to labor unions was to be kept secret and not avowed; e.g. " public opinion would be with us inasmuch as we had not attempted to crush labor unions but had simply accepted the various situations "; and " it would be a great mistake if it were understood that we had adopted a policy of antagonism."
5. Opposition to labor unions was to be through " the ordinary means " with final reliance on shutting down union mills where agreements had to be signed and turning the production over to the corporation's non-union mills; e.g. " to sign the scale for McKeesport mill and to keep it shut down."
6. Subsidiary presidents and superintendents were responsible for any methods of their own, which must " not be antagonistic to the views " of New York and which included discharge of workers for forming labor unions.

Methods were questioned only when the results threatened to be " disastrous," i.e. strikes.

7. Opposition to union labor included " temporizing," " finessing " and opportunistic reliance on subordinates with concern only for " results."

8. Workmen were not consulted and no systematic aboveboard means of hearing workmen's views was considered. Workmen's right to organize was considered a " natural " thing, to be repressed.

9. Final decision on labor policy rested with Wall Street which was ready to support the anti-union policy.

The sole concern of the Steel Corporation was whether the anti-union policy could be carried out, without too great damage to immediate profits. The decision was on a weighing of chances; the decision did not concern the rights of man.

The history of the Steel Corporation's dealings with labor since 1901 shows a consistent and successful carrying out of the anti-union policy. Largely by shutting down mills " conceded " to be " union" and by discharging workmen for forming other unions this result has come about: whereas in 1901 one-third of the Corporation's mills dealt with unions, in 1919 these and all other unions had been ousted; no unions were dealt with. Besides the stockholders' report of 1912 hitherto quoted, which " justifies " the Corporation's " repression of the workmen," Mr. Gary made plain to the Senate Investigating Committee that the same ideas and the same methods held all along.

He told the Senate Committee that " unionism is not a good thing for employer or employee." At the same time he declared that the Corporation did not carry this belief into practice by " opposing labor unions as such "; that no workman " was discriminated against because he was a union man "; that the Corporation did not attempt to crush unions. All this was in accord with the principles of 1901 of disclaiming the opposition, in the belief that "it would be a great mistake *if it were understood* that we had adopted a policy of antagonism."

Decisions in 1919 were made the same as in 1901, on the basis of what the Corporation might *have* to do, not what ought to be done. Mr. Gary said, "Now of course when there is only one thing to do or when there are various evils confronting us, the position to take is the one least unfavorable." His judgment on the vastly different conditions in England in no way concerned whether labor had reached power there because of any *justice* in labor's position; "I think England is inclined to go further than the people of this country would go, simply because she is compelled to." So far the Steel Corporation has not been "compelled to;"— "we are not obliged to contract with unions if we do not choose to do so."

It is necessary to keep in mind the distinction between Mr. Gary's arguments based on possible evils,—the "closed shop" argument,—and his arguments based on the Corporation's actual practice. The difference was illustrated in this statement by Mr. Gary to members of the Commission of Inquiry on December 5: "I am just as much opposed to one big union of all the steel companies of the country as to one big union of all the steel workmen. Both would be bad for the nation." Mr. Gary was not brought to a discussion based on *the actual fact:* whether one big union of *half* the steel companies of the country, with no recognized union among that half's steel workmen, was "bad for the nation." An analysis of fact, such as attempted in this report, must deal with the badness or justice of what actually exists,—with the alternative enforced by the Corporation's practice.

In sum, then, Mr. Gary could tell the Senate Committee

in the same breath that " of course workmen had a right to belong to unions " but that " it is my policy and the policies of the Corporation not to deal with union labor leaders at any time." The Corporation never proposed any plan between the horns of this dilemma. The dilemma was actually resolved by the Corporation's practice. What the Corporation actually did, and does, is dealt with here.

The Commission's data show that the practice of the anti-unionism alternative by the Corporation and by a large number of independents entailed in 1919—

1. Discharging workmen for unionism, just as the twelve men were discharged at Wellsville in 1901 " for forming a lodge"; also the eviction of workmen from company houses and similar coercions.
2. Blacklisting strikers.
3. Systematic espionage through "under-cover men."
4. Hiring strike-breaking spies from "labor detective agencies."

These will be considered before passing on to the wider social consequences affecting governmental and social institutions. In 1919 the Corporation had no further need for the practice of signing up agreements with unions in certain mills and then shutting those mills down. The threat of this practice, however, was well understood in 1919. In half a dozen towns investigators found evidences of it; for example, this remark made by a roller in New Kensington, once a union man but, in October, 1919, no union man and no striker, " If the union is started again you've got to remember that there is nothing to keep the company from starting its old policy of shutting down the mills. Then where'd you be with your better wages and shorter hours? "

1. *Discharge for unionism.*

The Commission's special evidence consists of hundreds of signed statements by steel workers who were discharged.

Mr. Gary flatly denied to the Senate Committee that such was the practice. He said:

" If that has been done in a single case or a few cases, if it has ever been done, which I deny, it has been contrary to our positive instructions and would not have been permitted, and the man would be disciplined if he disobeyed these instructions the second time. . . .

" Now, it is quite possible that a man, or more than one man, who is a member of a labor union, unknown to us or known to us—that is unimportant—has gotten up some proposition, has built up some straw man, for the purpose of making trouble, and of reporting that he was discriminated against because he was a union man. Or, it is possible, though I do not think probable, that some foreman may in some instances have shown some feeling against a union man when he discovered it. I do not know of any such case. It would be directly contrary to our orders, contrary to all our reports and contrary to the information I have. I have denied the proposition emphatically. It is not true." [1]

It is true and Mr. Gary's subordinates explained one phase of how it works. Mr. Buffington of the Illinois Steel, also Mr. Williams' representative for the Carnegie Steel and other officers put it uniformly in these words: " We don't discharge a man for belonging to a union, but of course we discharge men for agitating in the mills."

Who settles what constitutes agitating in the mills? The foreman. Two men during a breathing spell in the mill converse for a moment. One has been found out to be a union man. That talk, a word in passing, a gesture (which may be a union lodge secret sign in the foreman's belief) is sufficient for the foreman's judgment, once he has learned that the company wants the man got rid of.

---

[1] Senate Document No. 202. Vol. I, p. 166, p. 174.

Mr. Burnett, assistant to the President of Carnegie Steel, volunteered the information in a conversation that the discharge of eight men at a shears in their works was because "they were agitating in the mill" by having invited labor leaders to come and organize them. The practice varied widely: it was worst in the Pittsburgh District. And this fact must be borne in mind in considering the *number* of men discharged: the discharge of a single man in a department may be enough to stop unionizing among the five hundred men left. The spectacle of one old employee summarily fired, and the union he belongs to helpless to give him a job, may settle the fate of that union for a whole works. Only where "examples" fail to deter was discharge by the hundred resorted to, as at Johnstown.

The statements of discharged workers included cases where the foreman admitted the cause of the discharge and told who gave the order; cases of men secretly elected officers in a new union local and fired the next day; cases of men thirty-five years in companies' employ and fired after admitting joining to some man later proved a spy.

These are specific cases. More important is the feeling throughout the Corporation's workmen that the price of joining a union *may be* discharge at any minute. All workmen know it. Their first concern after secretly signing up is "protection." Moreover discharge is only the symbol for a whole system of opposition just as persistent and almost as effective as the more drastic act. The system works in discharge from a job, but not from the plant, i.e. in transfer of known union men from good jobs to worse ones, even from skilled jobs to common labor, until the man discharges himself from the industry. Finally, discharge is peculiarly effective in steel towns because generally no other jobs exist there. The discharged man must move himself and his family.

"Agitating in the mill" may include the mail a man receives at his home. At the Jones & Laughlin plant in Woodlawn, Pa., one department had twenty-four Finns. Finns are known as especially intelligent workmen and especially likely to join unions. In February, 1919, the plant management learned that these Finns were visiting a great deal with each other at night, meeting in the cellars of their own houses. Finally it was observed that the Finns seemed to be getting more mail than the other "foreigners," including newspapers and pamphlets. The twenty-four were called up one morning and fired without explanation. In September, 1919, the plant management were congratulating themselves: they observed in the list of union workers deported by plant guards from Weirton the names of some of their Finns. The plant had "spotted 'em all right."

Discharges for joining the union were so common in the months before the strike that the union organizers did not even keep records of the cases. Cases were too common to need proving and the organizer could only say to the victim, "After we're recognized you'll get your job back."

Pencil marks on a typewritten slip of paper in the Monessen "labor file" illustrated the principle of discharge. The paper was the report of a spy, plainly inside the union, and contained a list of names which were referred to in a letter, also in the file, from a labor detective agency. The appearance of the paper with the first five names crossed out, was as follows:

## MONONGAHELA LODGE NO. 127, PA.

The employees of the Page Steel and Wire Fence Company, Monessen, Pa., have formed a strong lodge of the A. A. Organizer M. E. Donehue acted as master of ceremonies in instituting this new addition. The officers of Monongahela Lodge No. 127, Pa., are:

President, Anthony Paulsweski, wire mill.
Vice-President, Joseph Pirer, wire mill.
Recording Secretary, Yudy Gladysz, wire mill.
Financial Secretary, Joseph Kissell, wire mill.
Treasurer, Frank Stockus, wire mill.
Guide, Nick Bachovchese, open.hearth.
Inside Guard, John Uring, page.
Outside Guard, Akym Cymbale, page.
Journal Agent, John Baran, wire mill.
Corresponding Representative, Paul Kissell, 216 Knox Ave., Monessen, Pa. _____

It is the Capuan punishment principle—strike off the heads of the leaders. The " examples " will take care of the rest of the would-be unionists.

In Johnstown where unionism spread through the entire Midvale-Cambria works, including even the office force, " examples " were not sufficient and literally thousands of men were summarily discharged. An investigator in November, 1919, obtained in two days about two hundred signed statements and sworn affidavits of discharged workmen who had been told or who believed that the cause was union affiliation. The forty pages of these statements make monotonous reading; specimens follow:

Joseph Yart, 216 Woodville Ave., Johnstown, was employed by the Cambria Steel Company for forty years in the car works and was never discharged before. He became a member of the union on February 3rd, and was discharged on May 12th by Superintendent Hill. When Mr. Yart asked him for the reason of his discharge, he was told " there is no more work for you here." He went to the employment agency to apply again in June and was told by Agent McGrew, " You can't work for Cambria any more, better look for something outside." Mr. Yart protested that he had worked there for forty years, that he is now 54 years of age and can't work very well on the outside and the only reply he got was "You can't work here any more—you are an agitator and a disturbance maker in the car department." Mr. Yart denied this charge and protested that he never spoke to anyone there about his union affiliations, but no attention was paid to his protest. Mr. Yart has been unable to find another job ever since and has been out of work now for the past eight months, as every place he goes to his age handicaps him in securing a job. Mr. Yart was born and lived all his life in Johnstown and was one of the first employees that helped to organize the Cambria Employees' Beneficial Association. One of Mr. Yart's sons was in the army of occupation, and Mr. Yart now complains: "My son went to fight for democracy and I am thrown out on the streets without any means of livelihood."

(Signed) Joseph Yart.

---

Charles Bacha, 811 Virginia Ave., Johnstown, was employed by the Cambria Steel Company for seven years and never discharged before. On April 1st he participated in the miners' parade, and although he was not a member of the union at that time, he was discharged on the 2nd of April by Superintendent Donk May. The foreman, May, gave him no explanation for his dismissal. He tried to find further employment with the Cambria and when he saw Mr. Lumpkin, the General Superintendent, he was told, "My boy, if you want union work, go down to a union town and get it—no work for you here."

Mr. Bacha applied again four times, but was refused work continuously. Mr. Bacha is a U. S. citizen and has been out of a job now for eight months, as he could not find another job.

(Signed) Charles Bacha.

---

William Barnhart, 50 Messenger St., Johnstown. On October 24, 1918, he was hired by Telford & Jones Coal Company and started to work, when the foreman came over and said, "I'm sorry, I'll have to take you off—they telephoned me from the main office to take you off." He asked the foreman whether this was because he belonged to the union, to which the foreman replied, "I have nothing against the union, but I got to be on the other side." Mr. Barnhart is a U. S. citizen.

(Signed) William Barnhart.

---

Bernard Heeney, 336 Honnan Ave., Johnstown, worked for the Cambria Steel Company for seven years and was never discharged before. He joined the union on March 24, 1919, and was discharged on June 6th by Assistant Superintendent F. W. Bryan. When he asked the Assistant Superintendent why he was laid off and explained to him that he was in charge of about twelve men and was the oldest employee in the department, Bryan said, "I don't know—we have orders here to take you off." When he asked him where these orders came from he said, "They may have come from New York, Philadelphia or Chicago." Mr. Heeney is a native of the U. S.

(Signed) Bernard Heeney.

---

Joe Mandorgotz, 1320 Virginia Ave., Johnstown. Worked for the Cambria Steel Company on and off for about twenty years. He joined the union about March, 1919, and took part in the miners' parade on April 1st. About April 7th, Davie Malcomb, foreman, asked him whether he belonged to a union. He admitted he did and was discharged two days later. Mr. Mandorgotz is a U. S. citizen, lived in Johnstown for twenty-seven years and has a wife and three children to support. He could not find another job for four months.

(Signed) Joe Mandorgotz.

---

Theodore Salitski, 206 Broad Ave., Johnstown, Pa., worked for Cambria seven years—never discharged before. Was discharged by foreman, Donk May. Joined the union March 17th and was discharged April 7th. Took part in parade held April 1, 1919. When asked for reason, told him "Because you stayed home April 1st." Applied again and was told by May that "There is no work for a Bolshevist." Out of work six weeks. Married man—wife and one child. Lived in Johnstown eight years.

(Signed) Theodore Salitski.

---

I, the undersigned, do hereby testify that I have been employed by the Cambria Steel Company for almost eight (8) years in the capacity of unloading steel.

I have at all times been an efficient and reliable employee.

W. H. Walter, the Foreman of the stockyard Department called me into his office this morning and then he asked me if I belonged to the Union. I answered "Yes." He then asked why I joined the Union. I told him the men were joining and I thought I should belong. Mr. Walters then asked "If the men jumped into the furnace would you follow them?" I answered "Yes, if they would I would." I did not believe it was any of his business, as I believe I have a right to join a labor organization for my protection.

I asked Mr. Walters why he discharged me. He answered "Because you joined the Union."

The foregoing occurred the forenoon of February 22nd, 1919.

his<br>(Signed) Nick (X) Poppovich.<br>mark

---

Witness to mark: Thos. A. Daley.

State of Pennsylvania, } ss.:
County of Cambria,

Before me, a Notary Public, in and for said County personally came Nick Poppovich, who being by me duly sworn according to law deposed and said that the foregoing statement is true and correct.                                         his

(Signed) Nick (X) Poppovich.<br>mark

Witness to mark: Thos. A. Daley (Signed).

Sworn and subscribed, before me
this 22nd day of February, 1919.
Ray Patton Smith (Signed),
Notary Public (Seal).
My commission expires March 12, 1921.
Paper not drafted by Notary.

---

State of Pennsylvania, ⎰
County of Cambria, ⎱ ss.:

Personally appeared before me, Myrtle R. Johnston, a Notary
Public in and for said County and State, John Kubanda, personally known to me, who being by me first duly sworn deposes
and says:

That I worked for the Cambria Steel Company for nine
(9) years, the 1st two (2) years in the blast furnace department,
always was a steady and dependable man. On Thrusday, February 13th, 1919, Peter Riley, Foreman, sent a man to tell me
to come and get my time. I went in to the office and asked
him why I was laid off. He said " I got my orders from the
office." I told him I don't belong to the Union. He said,
" What were you doing at the meeting? " I said, " Anyone
can go over to the meeting." He said " go down to the general
office and fix it up with them."

I verily believe that it was through Union affiliations that
I was discharged.

(Signed) John Kubanda (Seal).

Sworn and subscribed, before me
this 24th day of February, A. D. 1919.
(Signed) Myrtle R. Johnston,
Notary Public (Seal).
My commission expires February 27th, 1921.

---

Affidavit on affidavit, the cases prove incontestibly the ter-
rorism, sometimes with purpose avowed, more often with
purpose disavowed, so that the discharged man has nothing
left even for argument if argument would be heard. The

nameless terror was more commonly applied, the answer, "You know why," as if the cause were some secret unspeakable disease in the victim, like leprosy.

It was much the same in Corporation mills:

Joe Mayor, 440 Beach Way, Homestead—Aug. 15, 1919.

Mayor said that he had worked for the Carnegie Steel Co. in the car wheel shop 12 years and had never been discharged before.

He joined the union on August 5th. He was discharged August 15th by Supt. Munle, who called him into his office but said "Were you at the meeting Tuesday night?"

M.—I was. How do you know?

Supt.—Somebody turned your name in and I am going to discharge you.

M.—What's matter? what I do, rob company of couple of dollars?

Supt.—We don't want you to attend union meetings. I don't want union men to work for me.

When the Superintendent inquired what they had told him at the meeting, he refused to answer and further refused to answer when the Superintendent asked him for the names of others present at the meeting. The Superintendent then called a policeman and he was taken out of the shop.

M. got a job for two weeks under a different name, as he knew himself to be blacklisted. Is a citizen and married; has lived in Homestead 14 years.

John Dablonski, 320½ Syria St., Duquesne, Pa.

Dablonski said that he had worked three years in the Carnegie Steel Plant and had never before been discharged. Early in September, he attended a Sunday meeting, at which Mother Jones spoke, in Duquesne, a few days later, Mr. Buswick, a foreman of the Carnegie Steel Co., told him he was discharged. D. asked why but Mr. Buswick would not tell him.

He is married and has taken out his first papers.

These are examples. The range of the Commission's data is given in a sub-report. The Pittsburgh District saw the most extensive use of this weapon.

2. *Blacklists.*

Blacklists as an integral part of the anti-union alternative of course are ordinarily kept secret by the companies. The steel plant in Monessen, however, which freely lent its " labor file " to an investigator to study, included among the detectives' reports, etc., several blacklists. To most actual plant managers, as distinguished from Mr. Gary, blacklists seem after all too common to be deeply concealed. With the lists examined by the Commission are evidences of the system of inter-company exchange like the detective reports where the names of " independent " and Corporation mills were mixed together.

PITTSBURGH STEEL PRODUCTS COMPANY
Mill Office

M. Wikstrom,
  Gen'l Supt.
Jas. H. Dunbar,
  Ass't to Gen'l Supt.

Monessen, Pa., November 7th, 1919.

George A. Paff, Supt.,
  Page Steel and Wire Company,
    Monessen, Pa.

Dear Sir:

Attached hereto is list of former employees who have failed to return to work in our Plant.

This list is forwarded to you so that proper action can be taken—should they apply for employment at your Plant.

We would ask that you kindly consider this as confidential.

Yours very truly,

PITTSBURGH STEEL PRODUCTS COMPANY,

(Signed)   M. Wikstrom,

SW/F
Gen'l Superintendent.

November 20, 1919.

Mr. M. Wikstrom, General Superintendent,
   Pittsburgh Steel Products Company,
      Monessen, Pa.

Dear Mr. Wikstrom:

In compliance with your request, we are submitting herewith a complete list of our employees who have not as yet returned to work.

Naturally, we expect to re-employ the larger portion of these men, although we have underscored the names of some radicals who, I believe, nobody would want around a plant.

Very truly yours,

PAGE STEEL AND WIRE COMPANY,

GAP/M                              General Superintendent.

---

MONESSEN FOUNDRY AND MACHINE COMPANY
Monessen, Pa., November 4th, 1919.

Mr. Geo. Paff,
   Page Steel and Wire Co.,
      Monessen, Pa.

Dear Sir:

We attach herewith list of former employees, who are striking for Closed Shop. This list is forwarded to you at this time, as we understand several of these men are applying for work at your plant.

Very truly yours,

MONESSEN FOUNDRY & MACH. CO.,

(Signed) Louis X. Ely,

LXE/OH                                    Secretary.
Copy to PMW 11/15

---

It is a regular system; "in compliance with your request." It is secret; "consider confidential." It is disingenuous; "striking for closed shop." The attached lists, principally "hunkies," run from fifty to two hundred names apiece. A sub-report gives the range of the Commission's data, of which the above are samples.

3. *Espionage.* ("Under-cover" men.)

Great systems of espionage are an integral part of the anti-union alternative; spies are integral to warfare.

Espionage was of two general classes: spies directly in the employ of the steel companies; and spies hired from professional "labor detective" agencies. The Steel Corporation plants have their own detective forces; one case of hiring outside agencies by a Corporation subsidiary was charged publicly during the strike.

Espionage was of two general characters: spies pure and simple who merely furnished information; and spies who also acted as propagandist strike breakers, mingling with the strikers and whispering that the strike was failing, that the men in other towns had gone back, that the union leaders were crooks, etc. The Monessen "labor file" contained some six hundred daily reports by "under-cover" spies of both characters, mere detectives and strike-breaking propagandists.

*These company spy-systems carry right through into the United States Government.*

Federal immigration authorities testified to the Commission that raids and arrests, for "radicalism," etc., were made especially in the Pittsburgh District on the denunciations and secret reports of steel company "under-cover" men, and the prisoners turned over to the Department of Justice.

The Monessen "labor file" enabled the student to follow one such paper through to the government. It is given here as offering light upon the question why many workingmen, especially steel workers, have come to suspect that the government, *as government,* has taken sides in industrial warfare; has taken sides against workingmen.

In this freely offered "file," among the blacklists, detective agency contracts, "under-cover men's" reports, typed letters of big concerns on high grade paper with luxurious letter-heads, there was a scrap of dirty paper the size of one's palm. Scribbled on both sides it read exactly as follows:

Charleroi, Pa., Oct. 13th, 1919.

Dear Sir:

I am an employee of the Pitts Steele Proct of Allenport I went to work last Fri and would like to work so I will give you some names of some Belgian dogs that made it so hard for me and my family I had to quite they are a menace to our country so Please keep there names in mind

Yours truly

Over

Charle Ballue
    209 Shady ave    Charleroi Pa
Arthur Ballue
    Oakland ave between 3 and 4 st    Charleroi Pa
Tony Jarruse
    208 Shady ave    Charleroi Pa
Gus Vanduzene
    312 Shady ave    Charleroi Pa
Albert Balue
    3 st    Charleroi Pa

Make these suffer as they are making other just now when you start your mills.

The investigator of the file wondered what happened to spiteful scraps of paper in the steel industry. Beside the scrap was a letter as follows:

PITTSBURGH STEEL PRODUCTS COMPANY

Mill Office

Monessen, Pa., October 15, 1919.

M. Wikstrom, Gen'l Supt.

Jas. H. Dunbar,

Ass't to Gen'l Supt.

Messrs:

George A. Paff,

C. J. Mogan,

U. S. Smiley,

W. S. Bumbaugh,

W. C. Sutherland,

J. W. Connery,

Gentlemen:

We are in receipt of an anonymous communication under date of October 13th, which reads as follows:

" I am an employee of the Pittsburgh Steel Products Company of Allenport. I went to work last Friday and would like to work, so I will give you some names of some Belgian Dogs that made it so hard for me and my family, I had to quit. They are a menace to our country—so please keep these names in mind when you start your mill.

Charles Ballue,

209 Shady Ave., Charleroi, Pa.,

Arthur Ballue,

Between 3rd and 4th Sts., Charleroi, Pa.

Tony Jarouse,

208 Shady Ave., Charleroi, Pa.,

(Formerly worked in our mill under Check No. 5321).

Gus Vanduzen,

312 Shady Ave., Charleroi, Pa.

Albert Ballue,

3d St., Charleroi, Pa.

Make these men suffer as they are making me suffer just now when you start your mill."

This is for your information and files.

Yours very truly,

PITTSBURGH STEEL PRODUCTS COMPANY,

(Signed)    Malcolm Wikstrom,

JDH/W                              General Superintendent.


The list at the top of the letter represented every steel concern in Monessen.  The promptness with which the list of names was speeded back and forth among the companies was illustrated in another letter in the file, sent out the same day the above was received.


PITTSBURGH STEEL COMPANY

Mill Office

Monessen, Pa., October 15, 1919.

C. J. Mogan, Gen'l Supt.

D. P. King, Ass't Gen'l Supt.

A. Allison, Ass't Gen'l Supt.

Messrs.,

M. Wikstrom, Pgh. Steel Products.

U. S. Smiley, American Sheet. & Tin Co.

F. D. Bumbaugh, Monessen Fdry. & Mach. Co.

J. L. Hoffman, Carnegie Steel Co.

G. A. Paff, Page Steel & Wire Co.

Dear Sirs:

Enclosed is a list of men who are some of the leading agitators in keeping the men from going to work by all kinds of threats.

Yours very truly,

(Signed)    C. J. Mogan,

CJM/C                              General Superintendent.


Attached to this letter was a copy of the same little list, with one additional name.  Of the mills catalogued, beneath the letterhead, as on the circuit of vital information, two were Corporation subsidiaries,—American Sheet & Tin, and

Carnegie Steel,—the rest "independents." The letters crossed and recrossed, so that the Pittsburgh Steel Products Co. officer who started the list out got the same list back from the Pittsburgh Steel Co. (another "independent") the same day.

Finally in the file was the carbon of a letter transmitting the same list to the Department of Justice at Washington, asserting that the men named were "leading radicals."

From a scrap of dirty paper, rising through stages of typed and embossed letterhead dignity, to those dossiers, marked "*Important*—VERY SECRET," in Government Bureaus in Washington! The circumstances at either end of the chain were not investigated.

The testimony of a Federal officer of long official experience, made at a hearing of the Commission of Inquiry in November in Pittsburgh was:

. . . 90 per cent. of all the radicals arrested and taken into custody were reported by one of the large corporations, either of the steel or coal industry. I mean by that, that these corporations are loaded up with what they call "under-cover" men who must earn their salaries, and they go around and get into these organizations and report the cases to the detectives for the large companies. The detectives in turn report to the chief of police of the city. Generally, the chiefs of police in these small cities around Pittsburgh were placed there by the corporations.

The corporation orders an organization raided by the police department, the members are taken into custody, thrown into the police station and the department of justice is notified. They send a man to examine them to see if there are any extreme radicals or anarchists among them. They usually let all but a few go. In one instance seventy-nine were taken. The Department of Justice let all go but three; of those we asked for warrants for two, and at the hearing we made a case against one of them.

The Steel Corporation has been using every possible endeavor for the last 20 years to fill its mills with foreigners, and to a large extent has done so; then you must see why the foreigner is taking the front of the stage in this conflict. When the large corporations put these foreigners in they thought they had a class of men who wouldn't strike. Now they want to get rid of some of them.

During the war a number of able patriotic American citizens, lawyers, etc., as officers in the army or as Federal officials under the Department of Justice, became acquainted with this widespread intimate connection between "undercover" systems and Federal authorities and became seriously disquieted, partly because of the possibility that, in such a system, governmental power might be put at the mercy of mercenary and interested men, or might lead to the flagrant misuse of such influence in behalf of private ends. Since the armistice several of these ex-officials have publicly criticized the whole system, without visible reform resulting. During the steel strike the same system, a year after the armistice, was worked hard. The undoubted existence of a fractional percentage of "alien radicals" was capitalized, with Government assistance, in order to disorganize bodies of strikers whose loyalty was of unquestionable legal standing.

Before considering the data on this phase of the inquiry, reference should be made to the character of the under-cover organizations.

Two extensive labor-detective strike-breaking corporations, with offices in a dozen cities, had a hand in fighting the steel strike. Documents and reports from one of the concerns filled half the Monessen "labor file." Affidavits and documents were obtained from the other, which operated chiefly in the Chicago District. Also in the Monessen "labor file" were the reports furnished by two other " detective " agencies. In the file were the forms of contracts under which these concerns were hired and operate. Their " operatives " reports run from the illiterate scribblings of professional parasites to the most accurate transcriptions of union locals' secret meetings. Interviews with the officers of these strike-breaking concerns gave further insight into the range of their " work " in the steel strike. A sub-report furnishes the material for building up a day by day story of the strike in Monessen. The other documents and the interviews show the extent. It is all of a piece and it is the least noble side of the war waged for the " open shop " in steel.

The manager of the detective strike-breaking corporation whose reports and contracts appeared in the Monessen " labor file," when interviewed spoke fairly freely of his concern's views and activities. He had over five hundred " operatives " at work in the steel strike. Some of his operatives had been injected into the steel plants a year before. Many of his operatives had become officers of labor unions. He said that there was on the National Strike Committee a labor leader who took his money. He denied that his concern was a mere detective or strike-breaking concern.

He used the same arguments as Mr. Gary in explaining why he supported Mr. Gary. He said workmen had a right to organize but the " open shop " must be preserved. He said that labor unions had rights but that the unions had fallen into the hands of radical leaders.

Like Mr. Gary he denied that he wanted to crush unions. He denied that his operatives were really strike breakers; though the " labor file " contained full details of his operatives' strike breaking activities and the following letter:

New York Office, 680 Hudson Terminal.
Chicago Office, 1051 Peoples' Gas Bldg.
Cleveland Office, 1835 Euclid Ave.
Pittsburgh Office, Wabash Bldg.
St. Louis Office, Chemical Bldg.
Cincinnati Office, Union Trust Bldg.
Detroit Office, Book Bldg.

THE CORPORATIONS AUXILIARY COMPANY

Wabash Building,

Pittsburgh, Pa.

J. H. Smith, Pres. & Treas.
John Weber, Secy.
D. G. Ross, Gen. Mgr.
H. C. Breton, Res. Mgr.
—— ——, Gen'l Mgr.,[1]                    October 11th, 1919.
—— —— Co.,
    Pittsburgh, Pa.
Dear Sir:

Confirming conversation between your Mr. —— ——[1]
and the writer on yesterday, we will furnish you as quickly as
possible with two Slavish speaking operatives to work along the
lines as agreed between the writer and Mr. —— on yesterday.

This is as per the terms of our regular $225 monthly contract
with the usual wage credits of $3.00 per day allowed as per
the copy of attached contract, with the exception that it is understood that this service will terminate at the end of 30 days from
commencement of same unless otherwise extended.

We wish to thank you very much for this business and will
endeavor to make same as valuable to you as possible and trust
that it will be instrumental in having the morale of your foreign
strikers broken.

We will thank you very much for your cooperation in the

[1] Deleted names are in original letter; copy in possession of Commission.

handling of this service and will appreciate your calling upon us at any time we can be of special service to you.

Yours very/truly,

THE CORPORATIONS AUXILIARY COMPANY,

By (Signed) S. Dewson,

Resident Manager.

B-W: P-11

No other country in the world has such large widespread, well-financed, strike-breaking corporations, making money out of "labor trouble" as America. Their existence is an integral part of the industrial corporations' policy of "not dealing with labor unions." The steel strike was harvest-home for them. Outside the plants and inside, outside the strikers and inside the labor unions, their "operatives" spied, secretly denounced, engineered raids and arrests, and incited to riot. The concerns' managers spoke the same arguments as Mr. Gary in justification of their activities. The companies concealed but were not ashamed of hiring "operatives"; it was a customary inevitable part of the anti-union alternative.

Nor was it the custom of certain strike-breaking concerns to wait for "labor trouble." When business was slack they made "trouble." The sub-report details, from affidavits of former operatives, how certain concerns provoked strikes in peaceful shops in the past to create "business," set union to fighting union, organized unions in order to be called in to break the unions. They bled both sides; and the Federal Government files contained their patriotic reports.

In the Chicago-Gary District one such great strike-breaking concern became so active in the steel strike that its offices were raided and one of its officers was indicted for "intent to create riots" and for intent to "kill and murder divers large numbers of persons." This officer after five months had still not been brought to trial. A sample of the riot-inciting instructions given to this concern's operatives in the South Chicago steel mills follows:

A 563-D                                        October 2, 1919.
Rep.——
Dear Sir:
We have talked to you and instructed you. We want you to stir up as much bad feeling as you possibly can between the Serbians and Italians. Spread data among the Serbians that the Italians are going back to work. Call up every question you can in reference to racial hatred between these two nationalities; make them realize to the fullest extent that far better results would be accomplished if they will go back to work. Urge them to go back to work or the Italians will get their jobs.

Daily Maxim—Send to every representative today:

Conserve your forces on a set point—begin before the other fellow starts.

Remail.

This operative's duties, according to *The New Majority* (November 11, 1919), were as follows:

He was assigned to the client whose code was A 536 D, the number appearing at the top of the Italian-Serbian letter. This code means the South Chicago plant of the Illinois Steel Company.

Then he received the regular course of instruction given "representatives." He was told to move around among the strikers and get them to go back to work. He was told to go to Indiana Harbor, Ind., and get strikers from the Inland Steel Company plant there to go to South Chicago and go to work as strike breakers for the Illinois Steel Company. He was told to go to the vicinity of employment agencies and get strike breakers and to take them into the plant by automobile or otherwise, at night.

He was also instructed to move around among the strikers for the purpose of reporting what conversations he heard, as well as urging them to go to work. He was given a union card in a local of one of the international unions affiliated with the American Federation of Labor, and told to use it to pass himself off as a union man.

The Illinois Steel Company is the Steel Corporation's biggest western subsidiary. Its president, Mr. Buffington, declared to the Commission of Inquiry that the first he had heard of the matter was when he saw it in the Chicago papers; that the Illinois Steel Co. did not hire this strike-breaking concern; that he was " confident that at the trial no evidence involving the Illinois Steel Co. would be brought out."

The manager of the strike-breaking concern, with offices in the same building as Mr. Buffington, declared to Commission investigators that their operatives were hired by the Illinois Steel Co.

Meanwhile the raided concern was defending itself in page advertisements in papers in many cities as follows:

### WHY IS SHERMAN SERVICE BEING ATTACKED?

Sherman Service is a national institution composed of men and women who have made Industrial Relationship their life work   .   .   .

They cause the employer (their client) to recognize and practice the basic principles of " square dealing " in his relations with his employees.   A spirit of sympathetic understanding follows—the result is harmony, cooperation, maximum production, high quality and lessened waste.

The community, which comprises both employee and employer and invested capital, is able, through such harmonious and productive relationship, to provide the greatest opportunities afforded under our free form of government, to the advantage of all agreeably concerned. Americanization, in its fullest sense, is made possible and does follow; our national structure is preserved and enforced, and we are all better off for it.

SHERMAN SERVICE, INC.

John Francis Sherman, Chairman Executive Board New York City Boston St. Louis Chicago Philadelphia Cleveland New Haven Providence Detroit Toronto.

Postscript: Sherman Service is not a detective agency. It renders no detective service of any description whatsoever.

Concerning the last line, investigators noted that the Sherman Service Co. was elsewhere carrying on suit in court to protect its " rights as a detective agency." According to the private " house organ " of this concern it also serves the government; for this purpose its operatives become " apparent reds."

" Wherever such organizations exist in the community and try to influence the workers it becomes the duty of the Sherman representatives to pretend sympathy and join so as to learn who the leaders are. Such information is then supplied to the government."

Some steel companies placed implicit confidence in the reports and advice of these strike-breaking spy-corporations. Other companies were skeptical and dissatisfied but puzzled as to what else to do. But no managers doubted what they wanted the detective agencies to accomplish—to keep workmen from organizing and if they organized to break up or nullify the organizations. The attitude of steel company managers was the same; it was illustrated by the reply of a general superintendent in Monessen to an investigator's request to be allowed to talk with the men in the plant (during the strike). He said: " We've got about 300 men in there now; generally we have 3,000. And those 300 men have cost us just about $500 apiece to get. Now if you go in there and ask them questions they may all get nervous and walk out again."

Just as in this plant in Monessen where, as the superintendent and the investigator knew, two " detective agencies " had propagandist-spies mixed with the real workers, so throughout the domain of steel, watchers—from subsidized workers to hired detectives—peek and glower at the labor force and try to guess, by the way men walk or look or talk or stay silent or spit, what they are thinking.

The reach of the industrial spy system and the reliance placed on it were brought home to the Commission of Inquiry by the spy report on the Commission which was sent to Mr. Gary. It has been referred to before; the Commission in November read the report, knew that it was being distributed in the territory of the Steel Corporation's plants, and disregarded so amusingly false a document; in December when the Commission made its effort to settle the strike, Mr. Gary exhibited it and cross-examined the Commissioners on its charges. Someone had set a spy on the Commission and on the Interchurch World Movement. The anonymous " special report " was dated November 12. The Commission's first interview with Mr. Gary had been on November 10.

The " special report " names (misspelling the names) some of the Commission's investigators, names others as investigators who were not, and calls all named " radicals," " members of the I.W.W.," " Reds " and " active in the organization known as the People's Print . . . formerly known as the People's Peace Council, better known as the National Civil Liberties League." No statement made about the investigators was true. The capacity of the spy and the purposes of the persons who hired him are indicated in the following excerpt:

In fact none of these people that are now here in Pittsburgh investigating for this Church movement should be told anything at all, nor should they be allowed to get any information from the Mills in any manner.

After paying a visit to their offices in New York and talking to a large number of the officials there I find that this organization could be used to a very good advantage if handled by the right parties. This organization could become a power in both the Industrial Field and the Church Field.

There are a large number of the men and women connected with this organization that are know as Pink Tea Socialists and Parlor Reds, and are not considered dangerous. I would suggest that these kind of people be weeded out of the organization. These are the worst kind of Reds to be connected with as they are to a certain extent high up in circles that are hard to reach and they can spread propaganda that hurts the work of others.

I found that this Organization is now making a canvass for money among the rich and the Corporation in the East, and that they have already had a Committee see Judge Gary, asking for money to carry on their work with.

A Mr. Blacenhorn will arrive in Pittsburgh on Thursday morning to assist the ones that are already here on the Steel Strike investigation.

No money should be given or any assistance granted this organization until they recall all of the ones that they have in the Pittsburgh District, and furthermore if there is any way at all of forcing them to get rid of the ones that I have mentioned they should be let go.


The literary qualities of this report can be profitably studied by comparison with the reports in the Monessen " labor file."

The maintenance of the non-unionism alternative, therefore, entailed for the steel companies activities running from spies in church offices in New York to sealed carloads of negroes shipped into Pittsburgh plant yards at night. For

communities and for states the alternative entailed activities
of greater import and greater menace.  These affected civil
liberties in whole communities, local legislative bodies, police
authorities, judges, state police troops, Federal government
departments and the U. S. Army.

The consequences (which are studied in sub-reports) are
perhaps most important in regard to the abrogation of civil
liberties.  War-experiences especially have accustomed the
American people to the thought that the right of assembly,
the right of free speech, and traditional personal rights can
be abrogated when the cause is deemed sufficiently great.
The practise of western Pennsylvania proved that these rights
were abrogated for the purpose of preventing the organization of trade unions among steel workers, or of defeating
organized unions.   The abrogations largely persist four
months after the strike.

The salient fact is as follows:

Denial of the rights of assemblage and free speech did not
primarily grow out of the strike but was a precedent
fact, directly related to the policies of preventing labor
organization maintained by the Steel Corporation and
certain " independents."  It was for years the rule in
towns about Pittsburgh that labor organizers could not
hold meetings.

To quote from the sub-report: [1]

Local public officials assert that it was necessary to prohibit
meetings in order to prevent violence.  This statement is open
to question, but if it is accepted, still the connection between
labor policy and absence of civil liberty remains.  Whatever
danger of violence there was, arose from the industrial conflict.
On account of the long-continued refusal of the employers to deal
with organized labor, industrial conflict became inevitable the

[1] From " Civil Liberties," in Western Pennsylvania, by George Soule.

moment workmen began to assemble for the purpose of forming unions. If, therefore, the right to assemble led to the forming and strengthening of unions, and unions led to industrial conflict, and industrial conflict led to breaches of the peace, the only way to prevent violence was, in the minds of the local officials, to prevent meetings. In other words, if the officials were right, the industrial situation was such that civil peace could be preserved only by interference with the exercise of ordinary civil liberties on the part of a large proportion of the population.

To maintain steel companies' non-union policies, communities lost their rights of assembly so completely that in some towns government agents, sent to give patriotic lectures, were denied the right to hold meetings; one such was arrested.

The extent to which rights were abrogated depended largely upon the extent to which non-unionism was endangered. If labor organizers were aggressive and local restrictive ordinances were insufficient the most arbitrary executive acts were resorted to. During the strike the repression was complete. Legally the Interchurch Commission of Inquiry being composed of " three or more persons " broke the Sheriff's orders by the simple act of assembling and " loitering " in the streets of Pittsburgh. A Commissioner conversed with strikers in the office used as their headquarters in Braddock; five minutes after his departure State troopers broke into the place demanding " that speaker " and started to close down the office because " a meeting " had been held.

Concerning the " violence " justification for such abrogations the following facts were noted:

The argument that the right of assembly would lead to violence met this contradiction in McKeesport; a riot there, the only one, resulted from the authorities' cancellation of a meeting for which a permit had been granted.

In Johnstown no restriction was ever laid on meetings and no violence ever resulted; the only attempt at violence was the action of a Citizens' Committee, led by a Y. M. C. A. secretary, which drove labor organizers out of town.

In Sharon and Farrell the workers, prohibited from assembly marched weekly across the state line into Ohio where they held great mass meetings without a sign of violence.

Comparison of the Pittsburgh District with Wheeling, West Va., and Ohio districts proves that the reasons given by the Pennsylvania authorities were without basis in fact.

The progressive nature of the restrictions imposed was illustrated in the South Side of Pittsburgh where labor organizers obtained a hall after every pressure had been put on the owner to cancel the lease. Thereupon the Mayor of Pittsburgh forbade outright all meetings on the South Side.

The whole case for the abrogations is epitomized in the preamble to the Sheriff's proclamation issued September 20 (two days before the strike):

Whereas I, William S. Haddock, sheriff of Allegheny County, have been formally notified by many citizens, industrial corporations, and employers that printed inflammatory circulars and other information have been distributed and disseminated among the people calling a general strike of all employees of various industrial manufactories throughout Allegheny County, with the request that they cease work and leave their places of employment and by reason thereof there now exists among the people great unrest, uncertainty, and doubt as to the safety of life, liberty, and property: Therefore . . .

Now Sheriff Haddock has admitted that he never saw the "printed inflammatory circulars" alleged to have been distributed; neither did any "citizens, industrial corporations and employers" produce any such circulars issued by the strike leadership in the period immediately preceding September 20.

These abrogations, before, during and after the strike, must be considered with this fact:

" Free elections " were customarily impossible in steel towns in Western Pennsylvania due to clearly understood manipulations by steel company officials or by steel company officials who were also public officials.

That is, democratic practises as well as constitutional rights are decisively modified by the steel companies in western Pennsylvania and the " modifications " are for the purpose of defeating labor organization.

During the strike violations of personal rights and personal liberty were wholesale; men were arrested without warrants, imprisoned without charges, their homes invaded without legal process, magistrates' verdicts were rendered frankly on the basis of whether the striker would go back to work or not. But even these things would seem to be less a concern to the nation at large than the degradation, persistent and approved by " public opinion," of civil liberties in behalf of private concerns' industrial practices.

To the steel workers the import of the violations of civil and personal rights resulted as follows:

Great numbers of workers came to believe—
> that local mayors, magistrates and police officials try to break strikes;
> that state and Federal officials, particularly the Federal Department of Justice, help to break strikes, and that armed forces are used for this purpose;
> that most newspapers actively and promptly exert a strike-breaking influence; most churches passively.

Workers generally attributed such strike breaking to the men filling the offices rather than to the Governmental and social institutions *per se*.

The above beliefs were undoubtedly widespread among steel workers; many expressed the beliefs with ferocity; many more in a dumb, deep-seated suspiciousness of everything and everybody connected with public executives, courts, Federal agents, army officers, reporters or clergy. *The steel strike made tens of thousands of citizens believe that our American institutions are not democratic or not democratically administered.*

The basis of such beliefs (detailed in sub-reports) will be hastily summarized here. The data concern chiefly western Pennsylvania, secondarily Indiana and Illinois.

*Local magistrates, police authorities, etc.,* around Pittsburgh were very frequently steel mill officials or relations of mill officials. In other cases steel mill officials exercised police authority without the excuse of having been previously elected to public office. For example, besides Sheriff Haddock of Allegheny County whose brother was superintendent of an American Sheet & Tin Plate plant (Corporation subsidiary), Mayor Crawford of Duquesne was the brother of the President of the McKeesport Tin Plate Co.; President Moon of the Borough Council of Homestead was chief of the mechanical department of the Homestead mill; Burgess Lincoln of Munhall was a department superintendent in the same mill. The Burgess of Clairton was a mill official; etc., etc. When a striker was taken before mill-official public-officials he was likely to suspect connections between his fate and the steel company's desires. In many other cases officials of mills only, personally, gave the orders for arrests, and the decisions as to whether the arrested should be jailed or not, generally after learning whether the striker would return to work or not.

The charges on which strikers were arraigned before local magistrates, then imprisoned or fined, were often never recorded and never learned by the prisoners. Recorded formal specifications included " stopping men from going to work," " cursing " (the state police or deputies), " abusing," " refusing to obey orders " (to move on, etc.), " going out of his house before daylight," " laughing at the police," " throwing strike cards out on the street," " smiling at the state police." Fines ran from $10 to $50 or $60. Imprisonment terms ran up to months. Arrested men were frequently taken, not to jail, but inside the steel mill and held there. The charges of beatings, clubbings, often substantiated by doctors' and eye-witnesses' affidavits, were endless and monotonous; in most communities the only public official to appeal to turned out to be another mill official.

*Federal officials'* active intervention concerned chiefly (1) the Department of Justice, whose connections with steel company " under-cover men " were referred to earlier, and whose public activities dealt with raids in search of " reds " and Attorney General Palmer's statements about " reds " in the steel strike; and (2) the U. S. Army. Both cases contributed to steel workers' beliefs about strike-breaking activities. The Administration left the field to the Department of Justice and the Army, so far as the steel workers could see. Congressional intervention in the shape of the investigation and report of the Senate Committee on Labor and Education filled the strikers with a bitterness only to be understood by detailed comparison of the Committee's report and the facts.

The principal *use of armed forces* outside of Pennsylvania was at Gary, Ind., occupied first by the State militia, then by the U. S. Army under General Leonard Wood. Previous to these occupations newspapers throughout the country printed stories of " bloody riots " in Gary and that the city was a " hotbed of reds." The facts were as follows:

The walkout on September 22 at Gary was almost complete. Agreements, subject to various disputes over interpretation, were reached with the city authorities concerning picket line rules. Huge mass-meetings were held in the open air. The strikers made frequent complaints of violent raids carried out by bands of citizens calling themselves " Loyal American Leaguers " who were charged with clubbing groups of strikers on street corners at nights. A crowd of strikers leaving a mass-meeting tried to pull a negro strike breaker off a street car: the negro was slightly injured and a number of strikers were clubbed. On this case of " mob violence," the only one alleged, Indiana state guards were sent in. Parades were forbidden. Ex-service men among the strikers, independently of the strike leadership, put on their old army uniforms and started a march to exhibit the uniforms to the guardsmen. There were about two hundred of these ex-soldiers and about ten thousand strikers in the streets fell in behind the procession which wound through the town in disregard of the guardsmen and quietly disbanded in the park where meetings were held. On this second case of " mob violence," known as the " outlaw parade," the U. S. regulars occupied Gary, with General Wood in personal charge, proclaiming martial law. The regulars were equipped with bayonets and steel helmets and the force included many trucks mounting machine guns and bringing field artillery.

General Wood declared that "the army would be neutral." He established rules in regard to picketing. These rules were so interpreted and carried out as to result in breaking up the picket line. One picket, for example, would be permitted at a certain spot; if the striker who came up to relieve the picket stopped to converse with him and to receive reports and instructions, both strikers would be arrested. Delays and difficulties would attend the release of these men from jail or " bull pen." The picket line thus dwindled and its disappearance signalled to the Gary workers that the strike was breaking. Army officers sent soldiers to arrest union officers in other trades, for example, for threatening to call a strike on a local building operation. Workers throughout the city believed that the Federal Government opposed them and that the regulars would stay as long as the steel workers remained on strike. The army was not withdrawn until the strike was declared off.

The maintenance of the Steel Corporation's non-union policy in Gary, therefore, entailed the use of the Federal army and the expenditure of public money with results which helped to break the strike.

The feeling of the steel workers, then, might be summed up thus: that local and national government not only *was not their government* (i.e. in their behalf) but was government in behalf of interests opposing theirs; that in strike times government activities tended to break strikes. So far the steel workers' suspicions concern the administrators, rather than the institutions, of government.

Finally *the press* in most communities, and particularly in Pittsburgh, led the workers there to the belief that the press lends itself instantly and persistently to strike breaking. They believed that the press immediately took sides, printed only the news favoring that side, suppressed or colored its records, printed advertisements and editorials urging the strikers to go back, denounced the strikers and incessantly misrepresented the facts. All this was found to be true in the case of the Pittsburgh papers (as analyzed in a sub-report). Foreign language papers largely followed the lead of the English papers. The average American-born discriminating citizen of Pittsburgh could not have obtained from his papers sufficient information to get a true conception of the strike; basic information was not in those papers. The steel worker-reader, moreover, gave attention not only to the omissions of the press but to commissions plainly directed against the strike. In the minds of workingmen outside steel areas the newspapers' handling of the steel strike added weight to the conviction that the press of the country is not the workingmen's press.

The *pulpit* as carefully analyzed in the Pittsburgh district proved itself largely dependent on the press. The sub-report finds that a fair and comprehensive history of the strike would not require mention of either the Protestant Church or Catholic Church as organizations in Allegheny County. In one or two communities individual clergymen were the heart of either the support of the strike or of the opposition to it. Research among clergymen revealed a large minority deeply suspicious of the newspaper version of the strike but ineffective for organizing concerted action, even for purposes of self-information. The workers' attitude to the church followed mainly these few individuals, deeming the church another strike breaker where some clergyman preached or wrote against the strike or where another gift to a local church by a steel company became public, or deeming it a comfort at least, where some clergyman worked for the strike. The great mass of steel workers paid no heed to the church as a social organization.

This difference in workers' attitudes to press and to pulpit was noted: after the strike workers generally were making no effort to make the church their church; but workers in many sections of the nation, in steel towns and out, redoubled efforts to set up their own press and inaugurated their own federated news service.

To sum up the social consequences of a non-union labor policy, especially that of the Steel Corporation, is plainly difficult; the manifestations were so wide and so various. The Corporation's policy dominated the industry. The industry's practise entailed discharge for unionism, coercion, espionage, the use of under-cover men and strike-breaking detective agencies. Maintenance of the industry's practise changed the complexion of governmental and social institutions. In the eyes of the strikers and a host of their fellow-workingmen these changed governmental and social institutions tended, in greater or less degree, more or less promptly, to strike breaking. In the eyes of less interested observers the facts at least raised the questions:

Whether there is any influence at present more powerful in American civilization than the influence of great industrial corporations or trusts?

Whether any single influence works more effectively on our national life than the non-union policy of our greatest Corporation for vicious or beneficial results?

For the great part of the country's beaten steel strikers the answer was over-simplified. The steel worker went back to the twelve-hour day, earnings under a living wage, ruthlessly arbitrary anti-organization control. For escape he had turned to the A. F. of L. and in 1920 the A. F. of L. was not succeeding in freeing him. He hesitated to turn to the I.W.W., for the I.W.W. was "outlawed." He could not turn to the Steel Corporation or the other great companies for they were standing pat. He did not turn to the press. Among American democratic institutions he found none to fit his need, no Federal body or machinery for acting on his case nor even any governmental institution of inquiry, which in 1920 was reaching out to learn his grievances.

The beaten steel worker displayed little interest in governmental institutions; instead he had acquired a rather active distrust of them. While many of the "foreigners" began piling up money to get themselves out of America the great majority began waiting for "the next strike." That was the only resource thoughtfully provided for them among the democratic American institutions.

# CONCLUDING

The Summarized Conclusions and Recommendations of the Report have been transferred for convenience to pages 11-19 in Chapter I (Introduction) from the end of the book, where they belong naturally, inasmuch as they were formulated after all the foregoing analyses and discussion had been drafted.

The gist of the Conclusions is that conditions in the steel industry " gave the workers just cause for complaint and for action " and that " these unredressed grievances still exist."

The gist of the Recommendations is that the Federal Government set up a commission for the industry, in order to initiate free, open conference between those who must always be chiefly responsible for settlement of the industry's problems:—its owners and its workers. To this is added recommendation for persistent investigation and publicity.

In pursuit of its recommendations and in concluding its immediate task, the Commission put this report before the American people and the American people's government, in the person of President Wilson. The action of the Commission virtually raised this question of fundamental importance:

Is the nation helpless before conditions in a basic industry which promise a future crisis? Can our democratic society be moved to do industrial justice without the pressure of crisis itself?

As a part of the task of publishing the facts and as a means of expressing their judgment as Christians, the Commissioners requested a committee to draw up, for separate free distribution, if possible, a compact form of General

245

Findings based on the Conclusions of the Report. Necessarily they are in part repetitious, but they were designed to include expressions of moral judgment, such as were not the first concern of the Report. A sub-committee, of which Dr. Alva W. Taylor was chairman, drafted these findings, which were presented to the Executive Committee of the Interchurch Movement with the Report on May 10, 1920, as adopted by the Commission.

## FINDINGS

1. The fundamental grievances were found to be:
   (a) Excessive hours.
   (b) The " boss system."
   (c) No right to organize or to representation.

2. The remedies desired were:
   (a) Shorter day and week with a living wage.
   (b) Representation and conference, and an end to the " boss system " which so often subjects common labor to petty tyrannies.
   (c) Right to unionize and a substitution of industrial democracy for industrial autocracy.

3. These grievances were of long standing, but had found no expression because:
   (a) They were limited largely to foreigners of many races and languages without industrial tradition, education or leadership to organize.
   (b) Race prejudice effectually kept the more skilled, more intelligent and better paid American workmen from taking up the cause of the foreign-speaking workmen.
   (c) Labor unions have been accustomed to look upon the foreigner as an actual or potential strike breaker.
   (d) The steel companies have most effectually deterred men from joining labor organizations.

4. These long-standing grievances were brought to expression by:

(a) The part these workingmen played in the war and the treatment afforded them for the sake of war production which gave them a new sense of worth and independence.

(b) The fight for democracy and news of a larger workingmen's freedom in their native lands together with a growing sense of real Americanism, which brought a spirit of democracy to their ranks.

(c) The decision of the American Federation of Labor to organize them and its actual work of organizing them into Craft Unions.

5. We found:

(a) That the strike was regularly conducted in orthodox fashion according to the A. F. of L. rules and principles.

(b) That while radicals sympathized with the strikers, as was natural, they were effectually debarred by the strike leaders and that far from having influence in it, they often denounced and opposed those who conducted the strike.

6. We find the grievances to have been real:

(a) The average week of 68.7 hours, the twelve-hour day, whether on a straight twelve-hour shift or on a broken division of 11-13 or 10-14 hours, the unbroken 24-hour work period at the turn of a shift and the underpayment of unskilled labor, are all inhuman.

(b) It is entirely practicable to put all processes requiring continuous operation on a straight eight-hour basis as is illustrated by the Colorado Fuel and Iron Company. These processes require the services of only a fraction of the workers.

(c) The "boss system" is bad, the plant organization is military and the control autocratic. The companies' claims, that they accord the right to join unions and the opportunity of conference, are theoretical; neither is allowed in practice.

(d) The use of "under-cover" men is severely condemned. It breeds distrust, breaks down morals and stimulates ill-will; it is undemocratic and un-American.

(e) The refusal of the United States Steel Corporation to confer, to accept mediation and its attitude of hauteur as shown by its refusal to follow the recommendations of the War Labor Board incited labor strife and because of the strength and influence of this Corporation, forms one of the greatest obstacles to a just settlement of industrial grievances and unrest at this time.

7. The Strike was defeated by:

(a) The strike-breaking methods of the steel companies and their effective mobilization of public opinion against the strikers through the charges of radicalism, bolshevism, and the closed shop, none of which were justified by the facts; and by the suppression of civil rights.

(b) The hostility of the press giving biased and colored news and the silence of both press and pulpit on the actual question of justice involved; which attitudes of press and pulpit helped to break the strikers' morale.

(c) Public fear of a general labor war, to the coincidence of the coal strike and threat of the railroad strike, together with labor's failure to formulate and explain its purposes with regard to public service.

(d) The prevailing prejudice in the steel towns and in the general public mind and among the English-speaking workingmen against the foreigners who constituted the overwhelming number of the strikers.

(e) The ineffective support given the strike by most of the twenty-four affiliated Craft Unions through which it was organized, and by the A. F. of L.

8. Recommendations:

1. The adoption of the eight-hour shift on all continuous processes.

2. Limiting of the day to not more than ten hours on duty, with not more than a six-day and a fifty-four hour week, with at least a minimum comfort wage.

3. Recognition of right to join regular Craft Unions or any other freely chosen form of labor organization; recognition of right to open conference, either through shop committees or union representatives; recognition of right of collective bargaining.

4. A vast extension of house building—by the communities where possible; by the steel companies where community building is inadequate or impossible.

5. That organized labor:

   (a) Democratize and control the unions, especially in regard to the calling, conduct and settlement of strikes.

   (b) Reorganize unions with a view of sharing in responsibility for production and in control of production processes; to this end:

      1. Repudiating restriction of production as a doctrine.

      2. Formulating contracts which can be lived up to.

      3. Finding a substitute for the closed shop wherever it is a union practice.

   (c) Scrupulously avoid all advocates of violence.

   (d) Accept all possible proffers of publicity and conciliation.

   (e) Promote Americanization in all possible ways and insist upon an American standard of living for all workingmen.

   (f) Prepare more adequate technical information for the public in regard to all conditions bearing upon the calling and the conduct of a strike.

   (g) Seek alliance and council from the salaried class known as brain workers.

6. That the President's Industrial Conference's plan for standing tribunals of conciliation and publicity be given a fair trial. We believe that the most effective step to be taken for the obtaining of justice in a strike situation is through publicity, conciliation and a voluntary system of arbitration; and as a beginning we recommend the fullest publication

of these findings and of our more complete reports.

7. That minimum wage commissions be established and laws enacted providing for an American standard of living through the labor of the natural bread-winner permitting the mother to keep up a good home and the children to obtain at least a high school education.

8. That the Federal Government investigate the relations of Federal authorities to private corporations' "under-cover" men and to "labor detective agencies."

9. That the eight-hour day be accepted by labor, capital and the public as the immediate goal for the working day and that government provide by law against working days that bring over-fatigue and deprive the individual, his home and his community of that minimum of time which gives him an opportunity to discharge all his obligations as a social being in a democratic society.

---

We recommend to the press that it free itself of the all too well founded charge of bias, favoring capital as against labor and redeem its power as a promoter of truth and a formulator of public opinion by searching out all the facts in regard to industrial questions and publishing them without fear or favor.

We plead with the pulpit that it be diligent to discharge its legitimate prophetic rôle as an advocate of justice, righteousness and humanity in all such conflicts of human interest as those involved in industrial strife.

We condemn unsparingly those authorities who suspended the right of free speech and peaceful assemblage before, during and after the steel strike.

We recommend that the Industrial Department of the Interchurch World Movement and the Social Service Commission of the Federal Council of Churches continue this type of impartial investigation of industrial strife and unrest and extend it to studies of general conditions in industry affecting the life, peace, and welfare of all concerned and that their findings be published as a means of enlightening public opinion, begetting impartial judgment, and promoting industrial justice and peace.

*Conclusion.*

All the conditions that caused the steel strike continue to exist. We feel that unless changes are made approximating in some degree the findings here presented, further unrest is inevitable and another strike must come. In the measure that workingmen become intelligent and Americanized, will they refuse to labor under such conditions.

APPENDICES

## Appendix A

## MINIMUM OF SUBSISTENCE AND MINIMUM COMFORT BUDGET

From report made for this Inquiry by the Bureau of Applied Economics, Washington, D. C. (November, 1919.)

Various students of the subject have endeavored to establish the amount of income necessary to support a family in health and decency. In doing so several budget levels of living have been analyzed. The two most clearly distinguished are:

1. *The Minimum of Subsistence Level.* This level is based essentially on animal well being with little or no attention to the comforts or social demands of human beings.

2. *The Minimum of Comfort Level.* This represents a level somewhat above that of mere animal subsistence and provides in some measure for comfortable clothing, insurance, a modest amount of recreation, etc. This level provides for health and decency but for very few comforts, and is probably much below the idea had in mind in the frequent but indefinite expression "The American Standard of Living."

All of the studies have taken as a basis a family of five—husband, wife and three children. This is done (1) because the average American family is of this size and (2) because it is necessary that marriage should be practically universal and result in a minimum of three children of the race is to perpetuate itself.

The results of the various studies are closely similar and indicate that the annual cost of maintaining a family of five at a minimum of subsistence level at prices prevailing in the latter part of 1919 was approximately $1,575. This would be equivalent in purchasing power to approximately $885 in 1914.

The cost of maintaining the minimum of comfort level has not been so thoroughly studied. Prof. Ogburn's estimate as of

255

June, 1918, was $1,760. With an increase of 15 per cent. in living costs since that time the cost of this budget would now be approximately $2,000. This sum would be equivalent in purchasing power to approximately $1,125 in 1914. Prof. Ogburn's conclusions may be taken as a conservative minimum, as it is much below the estimate recently put forth by the U. S. Bureau of Labor Statistics as to the cost of maintaining a government employee's family in Washington at a level of health and decency. This budget, at August, 1919, prices, cost $2,262.

All of the studies referred to dealt with larger Eastern cities, chiefly New York. The costs would, therefore, not be strictly applicable to all cities and towns of the country. The differences, however, except in a few exceptional cases, would not be very great.

A more detailed analysis of these studies is made in the following paragraphs:

### 1. THE COST OF A MINIMUM OF SUBSISTENCE BUDGET.

Professor W. F. Ogburn, of Columbia University, and one of the best known authorities on cost of living, in a recently published article made a very careful analysis of all preceding studies of minimum of subsistence levels and also submits a carefully prepared budget of his own.[1] Professor Ogburn's calculations are all based on prices prevailing in June, 1918. Prices between that time and the Autumn of 1919 have advanced about 15 per cent., and these changes, of course, would have to be taken into consideration in arriving at the cost of the budgets at the present time. In order, however, to make the reasoning entirely clear the details of the various studies are first summarized from Professor Ogburn's article.

[1] Published in " Standards of Living," Bureau of Applied Economics, Washington, 1919.

## (a) Professor Ogburn's Budget

| | |
|---|---:|
| Food | $615 |
| Clothing: | |
|     Man | 76 |
|     Woman | 55 |
|     11 to 14 years | 40 |
|     7 to 10 years | 33 |
|     4 to 6 years | 30 |
| Rent | 180 |
| Fuel and light | 62 |
| Insurance | 40 |
| Organizations | 12 |
| Religion | 7 |
| Street-car fare | 40 |
| Paper, books, etc. | 9 |
| Amusements, drinks, and tobacco | 50 |
| Sickness | 60 |
| Dentist, occulist, glasses, etc. | 3 |
| Furnishings | 35 |
| Laundry | 4 |
| Cleaning supplies | 15 |
| Miscellaneous | 20 |
| **Total** | **$1,386** |

This budget is for a large eastern city and is the result of studies of 600 actual budgets of shipyard workers in the New York shipbuilding district.

### (b) Professor Chapin's Budget Brought Up to Date

Another way of estimating a minimum budget for the American subsistence level in 1918 is to take minimum budgets of past years that have been accepted as standard and apply the increases from the date of the budget to the present time in the prices of the various items of the budget, thus bringing them up to date. This method assumes no change in minimum standards. It is of course subject to possible inaccuracies in measuring the rising cost of living between specific dates for specific places. This inaccuracy is thought to be slight, however.

For instance, one of the most famous and perhaps most generally accepted budget estimates is that of Prof. Chapin, who made a study lasting several years of New York families, publishing his result in 1907. He said, "An income under $800 is not enough to permit the maintenance of a normal standard. An income of $900 or over probably permits the maintenance of a normal standard at least as far as the physical man is concerned." If we take the increase in the cost of living from 1907 to June, 1918, to be 55 per cent., then Chapin's $900 becomes $1,395. If we take the increase to be 60 per cent. then Chapin's $900 becomes $1,440. Probably the best estimates of increasing cost of living place the increase from January 1, 1915, to June 1, 1918, as 55 per cent.

(c) *Minimum Budget of New York Factory Commission Brought Up to Date*

In 1915 the New York State Factory Investigation Commission set a minimum budget for 1914 in New York City at the figure $876. Applying increases in items of the budget by classes from January 1, 1915, to June 1, 1918, we get, as seen from the following table, a budget of $1,356.

| | Budget New York Factory Commission 1914 | Increase in cost of living to June 1, 1918 Per cent. | New York Factory Budget Brought Up to Date |
|---|---|---|---|
| Food | $325 | 65 | $536 |
| Rent | 200 | 29 | 258 |
| Fuel and light | 20 | 44 | 28 |
| Clothing | 140 | 76 | 246 |
| Sundries | 191 | 51 | 288 |
| | $876 | | $1,356 |

MINIMUM BUDGET OF THE NEW YORK FACTORY INVESTIGATING COMMISSION, 1915

Estimate of Cost of Living of Normal Family of Five in New York City

| | |
|---|---|
| Food | $325.00 |
| Rent | 200.00 |
| Fuel and light | 20.00 |
| Clothing | 140.00 |
| Car fare | 31.20 |
| Insurance: | |
| Man | 20.00 |
| Family | 15.60 |
| Health | 22.00 |
| Furnishings | 7.00 |
| Education, newspaper | 5.63 |
| Recreation and amusement | 50.00 |
| Miscellaneous | 40.00 |
| Total | $876.43 |

## (d) Minimum Budget of New York Board of Estimate Brought Up to Date

In February, 1915, the Bureau of Personal Service of the Board of Estimate and Apportionment of New York City made a minimum budget estimate for an unskilled laborer's family in New York City of $845. Applying increases in items of the budget by classes from January 1, 1915, to June 1, 1918, we get, as seen from the following table, a budget of $1,317.

|  | Budget<br>New York Board<br>of Estimate, 1915 | Increase in<br>cost of living to<br>June 1, 1918<br>Per cent. | New York Board<br>of Estimate Budget<br>Brought Up to Date |
|---|---|---|---|
| Food | $384 | 65 | $634 |
| Rent | 168 | 29 | 217 |
| Fuel and light | 43 | 44 | 62 |
| Clothing | 104 | 76 | 183 |
| Sundries | 146 | 51 | 221 |
| Total | $845 |  | $1.317 |

It is possible to criticize this budget as being too low in allowances for health, furniture, and education, and very low indeed in other sundries.

### BUDGET OF NEW YORK BOARD OF ESTIMATE FOR 1915

| | |
|---|---|
| Housing | $168.00 |
| Car fare | 30.30 |
| Food | 383.81 |
| Clothing | 104.20 |
| Fuel and light | 42.75 |
| Health | 20.00 |
| Insurance | 22.88 |
| Papers and other reading matter | 5.00 |
| Recreation | 40.00 |
| Furniture, utensils, fixtures, moving expenses, etc. | 18.00 |
| Church dues | 5.00 |
| Incidentals—soap, washing material, stamps, etc. | 5.00 |
| Total | $844.94 |

## (e) Estimating the Budget from Food Expenditure

It is generally accepted that a man at moderate physical labor needs 3,500 calories a day and Atwater has estimated the needs of the individual members of his family in per cents of his needs. Thus his wife consumes 0.8 as much; a boy of 16 years of age, 0.9 as much; a girl 15 to 16, 0.8; a child from 6 to 9 years, 0.5; and so on. We thus express a family in terms of adult males. We say that a family of five—man, wife, and three children—will equal 3.3 adult males when the children are at a certain age.

The average food budget of 600 families of shipyard workers in the New York district collected by the Bureau of Labor Statistics was found to cost $607 for 3.6 equivalent adult males. This was submitted to calory analysis and yielded 3,115 calories of energy for man per day, not including any waste. This means that $607 did not furnish enough food for the New York families. A food expert might have bought the necessary amount, but the families in actual practice did not.

Dietaries should be well balanced also, but this analysis was not undertaken. So the important conclusion results that in the New York shipbuilding area $607 is not enough of an allowance for food.

Prof. Chapin's study shows that at the point where the families cease to be undernourished, food is 44 per cent. of the total budget. Now, if the low figure of $615 is taken as the food allowance for a family of 3.3 or 3.4 equivalent adult males and estimated at 44 per cent. of the budget, we get a minimum budget of $1,396.

*Summary of Estimates on Minimum Budgets for American Subsistence Level in 1918*

From three angles, therefore, an estimate may be formed of a minimum budget: (1) from study of actual budgets, (2) from applying increased costs of living to recognized standard budgets, (3) from estimates of adequate food allowance and its percentage of expenditures.

These estimates for New York district in 1918 are as follows:

1. Prof. Ogburn's detailed budget from family studies ........ $1,386
2. Chapin's budget brought to date .. ....................... 1,395
   New York Factory Investigation Commissions' Budget brought to date ................................ 1,356
   New York Board of Estimate budget brought to date ...... 1,317
3. From food allowance ................................... 1,396

### The Above Studies Brought Up to 1919

The above estimates were all made as of June, 1918, or, if made at an earlier date, were brought up only to that date in Professor Ogburn's analysis. Between June, 1918, and the present time (i.e. the latter part of 1919) figures compiled by the U. S. Bureau of Labor Statistics show an increase of about 15 per cent. in general cost of living. Applying this percentage increase to the figures compiled by Professor Ogburn in the preceding table, the following results are obtained:

VARIOUS AUTHORITATIVE ESTIMATES OF THE ANNUAL COST OF MAINTAINING A FAMILY AT A MINIMUM OF SUBSISTENCE LEVEL, BROUGHT UP TO AUGUST, 1919

|  | June 1918 | August 1919 |
|---|---|---|
| Ogburn's Budget | $1,386 | $1,594 |
| Chapin's Budget | 1,395 | 1,604 |
| New York Factory Investigation Commission .... | 1,356 | 1,559 |
| New York Board of Estimate Budget | 1,317 | 1,515 |
| Budget compiled from food allowance | 1,396 | 1,605 |
| Average of all five estimate | $1,370 | $1,575 |

Inasmuch as these various estimates are so closely similar, the average of the five—namely $1,575—may be taken as the approximate amount necessary to maintain a family of five at a minimum of subsistence level at prices prevailing in the latter part of 1919.

### 2. THE COST OF A MINIMUM OF COMFORT BUDGET
### (a) Professor Ogburn's Budget

Professor W. F. Ogburn prepared in 1918, for the consideration of the National War Labor Board and of Judge Samuel Alschuler, arbitrator in the Chicago Packing house industries, a budget for an average workingman's family of five which would include not only subsistence requirements but a minimum of comfort and recreation. The cost of this budget was placed at $1,760. This was at prices prevailing in June, 1918. Since that date the cost of living, as above noted, has increased 15 per cent. This would make the present cost of the budget $2,024. By major items, this budget was distributed as follows:

|  | Cost June 1918 | Cost August 1919 |
|---|---|---|
| Food | $625.00 | |
| Clothing | 313.50 | |
| Rent, fuel and light | 295.00 | |
| Sundries | 527.00 | |
| Total | $1,760.50 | $2,024.00 |

### (b) U. S. Bureau of Labor Statistics' Budget for Government Employee's Family

The U. S. Bureau of Labor Statistics has just published, after very considerable investigation, a quantity and cost budget for a Government employee's family in Washington, D. C. The budget level aimed at is one of health and decency—that is to say—a level at which the family will have just enough to maintain itself in health and decency, but with none of the "trimmings" and very few of the comforts of life. This budget had in mind primarily the clerical employee, but except possibly in the matter of clothes there seems no reason why the level of a clerical worker should be more costly than that of a mechanic or laborer. On the other hand, Washington prices were undoubtedly above the average for the country as a whole.

This budget, at August, 1919, prices, cost $2,262. The distribution of its principal items is shown in the following table:

### SUMMARY OF BUDGET
#### Cost of Quantity Budget at Market Prices

| | | |
|---|---|---|
| I. Food | | $773.93 |
| II. Clothing: | | |
| Husband | $121.16 | |
| Wife | 166.46 | |
| Boy (11 years) | 96.60 | |
| Girl (5 years) | 82.50 | |
| Boy (2 years) | 47.00 | 513.72 |
| III. Housing, fuel and light | | 428.00 |
| IV. Miscellaneous | | 546.82 |
| Total budget at market prices | | $2,262.47 |

Possible saving upon market cost by a family of extreme thrift, of high intelligence, great industry in shopping, good fortune in purchasing at lowest prices, and in which the wife is able to do a maximum amount of home work.

I. Food (7½ per cent.) ........................ $58.04
II. Clothing (10 per cent.) .................... 51.37
III. Housing ................................... 30.00
IV. Miscellaneous ............................. 97.50

Total economies .................................. 236.91
                                                   ——————
Total budget minus economies ..................... $2,025.56

*Savings.*—No provision is made in this budget for savings, other than the original cost of household furniture and equipment, which would average about $1,000 in value. No definite estimate, of course, can be made as to the amount which a low-salaried Government employee should be expected to save. But an average saving of 12½ per cent. of yearly salary during an employee's single and early married life would seem to be the maximum which could be expected. Over a period of, say, 15 years this would result in a total accumulation of about $2,000. Assuming $1,000 of this to be invested in household equipment, there would be a net sum of $1,000 available for investment in a home or in other direct income-producing form. In any case, it would represent an annual income of approximately $50 per year.

Recognizing the high prices prevailing in Washington, and recognizing also that the Government employee's family may have certain necessary expenses not falling upon the working-man's family, it would seem that the fact that this budget cost $2,662 would tend to confirm the $2,000 minimum comfort budget of Professor Ogburn as conservative for workingmen's families generally in the country as a whole.

## Appendix B

## WAGES IN IRON AND STEEL AND OTHER INDUSTRIES

From report made for this inquiry by the Bureau of Applied Economics, Washington, D. C.

Information regarding hourly earnings and full time hours per week in the iron and steel industry is presented in considerable detail in an article in the Monthly Labor Review of the U. S. Bureau of Labor Statistics for October, 1919. Similar information of recent date is not available for many other industries, but there is sufficient to make possible a valuable comparison of earnings and hours of labor in the steel industry with conditions in other lines of employment.

The data presented below are divided into four groups:

1. WAGES AND HOURS IN THE STEEL INDUSTRY COMPARED WITH OTHER INDUSTRIES, FOR THE COUNTRY AS A WHOLE

The following table gives the hourly earnings, full time hours per week and full time earnings per week, for specified classes of labor in the steel industry and in all other important industries for which information in comparable form is available. All figures are for 1919, and, with few exceptions, for the latter part of 1919. The sources of the information are given on a later page.

The full time hours per week, it is important to note, are the regular weekly working hours for the occupation. The actual hours worked by individuals and, in consequence, their weekly earnings may be considerably less.

264

AVERAGE HOURLY EARNINGS AND HOURS PER FULL TIME
WEEK IN VARIOUS INDUSTRIES

|  | Average Hourly Rate | Full Time Hours per Week | Earnings per Full Week |
|---|---|---|---|
| **IRON AND STEEL** |  |  |  |
| All employees .................. | 68.1 | 68.7 | $46.78 |
| Common labor .................. | 46.2 | 74.0 | 34.19 |
| Other labor (including skilled and semi-skilled) .................. | 78.4 | 66.0 | 51.74 |
| **MINING** |  |  |  |
| 1. Anthracite: |  |  |  |
| Company miners ................. | 58.1 | 51.6 | 29.98 |
| Contract miners ................ | 84.2 | 51.6 | 43.45 |
| Company miners' laborers ........ | 52.6 | 51.6 | 27.14 |
| Contract miners' laborers ......... | 63.9 | 51.6 | 32.97 |
| Laborers ....................... | 51.9 | 52.2 | 26.90 |
| Average for all inside occupations .. | 67.3 | 52.0 | 35.00 |
| 2. Bituminous: |  |  |  |
| Miners, hand ................... | 78.4 | 47.3 | 37.08 |
| Miners, machine ................ | 94.7 | 48.1 | 45.55 |
| Loaders ....................... | 80.2 | 47.4 | 38.01 |
| Laborers ...................... | 57.5 | 52.0 | 29.90 |
| Average for all inside occupations .. | 74.4 | 51.9 | 38.42 |
| **UNITED STATES ARSENALS:** |  |  |  |
| Common labor .................. | 46.0 | 4.80 | 22.08 |
| All other employees, average ...... | 76.1 | 48.0 | 36.53 |
| **BUILDING TRADES:** |  |  |  |
| Average for all building trades .... | 85.4 | 44.0 | 37.58 |
| Common labor .................. | 52.0 | 44.0 | 22.88 |
| Bricklayers ................... | 89.3 | 44.2 | 39.47 |
| Carpenters .................... | 78.2 | 44.2 | 34.56 |
| Cement workers and finishers ..... | 80.8 | 44.9 | 36.28 |
| Wiremen, inside ............... | 79.9 | 44.3 | 35.40 |
| Painters ...................... | 76.2 | 42.8 | 32.61 |
| Plasterers .................... | 89.5 | 43.6 | 39.02 |
| Plumbers ..................... | 92.4 | 44.0 | 40.66 |
| Sheet-metal workers ............ | 80.9 | 44.0 | 35.60 |
| Steam fitters .................. | 92.8 | 44.0 | 40.83 |
| Structural iron workers .......... | 94.2 | 44.0 | 41.45 |
| New York, N. Y. |  |  |  |
| Average for all building trades .... | 83.5 | 44.0 | 36.74 |
| **NAVY YARDS:** |  |  |  |
| Laborers, common .............. | 44.5 | 48.0 | 21.36 |
| All other occupations ........... | 79.9 | 48.0 | 38.35 |
| Boilermakers .................. | 80.0 | 48.0 | 38.40 |
| Coppersmiths .................. | 86.0 | 48.0 | 41.28 |
| Electricians .................. | 80.0 | 48.0 | 38.40 |
| Machinists .................... | 80.0 | 48.0 | 38.40 |
| Machinists, electrical ........... | 80.0 | 48.0 | 38.40 |
| Molders ...................... | 80.0 | 48.0 | 38.40 |
| Patternmakers ................. | 86.6 | 48.0 | 41.57 |
| Pipefitters ................... | 80.0 | 48.0 | 38.40 |

| | Average Hourly Rate | Full Time Hours per Week | Earnings per Full Week |
|---|---|---|---|
| **NAVY YARDS (cont.):** | | | |
| Plumbers | 80.0 | 48.0 | 38.40 |
| Riveters | 80.0 | 48.0 | 38.40 |
| Shipfitters | 80.0 | 48.0 | 38.40 |
| Shipsmiths | 80.0 | 48.0 | 38.40 |
| Toolmakers | 86.0 | 48.0 | 41.28 |
| Holders-on | 60.6 | 48.0 | 29.09 |
| **PRINTERS: Various Cities.** | | | |
| Linotype Operators | | | |
| Newspapers, day | ... | ... | 35.72 |
| Book and job | ... | ... | 30.50 |
| Compositors | | | |
| Newspapers, day | ... | ... | 35.59 |
| Book and job | ... | ... | 26.28 |
| **RAILROAD EMPLOYEES:** | | | |
| Shopmen | | | |
| Machinists | 72.0 | 48.0 | 34.56 |
| Blacksmiths | 72.0 | 48.0 | 34.56 |
| Boilermakers | 72.0 | 48.0 | 34.56 |
| Road freight | | | |
| Engineers and motormen | 82.5 | ... | ... |
| Firemen | 60.0 | 48.0 | 28.80 |
| Conductors | 69.2 | ... | ... |
| Road passenger | | | |
| Engineers and motormen | 98.7 | ... | ... |
| Firemen | 88.0 | 30.0 * | 26.40 |
| Conductors | 83.3 | ... | ... |
| Yard Service | | | |
| Firemen | 52.0 | 48.0 | 24.96 |
| Hostlers | 53.1 | 48.0 | 25.49 |
| Laborers | | | |
| Mechanics' helpers and apprentices | 47.1 | | |
| Section men | 37.2 | | |
| Levermen | 49.6 | | |
| Yard switch tenders | 34.7 | | |
| Other yard employees | 37.4 | | |
| Enginehouse men | 42.3 | | |
| Other unskilled laborers | 41.3 | | |
| **SHIPYARDS:** | | | |
| Pacific Coast District | | | |
| Laborers | 52.0 | 48.0 | 24.96 |
| Other occupations | 75.8 | 48.0 | 36.38 |
| Atlantic Coast District | | | |
| Laborers | 36.0 | 48.0 | 17.28 |
| All occupations (including laborers) | 72.7 | 48.0 | 34.90 |
| **STREET RAILWAY EMPLOYEES:** | | | |
| Average for various cities | | | |
| North Atlantic | 49.8 | 56.4 | 28.09 |
| South Atlantic | 39.8 | 56.4 | 22.45 |
| North Central | 49.6 | 56.4 | 27.97 |
| Western | 49.4 | 56.4 | 27.86 |

\* 5 hours per day.

2. PITTSBURGH DISTRICT. WAGES AND HOURS OF LABOR IN THE
IRON AND STEEL INDUSTRY COMPARED WITH WAGES IN
OTHER INDUSTRIES IN THE PITTSBURGH DISTRICT.

The next table compares hourly earnings, full time hours per
week, and full time weekly earnings in the iron and steel industry with other industries in the *Pittsburgh District* for
which information was available. As available information is
not very extensive the comparison was necessarily limited, but
is believed to be sufficient to indicate how wage rates and hours
of employees in the steel industry compare with other lines of
employment.

Inasmuch as the primary comparison desired is one which will
bring out the extent to which the relatively high full time weekly
earnings in the steel industry may be due to long hours, there
is added to a table a column showing how much would be
earned by each group for 44 hours per week, at the prevailing
hourly rates. In doing so, 44 hours is used as a base simply
because a number of trades in the table were already working
44 hours per week. For the purpose of the comparison, of
course, it would make no difference what base were chosen.

Again, it is important to emphasize that the weekly hours
here presented are the regular full time hours per week of the
occupation, not the actual hours worked by individuals.

COMPARISON OF EARNINGS PER HOUR, REGULAR FULL TIME
HOURS PER WEEK, AND EARNINGS PER FULL TIME WEEK
IN VARIOUS INDUSTRIES AND OCCUPATIONS IN THE
PITTSBURGH (PA.) DISTRICT

|  | Average Hourly Rate | Regular Hours per Week | Earnings per Full Week | Earnings for 44 Hours per Week |
|---|---|---|---|---|
| IRON AND STEEL: |  |  |  |  |
| All employees .............. | 72.8 | 74.2 | 54.02 | 32.03 |
| Common labor ............. | 48.0 | 77.8 | 37.34 | 21.12 |
| Other labor (including skilled and semi-skilled) ....... | 87.1 | 72.1 | 62.80 | 38.32 |

| | Average Hourly Rate | Regular Hours per Week | Earnings per Full Week | Earnings for 44 Hours per Week |
|---|---|---|---|---|
| **BITUMINOUS COAL MINING:** | | | | |
| Miners, hand | 78.4 | 47.3 | 37.08 | 34.50 |
| Miners, machine | 94.7 | 48.1 | 45.55 | 41.67 |
| Loaders | 80.2 | 47.4 | 38.01 | 35.29 |
| Laborers | 57.5 | 52.0 | 29.90 | 25.30 |
| Average for all inside occupations | 74.4 | 51.9 | 38.61 | 32.74 |
| **METAL TRADES:** | | | | |
| Blacksmiths | 70.0 | 48.0 | 33.60 | 30.80 |
| Boilermakers | 66.0 | 50.0 | 33.00 | 29.04 |
| Molders, iron | 75.0 | 48.0 | 36.00 | 33.00 |
| **RAILROAD EMPLOYEES:** | | | | |
| Shopmen | | | | |
| Machinists | 72.0 | 48.0 | 34.56 | 31.68 |
| Blacksmiths | 72.0 | 48.0 | 34.56 | 31.68 |
| Boilermakers | 72.0 | 48.0 | 34.56 | 31.68 |
| Road freight | | | | |
| Firemen | 60.0 | 48.0 | 28.80 | 26.40 |
| **BUILDING TRADES:** | | | | |
| Laborers | | | | |
| Building laborers | 50.0 | 48.0 | 24.00 | 22.00 |
| Hod carriers | 70.0 | 44.0 | 30.80 | 30.80 |
| Plasterers' laborers | 70.0 | 44.0 | 30.80 | 30.80 |
| Average for laborers | 63.3 | 45.3 | 28.67 | 27.85 |
| Bricklayers | 112.5 | 44.0 | 49.50 | 49.50 |
| Carpenters | 90.0 | 44.0 | 39.60 | 39.60 |
| Cement finishers | 82.5 | 44.0 | 36.30 | 36.30 |
| Granite cutters, inside | 84.4 | 44.0 | 37.14 | 37.14 |
| Wiremen, inside | 90.0 | 44.0 | 39.60 | 39.60 |
| Painters | 87.5 | 44.0 | 38.50 | 38.50 |
| Plasterers | 97.5 | 44.0 | 42.90 | 42.90 |
| Plumbers | 93.8 | 44.0 | 41.27 | 41.27 |
| Sheet-metal workers | 90.0 | 44.0 | 39.60 | 39.60 |
| Structural iron workers | 100.0 | 44.0 | 44.00 | 44.00 |
| **STREET RAILWAY EMPLOYEES:** | | | | |
| Motormen and conductors | 54.0 | 56.4 | 30.46 | 23.76 |
| **PRINTERS:** | | | | |
| Linotype operators | | | | |
| Newspapers, day | 87.5 | 48.0 | 42.00 | 38.50 |
| Book and job | 68.8 | 48.0 | 33.02 | 30.27 |
| Compositors | | | | |
| Newspapers, day | 77.0 | 48.0 | 36.96 | 33.88 |
| Book and job | 60.4 | 48.0 | 28.99 | 26.58 |

# APPENDICES 269

## SOURCES OF DATA USED IN COMPILING DATA ON WAGES AND HOURS USED IN THIS STUDY

Iron and Steel: Monthly Labor Review, U. S. Department of Labor, Bureau of Labor Statistics, October, 1919.

Mining: Press Report of U. S. Bureau of Labor Statistics, entitled "Hours and Earnings of Employees in the Coal Mining Industry," dated Nov. 2, 1919.

United States Arsenal: Monthly Labor Review, U. S. Department of Labor Statistics, October, 1910.

Building Trades: (1) Union wages for various trades for most of the larger cities of the country, as compiled by the United States Bureau of Labor Statistics and supplemented by data furnished by union officials; (2) Wage rates of building laborers under the scales of the Hod Carriers' and Building Laborers' Union, and (3) Prevailing wages in the building trades of New York as published by the Building Trades Council of that city.

Navy Yards: Data supplied by United States Navy Department.

Printers: The data presented were obtained from the wage scales and advances as published in the journals and Bulletins of the Typographical Union and from computations made by the United States Bureau of Labor Statistics.

Railroad Employees: From a Statement prepared by the U. S. Railroad Administration under date of April 8, 1919.

Shipyards: From the award of the Shipbuilding Labor Adjustment Board in October, 1918, still in effect. This award provided for two general scales of shipyard wages—one for the Atlantic Coast and one for the Pacific Coast.

Street Railway Employees: The compilation gives the hourly maximum rates of motormen and conductors in representative cities. The information was compiled from trade and labor publications and is believed to be closely accurate. The data for full time hours per week is based on an estimate made by Arthur Sturgis in his "Analysis of Electric Railway Operating Costs and the Cost of Living as Related to Wages of Conductors, Motormen, and Other Trainmen" and presented to the Electric Railway Commission, Washington, D. C., in October, 1919.

# APPENDIX C

The classification of unskilled, semi-skilled and skilled followed in this report is that used by the government survey in 1910 (Senate Document 110, 4 vols.), and is based primarily on wage rates. That division made all earnings under 18 cents an hour, unskilled; all 25 cents an hour or over, skilled; and those between, semi-skilled. The percentages of the three classes for the industry were derived from the table for a typical establishment. (S. D. 110, vol. III, p. 80.)

These percentages were, in Section IV of this report, applied to the exhaustive tables of full time earnings (S. D. 110, vol. III, pp. 550-551) in order to discover the corresponding percentages of total payrolls. The percentages thus applied and carried over to the column of weekly earnings made all below $12 weekly, unskilled (median wage $10.25); all over $15.50 weekly, skilled (median wage $19.10); all between, semi-skilled (median wage $13.50).

It is perfectly understood that this three-fold classification, with dividing lines drawn at percentages in decimal points, represents no corresponding precision of classification in the industry itself, either as organized or as possible. The gradations according to pay were used by the government (and by this report) solely because they formed the only accurate measurement existent of relative skill, a measurement which is very exact in the industry, meaning a hundred gradations in typical departmental payrolls. The usefulness of *any* precise classification is obvious; the use of the threefold classification is a makeshift, partly to conform to industry nomenclature, partly to distinguish the three chief differing types of worker, who may be described as being found clearly recognizable in the *middle* of each class. At the two edges of the semi-skilled class there is no definable dividing line in points of observable skill. These three clear types are (a) common labor, learning in a day how to do *something;* (b) skilled labor, unreplaceable by men who have not had many years of training; (c) semi-skilled labor, men of months or years of training, potentially able to do skilled work, but never having had opportunity actually to do it.

It is an indication of the backwardness of steel as an industry that no exact classifications of jobs have been generally worked out in it. Observation indicates that a classification much closer to facts would be five-fold, as follows:

(a) common labor;—shiftable, replaced by "anybody," learning the "know how" in from 1 day to 2 months.
(b) low-skilled;—common labor, but assigned steadily to set jobs requiring considerable "knack" and some responsibility.
(c) semi-skilled;—trained men, potentially able to take over a job, or occasionally doing it; of the next higher class (d).
(d) skilled;—men not only of many years' *training* but long experience on set jobs involving adeptness, judgment and responsibility.
(e) high-skilled;—long-experienced men, characterized by judgment amounting to "genius," and by executive ability.

That is a gamut of (a) yard labor; (b) "skip" operators; (c) melters' third helpers; (d) melters' first helpers; (e) rollers, blowers, etc.

# INDEX